THREE RADICAL
WOMEN WRITERS

GENDER AND GENRE IN LITERATURE
VOLUME 6
GARLAND REFERENCE LIBRARY OF THE HUMANITIES
VOLUME 1452

GENDER AND GENRE IN LITERATURE

BARBARA E. BOWEN, *Series Editor*

Three Radical Women Writers
Class and Gender in Meridel Le Sueur, Tillie Olsen, and Josephine Herbst

Nora Ruth Roberts

Garland Publishing, Inc.
New York and London
1996

Library of Congress Cataloging-in-Publication Data

Roberts, Nora Ruth.
    Three radical women writers : class and gender in Meridel Le Sueur,
Tillie Olsen, and Josephine Herbst / Nora Ruth Roberts.
        p.   cm. — (Gender & genre in literature ; vol. 6)   (Garland
reference library of the humanities ; vol. 1452)
    Includes bibliographical references and index.
    ISBN 0-8153-0330-0 (alk. paper)
    1. American literature—Women authors—History and criticism.
2. Radicalism in literature.   3. Feminism and literature—United States—
History—20th century.   4. Socialism and literature—United States—
History—20th century.   5. Literature and society—United States—History—
20th century.   6. Women and literature—United States—History—20th
century.   7. Radicalism—United States—History—20th century.   8. Le
Sueur, Meridel—Political and social views.   9. Olsen, Tillie—Political and
social views.   10. Herbst, Josephine, 1892–1969—Political and social
views.   11. Social classes in literature.   12. Sex role in literature.
I. Title. II. Series. III. Series: Garland reference library of the
humanities ; vol. 1452.
    PS228.R34R63   1996
    810.9'9287'0904—dc20   95-43538
                                                                          CIP

Printed on acid-free, 250-year-life paper
Manufactured in the United States of America

FOR FRANCES

in loving memory

Contents

Preface and Acknowledgments

In some respects this book is over fifty years in the making, at least as far as my participation in this process is concerned. I derive from a radical-progressive heritage that combines an American and immigrant socialist tradition that can be traced back at least three generations, and perhaps farther, if we broaden the scope of the term progressivism. Specifically, I had rather a difficult upbringing in the intellectually demanding and financially stinting working class socialist milieu of the Trotskyist organization, the Socialist Workers Party. My mother was public candidate on the SWP ticket for Board of Supervisors in San Francisco during the height of the Cold War period of the mid-fifties, and my father similarly ran for Mayor of Seattle, living separately, at nearly the same time. It was a difficult childhood in many ways, but this is not the time or place to shed light on that.

Suffice it to say that I came into a socialist-activist teen period immediately following the Khrushchev revelations of 1956, was in New York at the time, and was actively engaged, in whatever capacity I could muster, as a leader of the Trotskyist youth organization which became the Young Socialist Alliance. We were attempting to effect a unification or a reunification with forces disaffected from the Communist Party--those following John Gates out of the CP and those "fellow-travelers" allied to the readership of the *National Guardian.* Although the hoped-for reunification failed to materialize, despite some promising efforts, a concern for the revitalization of the family of the left has remained on my agenda, at times with more immediacy, at times with less. Specifically, when it came time to choose a topic for a dissertation after a late reentry into academic pursuits, I consulted the eminent Marxist literary scholar Dr. Annette T. Rubinstein, an abiding family friend from the "regroupment" period, whose name I think I can safely use. Annette recommended, as the three most important women figures to emerge from the thirties period of communist radicalization, the names of Meridel Le Sueur, Tillie Olsen and Josephine Herbst. Conversations with the late Hedda Garza and the distinguished radical journalist Elinor Ferry, whose friendships I also came to value from this period, corroborated my choice. As I began work on this project I found it was becoming a repository for all that I have been thinking, rethinking, discussing and writing about with regard to feminism, Marxism, the construction of identity and to some extent psychoanalysis. This thinking had been informed by the older generation but thought through in the context of a newer generation my age and a little younger not privileged to have had hands-on contact with the lost continuum of the American radical tradition. I hope this book will do justice not only to my thinking process, but to the reception I hope for it among a younger generation, to the writers in question themselves, and to the entire heritage which it seems to be my wont or my curse to appropriate.

As for my approach to the writers themselves, while I treat of all three as communists and as women, I hope most of all to respect their integrity as individuals and as writers. For that reason, my inquiry extends beyond the significant period of the thirties to examine the writers' entire productive lives.

As for acknowledgments, I feel I must abide by the old radical custom of withholding actual names of those who may obviously or not find themselves in sensitive positions when it comes to being associated with a book written by an avowed socialist. I make one exception, in the case of Morris Dickstein--he has tenure. Dr. Dickstein, my advisor and mentor, has been most supportive, interested, informed and generous with his time and approbation at nearly every step of the process. I trust if he were going to be disappointed in the results he would have told me by now. Dr. Rubinstein is a public figure, self-supporting and can probably stand the light. Meridel Le Sueur and her daughter were both most generous with their time when I visited them in Wisconsin, and I appreciate their permission to quote from Le Sueur's journals and letters, and the late Elinor Ferry, herself a public figure, along with Myra Page, gave valuable help in interviews on this project, Elinor both as a personal friend and associate of mine since 1957, and friend and one-time financial supporter of Josephine Herbst; Page as a radical novelist of the thirties who kindly shared with me her memories in the company of Dr. Rubinstein. I am grateful to the executor of Josephine Herbst's estate, Hilton Kramer, for permission to use unpublished archival material gleaned from the Beinecke Library collection at Yale.

I owe a deep debt to my mother and to my father, both deceased, and to the women, and few men--my stepfather and ex-husband included--of their generation who, by making a consistent struggle within the radical community for feminism, individuality, creativity, and an end to internecine factionalism, shaped within me an intellectual commitment to the human cause which, I think, has often rescued me from slipping into despair. While their concerns have not always been my concerns, at least not always in the same ways, they have shaped my thinking, indeed burrowed into the very marrow of my being.

In recent times I have been sustained by three important women in my family and two women friends in my community--along with a host of less long-standing acquaintances, colleagues, and fellow students. Importantly, I would like to give a special verbal hug to my two grown sons, who stood by me with some difficulty when the going was rough before I was able to get free of an unrewarding career in publishing and undertake more enjoyable academic pursuits. I hope these two stalwart young men will not feel they are too old to reap the benefits of my brightened mood and whatever rise to some modicum of public attention accrues. Lastly, I would like to acknowledge with gratitude the financial support of the Carolyn Heilbrun Dissertation Award Committee of the City University of New York, the Danforth Foundation, the Helena Rubinstein Foundation, the Jewish League for the Education of Women, the Theodore Goodman Fund of CCNY, and the generosity and patience of my ex-husband and my parents, all of whom contributed to my own determination to see my education through to this point.

I wanted to close this section with a joke and thank my devoted wife for typing, reading and editing my manuscript, but I was afraid that would convey the wrong impression. I have performed almost all the secretarial and editorial labor entirely by myself.

Tillie Olsen

Meridel Le Sueur

Josephine Herbst

Drawings by Herb Lebowitz

Introduction:

Three Radical Women

According to Eugene V. Debs's biographer Ray Ginger, the distinguished socialist leader confronted the duenna of the suffrage movement, Susan B. Anthony, on two occasions. The first was when Debs, as a young socialist organizer, attended an Anthony lecture and introduced himself afterward. The second time was in 1903, nearly twenty-five years later, when it was Debs who was the mature orator and Anthony, past eighty, greeted him afterward from the audience. Ginger reports their conversation after the meeting to be one of convivial confrontation. "Give us suffrage," Anthony is reported to have said laughingly, "and we'll give you socialism." Debs replied: "Give us socialism and we'll give you suffrage." (Ginger 224). In the twenty years that followed, suffrage was won and the Russian Revolution was to transform Debs's American Socialist movement, perhaps to his own dismay.

At the time, in the Midwest, there was a widespread socialist-populist movement which had its ramifications on the women's movement. The three women who are the subject of this study, Meridel Le Sueur, Tillie Olsen, and Josephine Herbst, came of age in that context. Shaped by the stirrings of progressivism among farmers, workers, and farm-community businesspeople in Kansas, Oklahoma, Nebraska, and Iowa, these three women took the socialism of Debs and the feminism of Anthony a step further and were to make of it an integral part of their work. By the late twenties and early thirties all three had pursued progressive politics to the extent of becoming part of the growing, intellectually important communist milieu. All three began their writing careers in significant ways by writing for *New Masses* and *The Daily Worker*, organs of the Communist Party in the United States. While

1

Josephine Herbst had already developed skills and prestige in the mainstream press, Olsen and Le Sueur were to get their initiation into publication through the radical press. As women writing about social issues, all three developed a uniquely feminine voice which has allowed them to figure importantly in dialogues in recent times, wherever radical feminist literature is discussed.

At the time the two aspects of socialist feminism were coming to fruition following the exchange between Debs and Anthony, Meridel Le Sueur, coming to maturity in a midwest socialist-feminist household, might well have known how to discuss those events from her avid reading of her parents' favorite newspaper, the Socialist Party's *Appeal to Reason*. Tillie Olsen, twelve or fourteen years younger, was no doubt overhearing debates on many related issues in her immigrant socialist household in Nebraska. Josephine Herbst, the only one of the three not from a socialist or feminist household, though the maternal line was important to her work, was older, committed to becoming a writer, finishing her studies at Berkeley, and preparing to make for Europe where she could live cheaply and develop her fledgling talent. She would be the only one of the four girls in her family to make a break from both the gender expectations and the political conservatism of her middle-class Iowa family. The confluence of the events is significant in that, while the speeches of Debs and Anthony are buried in archives, the writing of the heirs of their unification, Le Sueur, Olsen and Herbst, are at this writing in print and serving well to find a fresh readership among a new generation of socialists and feminists at a time when Debs and Anthony have been archaicized as figures of reverential awe who yet cease to resonate as ongoing participants in important discussions.

The basic position of socialists in relation to issues of women, family, and gender considerations did not fundamentally change from the original teachings of Marx and Engels until it was forced to meet the challenge of the rising feminist movement in the sixties. During the period when Le Sueur and Olsen and Herbst were developing as writers and beginning to attract their own followings, American radicalism was for the most part dominated by the American Communist Party, which took its positions on "the woman question" and on literature from orthodox Marxist-Leninist teachings. The three women writers who are the subject of this discussion knew each other's work, met at the all-important American Writers Congress of 1935, either joined or were sympathetic to the Communist movement and wrote in its press, but never did they forge a liaison with each other to discuss the situation of the woman writer in the American Communist movement. Part of the reason for that was the state of women's awareness of issues affecting their lives in the radical intellectual movement at the time. Specifically, a commitment to supportive bonding among women in the party would have been subject to suspicion among the party leadership and was not advanced by women intellectuals themselves. A more important reason undoubtedly resides in the very nature of the Marxist-Leninist interpretation of both feminism and the role of the writer, a question which was to place Le Sueur in opposition to Herbst, leaving Olsen uneasily in the middle. This is a question still unresolved in the feminist movement today as to whether class is a more important determinant of social imperative than gender or culture. Or to put it in terms of the Debs-Anthony exchange: Must socialism wait for feminism, or feminism wait for socialism? That question is at the heart of my inquiry.

In 1920, after the advent of woman suffrage, a bifurcation occurred within the socialist and feminist movements. The emphasis at the time was on active involvement in economic reform issues--strikes among the working class and demands for inclusion in the economic mainstream among the feminists. Looking back on the period with the advantage of hindsight, we can see that the significance of the work of the literary figures of the time, and especially of the three women writers I am discussing, is that they implicitly raise two major considerations which are central to the deliberations of the current generation. These issues relate to both the shaping of gender as it arises from sexuality and social determinants and the issue of how literature affects consciousness and how consciousness in turn affects social change. At the time these three were writing in the radical press these determinants of social change had not the relevance they have come to have in current intellectual discussions among leftist and feminist movements. In point of fact, both women's concerns and even literary considerations were marginalized in the communist literature of the period--both placed in subordinate positions while primary attention was given to what seemed of more immediate importance-- the victory of working class struggles and the fight against fascism. With the failure of that period to bring about the lasting transformation of social relations in the United States, and with the failure of socialist revolutions elsewhere to bring about important alterations in personal and material relations, the two issues of gender determination and of consciousness-formation in general have emerged as among the primary issues for those still concerned with the project of the amelioration of social ills and the progressive development of the human situation. The careers of Le Sueur, Olsen, and Herbst, as the three primary surviving women writers of the communist period of the thirties, offer an especially valuable way to assess the interaction among gender, sexuality and social consciousness. Just as their works could not have been written in any but the times in which they were most active or from any but a socialist perspective, so the full impact of those works could not be felt in quite so important a way on any but a new generation of readers infused with a sense of the contemporary discussion of consciousness, feminism, and the legacy of the imperative of social awareness.

In the early feminist movement, Crystal Eastman published a call in the December 1920 issue of *The Liberator*, the left-wing cultural journal she and her brother Max Eastman brought into being when *The Masses*, its predecessor, was confiscated by the U.S. Government as seditious material during World War I. Crystal Eastman's call, entitled, "Now We Can Begin," sounds distressingly familiar to the ear of a post-sixties feminist, distressing, in that the terms of the discussion are so little changed today. Crystal Eastman addresses her readers as follows:

> In fighting for the right to vote most women have tried to be either non-committal or thoroughly respectable on every other subject. Now they can say what they are really after; and what they are after, in common with all the rest of the struggling world is *freedom*. .... But as a feminist [woman] also knows that the whole of woman's slavery is not summed up in the profit system, nor her complete emancipation assured by the downfall of capitalism.
>
> Woman's freedom, in the feminist sense, can be fought for and conceivably won before the gates open into industrial democracy. On the other hand, woman's freedom, in the feminist sense, is not inherent in the communist ideal. ... What is the problem of women's freedom? It seems to me to be this: how to arrange the world so that women can be human beings, with a chance to exercise their infinitely varied gifts in infinitely varied ways, instead of being destined by the accident of their sex to one field of activity--housework and child-raising. And second, if and when they choose housework and child-raising to have that occupation recognized by the world as work, requiring a definite economic reward and not merely entitling the performer to be dependent on some man. ... I can agree that women will never be great until they achieve a certain emotional freedom, a strong healthy egotism, and some un-personal sources of joy--that in this inner sense we cannot make woman free by changing her economic status. What we can do, however, is to create conditions of outward freedom in which a free woman's soul can be born and grow. It is these outward conditions with which an organized feminist movement must concern itself. (Cook 75-76)

I have quoted Crystal Eastman at length both to indicate how dismayingly relevant her statement is to modern-day feminist agendas, and to indicate the parameters of the socialist/feminist discussion that was prevalent in the period in which I am placing the initiation of the careers of the three writers I am considering.

In point of fact, Crystal Eastman's agenda was not taken up by the left-wing movement generally. Instead, what occurred was a polarization. Feminists either stuck to an essentially liberal program of attempting to seek positions in business, academia and government or joined forces with the militant women socialists who allied their cause with that of the working class in the unionization drives of the socialist and communist parties. These movements also did not focus on women's issues so much as they utilized women's talents in organizing women workers, forming support movements in the form of women's auxiliaries and occasionally, but rarely, sponsoring women's special study groups.

Within the socialist/communist movement, the problem of whether capitalism can indeed accommodate the equalization of labor was not linked automatically to the feminist issues as it was to those involving race. Most of the questions brought forward by modern day feminists and even Marxist feminists--from the political economy of housework to *ecriture feminine*--were not on the agenda until the modern movement began with Simone de Beauvoir, Betty Friedan, the SDS women's caucuses, and Juliet Mitchell and the French psychoanalytically oriented feminist theorists.

At the time of Crystal Eastman's call, the liberal, primarily middle-class feminists were focusing their demands on issues of equal rights to political, educational, and economic points of access under capitalism, such as increasing the number of women professionals in publishing and business generally, in the universities and in government generally, and in organizing such groups as the League of Women Voters to lobby for legislation that would help alleviate women's dependency on men. At the same time, controversies over Margaret Sanger's incipient birth control movement were primarily confined to middle class "reformists." On the other hand, the radical press was extolling the virtues of their leading women figures who took their place alongside men on picket lines and organizing drives. If special attention was paid to women's issues, it was to their roles as wives and auxiliary helpmates to males in the movement.[1] The kind of definition of freedom Crystal Eastman made in her opening of the post-suffrage discussion was not even to become a matter of serious contention, either in the liberal women's movement, or in the radical heterogeneous movement until recent times.

To explore the questions of the time and to interrogate the work of the primary radical women writers of the height of the communist period in America, we must first of all correct for time and historical circumstance. To start with, we have to note that the socialist/communist movement of the pre-sixties era was never on the high theoretical plane that the European movement has been. Primarily a pragmatic working-man's movement since its inception in the Marx-Engels era, the various socialist organizations since the De Leonist/Marxist movement and the International Workers of the World tended to follow Marx rather than contend with him. The thrust of the early movement was on organizing labor into trade unions. The debates were on how to do this--through the existing conservative AFL and craft unions or through independent unions.[2]

Such women as Elizabeth Gurley Flynn, Kate Richards O'Hare and Rose Pastor Stokes played prominent roles in the IWW, in Debs's Socialist Party and in the opposition to World War I first of all because they were effective organizers and agitators for the causes they espoused, primarily industrial unionism. While they were not discriminated against because they were women, neither were they themselves especially significant as champions of women's causes. They were important representatives of that group of women socialist leaders who placed socialism higher on their agenda than feminism. While the three writers I am addressing, Le Sueur, Olsen, and Herbst, were not entirely in the same category, certainly social issues other than those associated with feminism made up their personal imperatives.

At the same time it would be wrong and perhaps inadvertently sexist to automatically minimize the influential positions even these few women held in otherwise male-dominated leadership bodies on the socialist/communist left. If their positions of authority did not lead to their espousal of feminist issues, that seems to have been due to their own choice to speak as the "vanguard" of a nominally degendered working class rather than to use their positions to advance women's causes. It is clear that all aspects of the socialist/communist essentially masculine leadership preferred things this way for a complexity of reasons that surely included bureaucratic self-interest as well as masculinist political bias. Crystal Eastman was to find no home in the communist hierarchy. Her latter-day descendant, Mary Inman, who raised similar issues within the CPUSA, was to find only deaf ears from both male and female leaders[3] but the problem of feminism within the organized left is certainly essential to an understanding of the women's literature the period produced.

For women writers in the socialist/communist milieu, the movement offered the opportunity to publish and develop a literature that, without forsaking a feminist perspective, was yet imbued with consciousness of social and historical process. The result in the case of Le Sueur, Olsen, and Herbst was the forging of an unambiguously feminine voice which was to give expression in a uniquely feminine way to the process of unfolding social event. Historical consciousness, the hallmark of Marxist theoretical underpinnings, was to take on new dimensions when translated by these writers into terms of women's experience of both history and of perception. No other moment in society was to provide such a peak for the development of women's social/historical consciousness until recent developments in the radicalized women's movement commencing in the sixties. Even at that, the 1930s, the period in which the voices of these three writers were at their most influential, offered a rare glimpse at the climacteric of large movements of working men and women waging daily battles for their rights as human beings. The Communist Party's membership of approximately 80,000 in that period does not begin to tell the story of the strikes, protests, unemployed councils and arts coalitions which that membership initiated. Men may have played dominant roles in these organizations, but there were many women who played key parts both in leadership positions and as activist organizers. If the thirties did not bring about the revolution that many felt the many recurrent uprisings promised, it was for many women as well as men a time when, oddly enough, even the most dismal of conditions seemed rectifiable by communal intercourse. Evictions called for tenant committees; milk shortages called for housewife committees; unemployment called for unemployed councils and demonstrations. If one wanted something done, in the testimony of Meridel Le Sueur, Myra Page, Dr. Annette Rubinstein, Elinor Ferry, Rose Chernin, Lillian Roberts, Eve Milton, and many other women activists of the period I've read and interviewed, one had merely to call in the Communist Party, and top-notch organizers, oftentimes women, would be dispatched to help the neighborhood men and women redress their grievances. It was a time, to paraphrase Trotsky, when the masses felt they could intervene in their own destiny.

It may seem ironic that while women and writers were frequently activists, the movement as a whole was not to consider their special needs as women or writers until the onset of the present generation. At the same time one must consider that the kind of theoretical discourse engaged in by today's feminist movement would have seemed idle and suspect to the women I have interviewed who were active in the period.

In point of fact, the very idea that women might have needs different from those of men was counter to the governing mythos of Marxist-Leninist ideology. The cornerstone of Marxist theory is that labor is exploited in the abstract in its commodity form as human labor power. That women and minorities may be unequally treated by the capitalist is the result of the peculiarities of history, a history that will be overcome by all human commodities joining forces to expropriate the exploiters and to overturn, for the first time in history, the exploitation of human by human. To say that Marx, Engels, and Lenin started from the need to unify the working class in their capacity as deracinated, non-gendered exploited masses is not to say that they took no interest in the conditions of gender or race, however erratically. Primarily concerned with the need to unify the working class, Marxists were to place a major emphasis on matters of race if not gender discrimination even against the prejudices of the most skilled workers whom they courted. The argument was made that the workers cannot allow the capitalists to divide their ranks and pit the more privileged against the more oppressed. It was further thought that those discriminated against racially would be all the more ripe for revolutionary leadership, and thus first the Irish, and then the African-American movements were eagerly wooed. It generally did not seem to occur to the revolutionary leadership that women might be subject to a similar dynamic. At the same time, it must be clear to those who have read Marx, Engels, and Lenin on "The Woman Question" that these communist leaders saw no validity in the current discussion of whether women (and at this point I shall jettison the question of race as more productively discussed elsewhere) have natures that are essentially and inherently different from male nature and therefore require special treatment in the communist proposal.

Clearly, Marx and Engels and their disciple August Bebel saw this as a question to be investigated after the initiation of the new society. In the meantime, the task was to engage as many men and women workers as possible in the struggle for socialism. As for women of the working class, they would find their equality as do all commodities, by entering the process of production and distribution. Virtually no attention was paid by Marx and Engels to the relationship of reproduction to production, of the "family wage" system as the locus of the oppression of patriarchy. Nor did those questions engage Le Sueur, Olsen, and Herbst. The point that I will address, however, is that all three writers, each in her own way, were creating a vision of woman in an historical social context that suggests an individuated feminist view that takes the question beyond that of the merely experiential, bordering on the essential, a discussion only now in our own time finding an ear.

On the question of woman's "essence"--a question important to my discussion of Le Sueur, Olsen, and Herbst--as with the question of man's essence--Marxism is peculiarly contradictory. The first gesture is one of deferral: "human nature" will not reveal itself until the abolition of private property and exploitation. On the other hand, it is clear that Bebel in his writings and Lenin in his show that the leading Marxists considered the normative position to be masculine and considered the feminine to be the deviant one (socially misgenerated) that must be made to align to the masculine in a position defined as equality. To explain what he means, Bebel writes:

> With woman . . . education, so far as at all attended to in a higher degree, is mainly aimed at the intensification of her feelings, at formality and polite culture--music, belles-letters, art, poetry--all of which only screw her nervous sensitiveness and phantasy up to a higher pitch. . . . The object must not be to develop still further the sentimental and imaginative side of woman, which would only tend to heighten her natural inclination to nervousness. . . . It would be of greatest benefit to both sexes if, in lieu of a superfluity of sentiment, that often becomes positively uncanny, woman possessed a good share of sharpened wit and power for exact reasoning; if in lieu of excessive nervous excitation and timidity, she possessed firmness of character and physical courage; in lieu of conventional, literary refinement, in so far as she at all has any, she had a knowledge of the world, of men and of the powers of Nature. (114).

One is reminded of the words of Henry Higgins: "Why can't a woman be more like a man?"

Contradicting this assumption is the position on self and society to be extracted from Marx's famous discourse on the fetishistic character of money.[4] In this passage the key observation is that under capitalism material relations between people become manifest as social relations between things. Once again we are in the situation that the essence of selfhood cannot be determined under capitalism. In point of fact if we consider masculinity to be more importantly shaped by the process of commodity production and exchange than is feminine identity, then feminine identity, existing as it does in an ancillary position to the process of production, is closer to the norm of "true human essence" than is masculine. Or, as the French feminists seem to be asking, "Why can't men be more like women?"

Although this point did not begin to be made until the advent of the recent feminist movement, the contradiction manifested itself within the socialist and communist movement which was a generative experience for the three writers I am investigating.

One of the ways the inherent gender contradiction made itself apparent in the lives of these three women was in their experiences as writers. It must be remembered that the options available to the socially conscious woman writer in the twenties and thirties were minimal. While there was an active women's reform movement, it was primarily concerned with finding ways to alter the existing system in order to alleviate women's economic inequality. Then there was the outright bourgeois women's marketplace consisting of journals and magazines promoting domesticity as a way of promoting domestic products merchandised by men to women consumers.

The socialist and communist movements were unique in recent history in offering both women and writers access to social forces in upheaval and to the opportunity to include discussions of those forces in their daily work. Most importantly, these movements offered avenues of publication to such writers for socially conscious work, avenues that might well not have been otherwise available to them.

To be sure, the question was not so simple. The point has been made in hindsight that the proletarian policy of the Communist Party enforced a rigorous masculinization. This position is problematical. The CP in the thirties both considered the needs of working women and provided forums for discussion among workingmen's wives. The fact that theoretical aspects of women's existence were not often attended to may well have been due to the fact that women as well as men placed the future of the whole race--which seemed at that moment in peril--higher on their agenda than items of isolated group concern.

Nonetheless, the Communist Party was undeniably a bureaucratically maintained organization and that bureaucracy, changing little over the years, was made up predominantly of males with an occasional non-quarrelsome woman. The reasons for this are multifarious, and, considering that they did not much affect Le Sueur, Olsen, and Herbst in their capacity as women writers, may be beside the point. To develop the points that are relevant, however, and give the matter its best expression, let me quote from the German Communist leader Clara Zetkin's discussion with Lenin on "The Woman Question." Lenin initiates the discussion with Zetkin by positing the need for a highly politicized woman's movement in the International Communist organization. Lenin asks Zetkin how she is getting along with her project to support this mission, but before she can make her report, Lenin intercedes:

> The record of your sins, Clara, is even worse. I have been told that at the evenings arranged for reading and discussion with working women, sex and marriage problems come first. They are said to be

the main objects of interest in your political instruction and educational work. I could not believe my ears when I heard . . . . I mistrust those who are always absorbed in the sex problems, the way an Indian saint is absorbed in the contemplation of his navel. . . . It springs from the desire to justify one's own abnormal or excessive sex life before bourgeois morality and to plead for tolerance towards oneself. This veiled respect for bourgeois morality is as repugnant to me as rooting about in all that bears on sex. No matter how rebellious and revolutionary it may be made to appear, it is in the final analysis thoroughly bourgeois. Intellectuals and others like them are particularly keen on this. There is no room for it in the Party, among the class-conscious, fighting proletariat. (Zetkin, "Lenin on the Woman Question" 101)

Two points are worth noting in regard to this passage. Lenin's essential puritanism, which he goes on to express more vividly in relation to the youth question, is a function of the jettisoning of the concern for the private sphere and privileging of the public. This is a question of primary importance to the current generation of Marxists and I will examine that issue at greater length in my discussions of whether there is indeed a uniquely feminine nature or whether there is at least a feminine sense of what creates consciousness and how that consciousness, if it does exist, affects social change. In this way I will be examining the relation of essentialism to historicism in the work of Le Sueur, Olsen, and Herbst. At this point I note the degree to which Lenin replaces personal prejudice for social process. While the onset of dictatorship in the Soviet Union was arguably occasioned by the demise of the power of the Soviets (workers councils) and Stalin's accession, the writings Marxist leaders addressed to their movements (those of Marx himself included) are fraught with dictatorial discourse. For women this meant that the last answer any Marxist was likely to give to Freud's upstart question, What do women want? would be, Why don't we let women decide for themselves what they want?

The problem of writers and artists in the movement of social change is perhaps more difficult than is that of women. It may be questionable to determine whether women were trivialized or subordinated in the communist movement, aside from their conspicuous absence in the top leadership. If the desirable proletarian was to *New Masses* writer Mike Gold a he-man roustabout decidedly masculine, the proletarian novels of women such as Clara Weatherwax, Grace Lumpkin and Mary Heaton Vorse were extolled, promoted and awarded prizes. If proletarianization did not necessarily mean the denigration of women--and there is much evidence to suggest that the issue is at least open to question--the issue of proletarianization wreaked havoc with the milieu of writers and intellectuals the Communist Party hoped to attract.

It must be remembered that in the twenties and thirties alliance with the working class was not for the radical movement the abstract issue it had been for Marx and Engels. The theory, as it relates to artists and intellectuals, was that it was the mission of the proletariat to overturn the capitalist class and establish socialism and the function of the intellectuals to ally themselves to the proletariat in an ancillary rather than leadership position. The function of literature was to be removed from the pure aesthetic and handed over to the service of raising the consciousness and self-consciousness of the working class. Writers and artists, then, were to take their cue (if not their orders) from the vanguard of the working class, the Communist Party.

To understand why this did not initially trouble Le Sueur and Olsen and for a time Herbst, one must look at two factors. One was the invitation, the desire, to become a significant player in a drama greater than any century had ever seen--the force that would overturn human exploitation once and for all was on the move in strikes, farm uprisings and unemployed marches all across America. Events in the Soviet Union, Spain, Cuba, seemed to proffer hope for a world socialist order within the lifetimes of those then writing. The excitement of the prospect is palpable in nearly all the work of the time, nowhere so evident as in the pages of *The New Masses* and *Partisan Review*, for which all three women wrote.

Secondly, key to the development of free literary expression within this proletarian context was Alexander Trachtenberg, whom some called the "cultural commissar" of the Communist Party. Trachtenberg, with international cultural connections that went directly to the Kremlin, was able through personal charisma to mediate the super-Bolshevik, perhaps overmasculinized, proletarian dictates to include overtures to such independently minded intellectuals as James T. Farrell, Nelson Algren, Jack Conroy, Muriel Rukeyser, Pablo Neruda, Andre Breton, Philip Rahv, William Phillips, and Josephine Herbst. Many of these were to balk at his efforts to subordinate intellectuals to the needs of proletarians. Meridel Le Sueur was to continue as a special protege of Trachtenberg's--he "nurtured her lyricism" she says despite or because of its femininity--and he no doubt was instrumental in providing the circumstances that made it possible for Tillie Olsen to initiate her career as well.

If, as I suggest, there was something inherently subversive of the

Marxist doctrine in the feminist aspect of the historically conscious import of the work of Le Sueur, Olsen, and Herbst that aspect seemed to have missed the attention of Trachtenberg and the Communist Party leadership. Several factors undoubtedly came into play to protect these writers from public condemnation. One undoubtedly was that they were women and did not seem to warrant theoretical scrutiny. At the same time it was important that Le Sueur and Olsen decidedly and unswervingly aligned themselves with the working class at a time when proletarian writing was questioned on all sides outside and within the CPUSA itself. This stance, certainly genuinely held, no doubt earned for these two the protection and unfailing publishing facilities of the communist movement. Josephine Herbst, in a letter to latter-day compiler David Madden, has rejected the label "proletarian writer." It must be remembered that she set out to be a mainstream writer, never wanted to be ghettoized within the communist milieu, and was regarded as an important sympathizer to the communist cause rather than as a member expected to follow party discipline. Even at that, her relationship to the communist literary milieu was always uneasy. She was most highly regarded for her reportage and her trilogy, which set out consciously to imbue a feminist vision with historical/social consciousness. That, as I claim, is the lasting contribution of all three of these women writers, and therefore it is their divergence from as well as their convergence with the communist experience of the twenties and thirties that makes for the substance of my inquiry.

Notes

1. For a full discussion of this aspect of communist movement life, see Elsa Dixler's dissertation, "The Woman Question: Women and the CPUSA,1929-1940." Yale University, 1974.

2. Several good general discussions of this debate exist. They include Theodore Draper's *The Roots of American Communism*. New York: Viking. 1957.

3. Mary Inman's feminist case within the CPUSA in the 1930s is discussed in fuller detail in Robert Shaffer, "Women and the Communist Party, USA, 1939-1940, *Socialist Review* No. 45 (Vol. 9, No. 3) May-June 1979, 73-119 as well as in Susan Ware, *Holding Their Own: American Women in the 1930s*. Boston: Twayne. 1982.

4. This discussion occurs in Section 4, Chapter 1, of Volume I of *Capital: A Critique of Political Economy*. New York: Random House, 1906 edition. 81-96.

Chapter One

Marxism and the Feminine Utopia

In the February 1911, issue of *The Masses*, the tongue-in-cheek commentator Eugene Wood wrote an essay entitled "A Highbrow Essay on Woman," in which he took issue with a scholar who identified woman's economic role as one of consumption merely. Seeming to uphold the importance of woman's place in the economic system, Wood maintained that her function as reproducer of the labor force is her ultimate *raison d'etre*:

> No, folks and friends, not Consumption of Commodities, not Production of Commodities, but Reproduction of Labor-Power is the main-top, all else being but side-shows of the snidest sort. This, which truly is the whole shooting-match, is The Economic Function of Woman. (11)

This argument seems remarkable primarily for its date. Although the position anticipates a whole wide-ranging discussion in modern times of an economic interpretation of housework given Marxist definitions of expropriation of labor and the function of labor power and commodities under capitalism, it triggered no such discussion in its own time. When Mary Inman was to raise similar questions in the Communist movement of the thirties, she met with a cold response. The very lightness of Wood's tone seems to signal a gentlemanly bantering that in some ways denigrates the seriousness of the question even while it poses questions of woman's role and capabilities in terms more sophisticated even than those of the typical suffragist exponent.

"No," Wood repeats, "there is no Economic Function peculiar to Woman but the one. Whatever the Man is able for, she also is able for, and then some." (11). To make the point, the editors of *The Masses* have accompanied the piece with a cartoon drawing of a moustachioed man holding an infant and cooking a meal over a wood stove. The implication is clearly that reproduction of the labor force as woman's function is not to be understood in its merely gynecological terms but includes the full range of housewifely duties. That man should undertake such duties is laughable. The cartoon is self-consciously captioned, "In such a case what is the economic function of man?" The implication is clearly that the division of labor that militates that woman is in charge of the reproduction of labor-power derives from biological necessity.

The issue of woman's relationship to the economic system of commodity production and consumption, or as the question is known, the relationship of reproduction to production, does not figure significantly in my consideration of the work of Le Sueur, Olsen, and Herbst; however, the question of woman's relation to history and social structure does.

For my primary theoretical orientation on this question, I draw, not without reservation, on the work of Jean Bethke Elshtain as presented in her major book *Public Man, Private Woman: Women in Social and Political Thought.* The metaphysics of the binary opposition Elshtain uniquely proposes suggests that although politics and mainstream economic functioning have been the domains of men, and the home and the "private sphere" has been that of women, the drive should not be to liberate women from the private sphere nor to collapse the private sphere into the "public" but to reconstruct the private sphere--including child-rearing, nurturing, feeding and education--as the shared domain of families which would be given a special consideration of importance in a humane society.

Elshtain distinguishes herself from contemporary feminists--from liberals to Marxists--by championing precisely the aspects of domestic life that have been rejected by feminist theorists. Wary of the conflation of the public and private realms, she implicitly overthrows the notion of the superiority of the public, or male-dominated political and economic purview. As she says:

> To attain and affirm an ideal of family life as the locus of humanization is, contrary to certain unreflective radical orthodoxies, to put pressure upon social structures and arrangements, not to affirm them. For to the extent that the public world, with all its political, economic, bureaucratic force, invades and erodes the private sphere,

it, not the private world, should be the target of the social rebel and feminist critic. To promote a politics of displacement that further erodes the terms of the private sphere and all that stands between us and a coarse power of market-ridden definition of all of life, is to repress discourse on public, political issues even as one simultaneously takes the symptoms of its destructive effects as the "good news" that radical change is just around the corner. (333)

Elshtain's thesis is important to my consideration of Le Sueur, Olsen, and Herbst because I find an identification of the private sphere as the primary locus of social action and a further linking of that sphere with the dominant voice of women to be the unifying factor in the works of all three writers. Other women writers wrote in the thirties, and others wrote of social issues and of the importance of women's roles in the working out of those themes, but what seems to be unique to the works of Le Sueur, Olsen, and Herbst, what makes them continue to resonate for a new generation, is that their sense of the primacy of the private realm within a social context speaks of a vision that is simultaneously linked to a particular time and suprahistorical.

To be sure, there are flaws in Elshtain's argument, flaws that bear upon its applicability to the three writers I am examining and their times. The aspect of her discussion I want to pay some special attention to is that which deals with Marxism and Marxist-feminism.

To begin with, although Elshtain does not devote much space to a consideration of the nature of housework in terms of the matrix of the commodity-production system--the paradigm into which we can fit the argument of Eugene Wood which begins this chapter--it is clear that Elshtain regards that primary economic system as the domain of the "public" or masculine, a sterile domain against which she promotes the family or "reproductive" domain of the feminine. By Elshtain's logic, equating the feminine role with that of a cog in the commodity-production machine is reductive and even destructive of the private or feminine sphere.

I hasten to indicate that this is not a reactionary "woman's place is in the home" argument. The confusion may arise from Elshtain's title which identifies the public with man and the private with woman. Elshtain goes on to assure her readers that both sexes can and perhaps should have both aspects to their lives and that the system of economic dependency as a means of holding women within the family is debilitating and crippling--even destructive of the integrity of private or family life, although this does not lead her to take on Angela Davis's militant pseudo-Marxist rejection of separate public-supported paychecks for housewives.[1] Since that question does not arise explicitly in the work of the three women I am considering, I, too, will, temporarily at least, jettison it.

My quarrel with Elshtain lies in her interpretation of Marx's utopian prognosis, which leads her to dismiss Marxism as a tool useful for feminist analysis entirely. I find myself sympathetic to her primary attack on Marxism, that it does not take into consideration the individual variations and mutual discords of collectives of various human selves. Some of this criticism can, to a degree, be leveled against the work under consideration here, especially that of Meridel Le Sueur. At the same time that Elshtain, rightly, I think, questions the "withering away of the state" fantasy in the light of the inherent individuality of members of the human community, she interprets Marx's conflation of private and public under communism with the subsuming of the private into the public that occurred under Stalinism. To be sure, in its most sophisticated application, as a device of literary critique, this charge can accurately be leveled against many of the literary products of the dominant proletarian or socialist realism prescriptions of the period, including some by women. This would be indicated by a subordination of private and personal causal factors and relationships to considerations of the workings of external social forces. In its largest sense, this construct is surely the dominant mode of the socially committed literature of the thirties and, as I will indicate, played an important part in shaping the social awareness of the characters created by Le Sueur, Olsen, and Herbst as well.

What saves the exceptional writers of the socially conscious period from being merely creators of knee-jerk automata is precisely the consideration of the private realm that Elshtain champions as the domain of women. In the case of the three women writers I am considering, it undoubtedly *is* the domain of women, although it can be well argued that no good work of fiction can hope to present any domain, masculine or feminine, without some development of the interaction between the public and private realms.

Elshtain is just as critical of the slogan "the personal is political," that rallying cry of women's consciousness-raising groups across the left spectrum as the result of the disillusionment of young women with the male-dominated political movements of the sixties. She sees in this feminist gesture, as with the Marxist move in utopian sloganeering, a conflation of the personal and the political that will jeopardize ultimately the personal rather than the superstructure by re-signifying the personal in terms of the political. Having had the experience myself, I find I am somewhat convinced by Elshtain's argument. Thus I tend not to interpret the work of Le Sueur, Olsen, and Herbst in terms of modern consciousness-raising movements, as do such modern discussants as Constance Coiner[2].

At the same time that I accept Elshtain's quarrel with Marx over the conflation of the private into the public on the question of individuation and the need for political organization no matter the economic circumstances, I take a different stance in relation to the ultimate conflation of public and private human beings. The missing term in the Marxist equation as Elshtain presents it is the question of the ultimate withering away of the production of exchange-value and surplus-value according to the delineations in the major body of Marx's texts. The commodity, in Marx's vision, would disappear under communism, to be replaced by an item that was no longer bifurcated and entered into existence solely as use-value. That is to say, in the Marxist paradigm, the commodity itself replicates the social split between public and private. The public domain, far from being the Aristotelian or Platonic expression of citizenship that so many liberal theorists from Betty Friedan to Gloria Steinem seek to crash, turns out to be in the Marxist lexicon, under capitalism, a nursery for the tending and developing of exchange-value and the reconnoitering of surplus-value. In this sense I agree with Elshtain's privileging of the private domain, which she identifies with the domain of women. My only addendum would be to note that in Marx's structure this domain is that of the use-value aspect of production, and as such stands as the gateway in and of itself to the development of communism, itself a society based on the production and consumption of use-values rather than market-oriented commodities.

In the sense that Marx foresees communism as the society which will be organized around the production of use-values rather than exchange values, a society which will allow for the first time the full development of consciousness in all spheres, emanating from the rational organization of the production and consumption of the socially determined necessities of life for all, he postulates the end of the dichotomy between the social and the individual, the personal and the political, the private and the public. Not foreseeing the tyranny of the subordination of the private to the public in the name of communism under Stalinism, he did not attend in his own work to the task of delineating the difference between *integrating* the social and the individual and *subsuming* the individual within the structure of the social. As the difference between integration and subordination can be seen in the difference between dialectical development and social imposition, it seems possible to include it within the realm of Marxist discourse.

The production of use-values as the sole rationale of the social order suggests the triumph of reason through a new definition of the Marxist concept of "socially necessary" determinations of utility. This suggests that men and women can together determine rationally what they need to reproduce a humane existence both personal and political and how much time and intelligence they want to devote to developing such ends. This may be a utopian suggestion, but it seems to be what Marx intended in his stress upon the rationality of the new order and an end of the subordination of the human species to its animal needs and to its commodity form. In this way, more importantly than what is to my mind a rather hopeless and useless fantasy about the end of conflict and alienation, Marx suggests the integration of the personal with the political through the reorganization of society from the production of commodities to the production of use-values. Much work has been done, notably by Althusser and Habermas on the project of rethinking the fantasy of the stateless order. As this does not seem essential to my project, I will not take it up here.

What is in order, with regard to Le Sueur, Olsen, and Herbst is the project of integrating the personal with the political in Elshtain's terms in a way that does not depart from Marxist thinking. If we accept Elshtain's understanding of the private sphere as being female-dominated we can lay the basis for understanding the importance of the work of these three writers. As I will show, a tracing of history and social force through the private, feminine-dominated field is perhaps the primary contribution of these three writers. By locating their work in the private domain within the context of significant forces of social change they place a unique focus on the interaction of the private and the public, of women and men.

Further, all three, as I will show, place a special emphasis on the primacy of the use-value over the exchange-value, even in consideration of the usual Marxist or quasi-Marxist interpretation of the problem of the reproduction of the labor force. The use-value becomes, in the work of these three writers, more or less what Marx intended it to be, a harbinger of the utopian future when all work will be the production of use-values. Specifically, I draw the conclusion from this work that in modern terms, women's work is itself the harbinger of such a utopian future. Not only Elshtain but Nancy Chodorow[3] suggest that the caring and nurturing of a family and the passing down of family values to succeeding generations must be interpreted not only from the point of view of capital, which can only consider such activity in the frame of the production and consumption of commodities and the need of capital for the commodity labor. We must also see, Elshtain and Chodorow suggest, that such activity is the key to the development of a humane, rational society. In that way, woman's work, despite its unnecessarily burdensome nature, shares a component with art and literature and crafts production in that it creates use-values only secondarily for exchange and calls on especially human qualities of nurturance and artisanship.

If such a thesis were to be presented without a social context, it might be construed as a reactionary admonition to all women to "go thou and get thee with child." The advantage of considering such a proposition in the context of Le Sueur, Olsen, and Herbst is that we can place the use-value aspect of women's work in the context of a larger political and social canvas. It turns out that what this suggests is that when the continuity of women's existence informs a social and historical imperative the resultant is a vector directing to a utopianism more viable than any Marx envisioned. The important term is the utopian projects of both Ernst Bloch and Herbert Marcuse. Both Frankfurt Marxists suggest that an element of utopianism is necessary to set goals and projects that reach beyond the reductionist materialism of capitalism. Or, in the words of Delmore Schwartz: "In dreams begin responsibilities." By contemplating the society of women in its use-value aspect, the three writers I am examining implicitly pose the utopian question--is it not possible for all of humankind to engage in use-value production and eliminate the repressive structure imposed by the transformation of humanity into commodities and of human society into a matter of circulation of commodities for the dubious benefit of the few at the expense of the many? In short, the question implicit in these works is: is capitalism a fit activity for the human species?

I note that the Elshtain position is not a popular one. Elshtain has been linked with Betty Friedan's book of rethinking and with Germaine Greer under the label of "backlash feminism."[4] The charge is now prevalent and has been fundamental to the women's movement since its inception. It is based on the difference in the assumptions of whether women will take positions of "equality" with men or will find an "essentialist" domain that will continue the peculiar contributions of women in what Elshtain refers to as the "private sphere."

Part of the controversy arises, in my opinion, from a misreading of the Marxist position. Such modern Marxist-feminist theoreticians as Margaret Benston, Heidi Hartmann and Annette Kuhn have been reading Marx's interpretation of the value of the reproduction of labor power in capitalist rather than socialist terms. Marx himself engaged in considerable debate with the "bourgeois" economists, especially Adam Smith and Ricardo, devoting three volumes in what is known as volume four of *Capital* under the heading *Theories of Surplus Value* to this debate. It is easy to surmise from Marx's own emphasis on an understanding of how value in its commodity form circulates and is reproduced that Marx himself viewed the worker and the worker's family only in the context of their place in the system of commodity exchange. This has been the dominant assumption of the Marxist-feminist theoreticians, but is, in my reading, a most un-Marxist assumption. Although Marx devoted considerable attention to the place of the human entity within the capitalist system, it was not he but the bourgeois economists with whom he argued who reduced human values to mere market values. It was Adam Smith and Ricardo who raised the question of "non-productive" labor and its role in a market economy. Marx may have been wrong to answer these theoreticians of capitalism in their own terms and thereby mislead his followers into the path of justifying all economic activity in terms of its position in the capitalist mode of production. Nevertheless, it is clear from Marx's early writings that he did not view men and women as mere cogs in a machine, nor did he reckon their value or the value of their activity in terms of their usefulness in the capitalist mode of production. If he erred, it was on the side of utopianism. While his own project was to uncover the dynamic of the capitalist system, and to free modern thinking about that dynamic from the mythos of naturalism in which it was enshrouded, he did not see capitalism as the arbiter of human nature. Quite the contrary. Marx's own view, as Erich Fromm has indicated,[6] foresaw in perhaps not well-worked out utopian terms a time when men and women would be free from the definition of humanity as a merely commodity-producing force. While Marx and Engels presented no blueprints for how such a society would function, they were adamant on the proposition that, freed from economic constraint to respond to capitalist market conditions, the human race would be free as well to explore new means of developing personal and "fully human" relationships. This was never intended to be the crass functionalism the Soviet interpreters gave to this proposition nor even the utilitarianism of modern-day Marxist feminists. For modern Marxist-feminists, it seems to me, subvert the Marxist project by interpreting the feminine dilemma in precisely the utilitarian terms that bourgeois economy employed to define all human activity. By saying that woman is an adjunct of male commodity reproduction and determining her liberation on liberation from that relationship, modern-day Marxist-feminists overlook precisely the nurturing, romantic, and solidarity-inspired relationships that make for the persistence of the human spirit in spite of rather than because of the capitalist mode. Such a view of the persistence of the human spirit, evidenced in the especially human relationships between men and women, as well as between adults and children, and same-sex bondings outside the marketplace may well be what can reinvigorate the Marxist promise of a future based on humanity rather than on commodity. It is for that reason that I am attracted to Elshtain's position, of the primacy of the private, non-market domain--a position which I find more in keeping with Marx's utopian writings than in opposition to them. It is also a position which I find especially productive to bear in mind in the project of reading the works of Le Sueur, Olsen, and Herbst in the context of the Marxist literary movement in which they were paramount spokeswomen.

In her very attack on Marxism, Elshtain seems to present the most cogent case for a re-examination of Marxist guidelines to the question of women, writing, and the place of both in society. Aside from Elshtain's work, little has been done to explore women's domain in antithesis to the political domain. Much has been done to discuss women's exclusion from the political domain and to make attempts to redress wrongs in that sphere. It remains to be seen whether a liberatory, rather than limiting critique can be developed on the premise that the womanly domain of the personal has values which either complement or supersede the purely functional values of the masculine body politic.

This position is not precisely the same as the New Left feminist position that "the personal is political." Elshtain may be correct in assessing that move as just another gesture that resulted in subordinating the personal to the political or politicizing the personal and thereby subordinating the personal values important to women's lives.

At the same time, one does not want to submit to the charge of "backlashism." If we do not read women's political work as "equal" to men's and we do not subordinate women's concerns to those of men, we need not wind up in the camp of the "bourgeois" women's magazines who preach that women must stay in their traditional value-roles.

To read the work of Le Sueur, Olsen, and Herbst in this context is to place them in a cross-grid between the masculinization of the proletarian orientation of the time they were writing, as Paula Rabinowitz elucidates that context in her book *Labor & Desire,* and the personalization of life as it is described in Elshtain's thesis. I maintain that all three writers crossed this difficult passage from proletarianization to personalization in ways that are uniquely meaningful for a modern generation interested in the period.

Two elements made these writers especially interesting to the readers of their own time aside from a feminist perspective, or as Rabinowitz argues, in spite of their feminist framework. A prime factor determining the publishing viability of at least Le Sueur and Olsen was their abiding commitment to the working class. As I will show, this alignment with the working class was a component as great as, if not greater than, their feminism in determining their decision to write for the communist press. Herbst adds to this dimension a commitment to historicity, which, in Lukacs's terms made her palatable to a communist audience. In all three cases, as I will show, the prose joined gender and class in a unique way, not in opposition, but in conjunction. The triumph of the feminine, in what was admittedly an overly masculinized genre, is the triumph of the personal in all three authors. In this way, to follow Marx's own paradigm, the triumph of the personal presupposes the time in the future when all production will be use-value production, the reproduction of the species will be the prime reponsibility of the species, and what is now undervalued as women's nurturing and concern for humane values will be extended to the society as a whole without subsuming one sex or the other into imposed roles.

It is my hope that a study of these three women writers, prime in a uniquely political way within personal domains, will further that project.

Notes

1. See Angela Davis's critique of Italian communist housewives' demand for compensation for household work in *Women, Race & Class*, New York: Vintage. 1983. Davis's argument is the fundamental Marxist-Leninist-Trotskyist point that women will only be liberated when they work alongside men at the site of production. Since housework is not commodity-production, in this view, compensation for it would be counterproductive. There is no evidence in Davis's text as to whether the Italian CP came to the defense of the housewives.

2. See Constance Coiner, "'Pessimism of the Mind, Optimism of the Will': Literature of Resistance," Ph.D. thesis, UCLA, 1987, and Coiner, "Literature of Resistance: The Intersection of Feminism and the Communist Left in Meridel Le Sueur and Tillie Olsen," in *Left Politics and the Literary Profession,* ed. Lennard J. Davis and Bella Mirabella (New York: Columbia

UP, 1990), 162-85.

3. See Chodorow, Nancy. *The Reproduction of Mothering: Psychoanalysis and the Sociology of Gender.* Berkeley: Univ. of California Press. 1978.

4. See Stacey, Judith. "Are Feminists Afraid to Leave Home? The Challenge of Conservative Pro-family Feminism." In Juliet Mitchell and Ann Oakley, eds. *What Is Feminism?* Oxford: Basil Blackwell. 1986.

Chapter Two

Delineating a Marxist Critique

The task of delineating a Marxist critique applicable to the women writers of the radical period involves the integration of two separate tasks. One is the need to understand the precepts of literary theory that were officially prescribed in the milieu in which such writers worked. This task involves such far-ranging investigations as the literary criticism standard in the *New Masses* and *The Daily Worker* and the major works of Granville Hicks and Joseph Freeman, themselves important thirties communist critics, and Mike Gold's almost single-handed attempt to define the desired proletarian literature in decidedly masculine terms. At the same time, while Gold may have been romantically idealizing the masculine ideal in the proletariat, there was among top CP leaders a theoretical premise on which the necessity for proletarian literature was based, emanating from Marx and Engels themselves and elucidated by Lenin and Stalin. I leave Trotsky out of consideration because, although he made important contributions to the question of the relationship of literature to revolution, he was, by the time the most important work I am considering was produced, not a significant actor in the Communist milieu. His work, in an ancillary way, influenced James T. Farrell, to be sure, and through him Josephine Herbst, and was no doubt a contributing factor to their ultimate split from the organized Communist left. Nonetheless, the ones deciding what was printed in the Communist press and how mainstream books were treated in that press were primarily Hicks, Freeman, Gold, and Trachtenberg, and a few others. It is therefore necessary to follow the logic of their ideology, if such a logic can be found, to understand the pressures on the three women I am considering and how they responded to those pressures.

At the same time, one must be aware that a rich discussion has emerged in the post-Stalinist era among Marxist theoreticians. Prime among such discussants have been Georg Lukacs, emerging from the Frankfurt School, and more recently, Raymond Williams, Terry Eagleton and Fredric Jameson. To be sure, Trotsky enters in as a germinal influence. If one were to approach the authors in question merely as historical artifacts, it might not be necessary to impose on their work the conclusions of this new group of theoreticians. It is because I consider that the work of Le Sueur, Olsen, and Herbst has special validity in the contemporary literary milieu that I undertake the task of reading across history and utilizing more modern insights to understand the particular dynamic of the period in which they did their most important work.

To the extent that both the critics of the left of the thirties and the more modern neo-Marxists shed light on the modern feminist undertaking, we must evaluate their work as well in the context of that of contemporary feminist literary theorists. In this chapter I can hope merely to indicate an approach to that task and to suggest how I will use this appproach in a closer reading of the texts of the three women that I have chosen to analyze.

In his book *Literature and Revolution*[1], Jurgen Ruhle indicates the transmogrification of theoretical overview into party dictate with regard to the development of a communist position on the question of literature and its social function.

The most famous statement of Marx's with regard to art and ideology is that in *The German Ideology*[2]. Here Marx indicates his fundamental argument:

> The ideas of the ruling class are in every epoch the ruling ideas, i.e. the class which is the ruling *material* force of society, is at the same time its ruling *intellectual* force. The class which has the means of material production at its disposal, has control at the same time over the means of mental production, so that thereby, generally speaking, the ideas of those who lack the means of mental production are subject to it. (64)

As Ruhle points out, Engels modified this statement of direct interdependence of art to economics to the more rounded point of view that too seldom held sway among post-Stalin-era communist literary commissars. As Ruhle quotes Engels:

The economic situation is the basis, but the various components of the superstructure--political forms of the class struggle and its results, to wit: constitutions established by the victorious class after a successful battle, etc., juridical forms, even the reflexes of all these actual battles in the brains of the participants, political, juristic, philosophical theories, religious views and their further development into systems of dogmas--also exercise their influence upon the course of the historical struggles and in many cases preponderate their *form*[3].

This statement, which Ruhle claims to be the more representative of Marx's and Engels's argument, leads to the modern Marxist view of ideology and art that they exist as individual expression of the class struggle, writ small. That is to say, every individual in capitalist society, every artist, functions as a cell within a unit. Just as each cell in an organism contains within it the genetic material necessary to re-create the entire body, so each individual contains within his or her psyche the entire social gestalt. The class struggle works on all of us in individuated ways and there is no way to contemplate a "pure" work of unattenuated working class or even capitalist class ideology.

In their utopian vision of the development of art Marx and Engels put forth a strategy for the fostering of artistic creativity that was to find no place in the Soviet or American Communist doctrine:

We have further shown that private property can be abolished only on condition of an all-round development of individuals, because the existing character of intercourse and productive forces is an all-round one, and only individuals that are developing in an all-round fashion can appropriate them, i.e. can turn them into free manifestations of their lives. (*The German Ideology* 117)

As for the "uniqueness" of artistic talent upon which so much aesthetic elitism rests, Marx and Engels proposed:

The exclusive concentration of artistic talent in particular individuals, and its suppression in the broad mass which is bound up with this, is a consequence of division of labour. If, even in certain social conditions, everyone was an excellent painter, that would not at all exclude the possibility of each of them being also an original painter, so that here too the difference between 'human' and 'unique' labour amounts to sheer nonsense. . . . In a communist society there are no painters but at most people who engage in painting among other activities. (*The German Ideology* 109).

To be generous, it might be assumed that it was to correct the "concentration of artistic talent in particular individuals, and its suppression in the broad mass" that the idea of proletarian art was born in the Communist movement, especially in the United States. In fact, as Walter Rideout has pointed out[4], there was a long tradition of working class fiction in America extending back to the middle of the nineteenth-century. Such figures as Jack London, Upton Sinclair, Claude McKay, Floyd Dell and Crystal Eastman and Charlotte Perkins Gilman crossed the borderline between the American working class tradition affiliated loosely with the Socialist Party and the more deterministically hard-lined preachings of the American Communist Party. A pivotal figure in this transition was Michael Gold, but he himself could not have promoted party-dominated art (primarily masculinized) without the approval of the top Communist leaders and, in turn, the Soviets themselves.

Once it was translated into conditions of social power and the struggle for social power, the dictates of socialist and proletarian realism became dangerous edicts. Ruhle cites Lenin on the question of artists even before the revolution:

> Lenin laid down the principle of partymindedness in 1905 in his canonical pamphlet *Party Organization and Party Literature*: "Down with non-partisan writers! Down with literary supermen! Literature must become *part* of the common cause of the proletariat a 'cog and a screw' of the single great Social-Democratic mechanism set in motion by the entire working class."[5]
>
> Thus by "partymindedness" Lenin did not mean merely partisanship, but subjugation to the party; it was, therefore, not a question of belief but of obedience. There is a school of thought to which Lukacs also subscribes which says that Lenin had in mind only reportage and publicistic writing, not belles lettres. But Lenin's own writings do not help to clarify matters. As far as I can see they merely prove that Lenin was unable to divorce art from politics. (132-133).

In point of fact, the discussions and calls for proletarian art in the pages of the *New Masses* appear innocent enough. Granville Hicks, in his 1935 edition of his major critical opus, *The Great Tradition: An Interpretation of American Literature Since the Civil War,* put forward a thesis, as Daniel Aaron discusses it, that attempts to link the proletarian realism of the Communist-dominated literary left with the tradition of American realism going back to Walt Whitman and the progressive era. While there may be some validity to this thesis, just as it is right to point out that for many, American communism was a natural outgrowth of the populist and socialist movements popular at the turn of the century, the argument is a bit disingenuous. In point of fact the difference between the American realist movement of the post-Civil War generation and the self-consciously proletarian products of the Communist-dominated era can be summed up in the words imperative and prescriptive.

A cursory reading of the fiction and poetry in *Appeal to Reason* and *The Masses* reveals the personally felt convictions and stylistic experimentation of individuated writers--writers such as Jack London, Upton Sinclair, Charlotte Perkins Gilman, and others that Hicks in his book does indeed cite. The turning point came with the Bolshevik Revolution of 1917 and the American response. No longer did writers of the left seek merely an avenue of expression; now they had a task. A crucial statement of this perspective is contained in Michael Gold's article in the *Liberator* of 1929, urging the young (male) writer to "Go Left." As Paula Rabinowitz points out, "Michael Gold declared that he had discovered a new path for American literature that would lead it 'toward proletarian art,' just as William Foster had declared that the CPUSA would proceed 'toward Soviet America.'" (21)

It should be pointed out that Gold himself played an exceptionally pointed and by no means clearly determinable role in the development of communist-oriented literature in the twenties and thirties. Principal organizer of the revitalized *New Masses,* Gold himself was more often would-be writer than actual literary figure, his *Jews Without Money* being the principal product of his output even in his own time. While he affected what would now be identified as a super-macho demeanor and was notably homophobic in his treatment of such "bourgeois" literary figures as Thornton Wilder, a close reading of his output suggests that his concern was more with class than with gender--and it is not entirely true that he identified the proletariat only with the masculine. Women who wrote from a working-class point of view such as Meridel Le Sueur, Mary Heaton Vorse, Agnes Smedley, Josephine Herbst, and many others one could name, were frequently featured and extolled in the pages of Gold's press.

The question of gender, as essential as it is to my study of the women writers of the period, is basically an aside in the problem of determining what caused the change from progressive working class expression to dictated proletarian imperative. A crucial document in this inquiry is the statement by Lenin, addressed to all artists who want to aid the revolution and translated and published in the *New Masses* in October of 1929. Here Lenin clearly indicates the necessity for writers to subordinate themselves to the need of the proletariat, and since he asserts that the Communist Party is the chief exponent of the proletariat, it follows that writers are to subordinate themselves to the Party. He says:

> Writers must belong to party organizations. Publishing houses and wholesalers, bookshops and reading rooms, libraries and other channels of distribution must be developed as party enterprises, subject to party control. . . . We must create a press free not only from police interference, but free of the capitalist competitive idea, free of bourgeois anarchistic individualism.[6]

As unpopular a figure as Mike Gold has become, especially among modern-day feminists commenting on the women's literature of the Communist era--and no doubt for good reason--I must come to his defense with reference to his implementation of Lenin's program. It is true he engaged in homophobic smearing of "bourgeois anarchistic individualism" as that was interpreted, but it is also true that part of his interpretation of the role of a proletarianized writer was to be a teacher and developer of heretofore disregarded working-class literary efforts. It was Gold who put forward in the pages of the *New Masses* the call for the organization of the John Reed Clubs, whose purposes included the nurturing of new working-class writing and the production and performance of dramatic works and festivals. While it may be seen from the evidence of the sampling of such work sent in to Gold's column that the results were not much more than one would expect from a good creative writing class in a modern-day inner-city community college, nonetheless the John Reed Clubs produced several noteworthy magazines, including the incipient *Partisan Review*, and were singularly responsible for bringing to light such talents as those of Richard Wright, Tillie (Lerner) Olsen and Meridel Le Sueur.

As I hope to investigate further the implications of this anti-bourgeois writing in the context of the modern-day concern for ideology as that has been promulgated in the post-Stalinist Marxist movement as part of the development of this book, after I have presented and discussed the work of the women I am investigating, let me turn at this point to the works in question, starting with the most representative writer of the generation, Meridel Le Sueur.

Several CP women I have interviewed, including some rather noteworthy ones, and including Le Sueur herself, have indicated that, for them, in the local clubs, engaged in organizing "mass" activities and developing as writers in that context, Party official dictates were frequently "filed and forgotten." I do not myself entirely believe that the sense of imperative and subordination to party dictate did not weigh upon most of the Communist-oriented writers of the period. At the same time, I would violate my own precepts about the indomitable nature of the human desire for "truly human" existence (in Marx's terms) if I did not suggest that nearly every writer I have read writing in the Communist press in the pre-war period expressed a certain measure of perhaps proletarian "anarchistic individualism." That is what makes the work of that period, at its best, continue to resonate with a new generation of readers today.

Notes

1. Ruhle, Jurgen, *Literature and Revolution: A Critical Study of the Writer and Communism in the Twentieth Century.* Trans. by Jean Steinberg. New York: Praeger. 1969.

2. Marx, Karl and Frederick Engels. *The German Ideology.* New York: International Publishers. 1970.

3. Ruhle quotes Karl Marx "Preface to 'A Contribution to the Critique of Political Economy.'" *Selected Works* (Moscow n.d.) p. 498. Quoted in Ruhle, p.131.

4. Rideout, Walter B. *The Radical Novel in the United States: Some Interrelations of Literature and Society 1900-1954.* New York: Columbia UP. 1992.

5. V.I. Lenin, "Party Organization and Party Literature," *Collected Works.* Moscow: Foreign Languages Publishing House. 1962, X, 45.

6. This passage appeared in an article entitled "Lenin on Working Class Literature," with a note of introduction signed by the editor, in the issue of October 1929 *New Masses* Vol. 5 (page number lost).

Chapter Three

The Political Writings of Meridel Le Sueur

I will begin my discussion of Meridel Le Sueur by giving primary consideration to three major areas, divided into several volumes. The first is the earliest collection of her stories, *Salute to Spring,* a compendium of Le Sueur's work that had appeared primarily in the Communist press. This was published in 1940 by International Publishers, the CPUSA's publishing branch, under the directorship of "cultural commissar" Alexander Trachtenberg. According to Le Sueur, it was Trachtenberg who was primarily responsible for bringing this collection together. As the focus of this collection is on stories of the radicalized proletariat (though not entirely) a study of this collection will allow us to assess Le Sueur's later individualistic viewpoint with regard to traditional and then-prevalent Marxist teachings about consciousness, gender, and their relation to the class struggle.

The second aspect of Le Sueur's work, her working class feminism, is the focal point both of her collection compiled by the Feminist Press in 1980 and of the recently recirculating novel written in the thirties, *The Girl,* published in 1978 by former *Daily World* editor John Crawford through his West End Press, which has in recent times consistently published Le Sueur's work. Both *Ripening,* the Feminist Press edition of Le Sueur's short pieces, primarily from the thirties, and *The Girl* indicate Le Sueur's concern with the place of women in the world at large and in the radical movement in particular. Both allow us to consider what she herself has discussed as her organicism, a view of women that relates birth-giving, nurturing and the life-giving forces of organic nature in a way that Le Sueur sees as anti-bourgeois and particularly feminine.

The final volume for consideration will be *Harvest Song,* the most recent collection of stories and short reportage and essays that Meridel Le Sueur herself compiled in her ninetieth year under the direction of her continuing publisher, John Crawford of West End Press. As this is Le Sueur's perhaps final collection, under her own supervision, we can assume that this, combined with several remarkable individual pieces she has recently published and, at last count, was continuing to write, is a significant part of the legacy with which she herself would want to introduce herself to younger generations of radicals and radical/feminists and general readers.   In that way it is important as a legacy of progressivism conveyed to the next generation, a torch passed on.

By starting with the earliest volume, *Salute to Spring,* we see Le Sueur at her most political.   Her lifetime abiding affiliation with the Communist Party becomes somewhat comprehensible. That these stories are "genuine" stories rather than "hack" work there can be no doubt. If Le Sueur followed a line, it was always, as we shall see, a line she herself genuinely adhered to.

By way of introduction, let me first say a few words about Le Sueur and how she came to write this particular work. Meridel Le Sueur was born in 1900 in Iowa and was raised by her mother and stepfather, Marian Wharton and Arthur Le Sueur, both professionals, occasional farmers, and full-time socialist activists. Both Meridel's mother and grandmother were active not only in the women's suffrage movement but in the temperance movement as well. Arthur Le Sueur, a noted lawyer who defended liberal and socialist causes, was for a time the socialist mayor of a small town in North Dakota during a period when a socialist mayor was not an uncommon sight, and Eugene V. Debs was pulling down nearly a million votes as the Socialist Party's presidential candidate. Meridel's mother, Marion Wharton, ran for office in her small midwestern town during the height of the McCarthy period in protest against the Korean War. She was then in her seventies.

The midwest, the farm, the neighboring farmers made a deep and lasting impression on Meridel, shaping what she came to see as an organic connection to a nurturing land. At the same time, both socialism and feminism were the gospels of her household. Meridel first turned to reading by picking up the *Socialist Call* and the *Appeal to Reason*, Socialist Party newspapers her family subscribed to. In my interview with her shortly after her ninetieth birthday, she confessed that she had only lasted one day in high school. She couldn't take it, she said. They were teaching rubbish. She left school soon after to return to the farm, to the land she loved and devoted her free time to reading all available books. (Her mother eventually sent her to a private "progressive" school.)

An important influence was the work of Walt Whitman and that work served to inspire her as she began to keep voluminous journals, writing every day, a practice which she was still continuing when I met her. The net catch of her journals is an enormous archive from which I have made selections, with her permission. I will discuss them as they relate to the development of her work. Another important influence was D.H. Lawrence, who, she said, blew a breath of fresh air into what had been, from a sexual standpoint, a cloistered midwestern puritanism. The effect of these two writers on her work will be an important aspect of my discussion. For reasons she has not explained in detail, she joined the then- incipient Communist Party in 1924 and began to write for its press.

The stance generally taken by modern-day feminist commentators-- from Coiner, to Hedges, to Pratt and Rabinowitz--is that the main import of Le Sueur's work was its opposition, either conscious or unconscious, to Communist Party dictate. The standard argument suggests that since the CPUSA interpreted the proletariat as a masculine domain, Le Sueur's attempt to resignify the masculine in feminine or feminist terms amounted to conscious or unconscious resistance to party policy.

The fallacy of this position is that it overlooks the degree to which proletarian concerns were of deeply felt interest to Le Sueur herself. It is clear from her WPA-financed study of her home terrain, *North Star Country*, as well as the stories in *Salute to Spring* and *Harvest Song*, that Le Sueur herself did not make the binary opposition between feminist and proletarian. Indeed, in Elshtain's terms, we see in Le Sueur's work an identification of women and the working class in that both operate excluded from the "public" domain of economic and political power. Le Sueur writes of both as the "oppressed," the "under classes."

It was from the proletariat, as well as from strong women, that she devised her theory of the liberating power of the return of the repressed. Making a translation that was virtually unique in the radical movement, which held no quarter for "masturbatory," "nihilistic," "bourgeois individualistic" psychoanalytic theory, Le Sueur constructed a view of the return of the repressed that would accommodate her Marxist communitarianism and would hopefully pave the way for a new world order under Communist leadership. That Le Sueur made this identification between the hidden or "private lives" that linked women and the working class can be seen in one of her early journal entries:

> I became a writer in Oklahoma when I was 8 because [nobody] told me anything and I couldn[']t find out much. Oklahoma was a new state and my friends were Indians, and a few pilgrims and I first felt the [tremendous] contradictions of american midwester[n] life and also its hidden potential strength and beauty. Later I lived in Kansas and on saturdays I would sit in the farmers market behind the water trough and [take] down the conversation of farmers which I handed in to my [English] teacher who called in my mother to know what kind of company I was keeping. In this frontier town the ladies had a Browning club and anything any speech or ribaldry not english was uncultural to them. So but then I thought the speech of cowmen farmers lost women sat[ur]day nigh[t] or any night speech more literature than anything I heard at school. (n.d.)

It is clear from the evidence that Le Sueur had forged her individual nexus before she joined the Communist Party. Women, for her, were strong women, sexual women, birth-giving women. They were allied with, in her work, not in opposition to, workers and men of the land. Together they composed an underclass, a manifestation of what Elshtain would call the "private" domain against the "public" men of power and authority. It is significant that Le Sueur devoted a good part of her adult life to collecting "found" speech from working class sources, both male and female, and extended her definition of "oppressed" voices to include many friends among American Indian tribes.

I personally feel too much is made among such modern feminist scholars of the period as Paula Rabinowitz, despite the enormous importance of her work, of the equation the CPUSA supposedly made between proletarian and masculine. The argument goes that since Marx predicted the revolution would be made by workers at the worksite, and statistics demonstrate that the majority of those worksite workers were male (though not all), the communist position necessarily privileged organization among male workers. This, according to the interviews I have held with men and women of the CP milieu, seems an oversimplification. Organizations prominent during the Depression years, such as unemployed councils, tenant organizations, consumers organizations, figured importantly on the CPUSA's agenda, as both my reporters and the pages of the CP press attest. Women, as both Elsa Dixler and my own informants report, figured prominently in many of these neighborhood and community activity groups. Furthermore, the CP press was as quick to report strikes among women at the workplace as it was to publicize male workers' actions, albeit sometimes with notes that may be interpreted as condescension. At issue is the indubitably overmasculinized super-prol prose of flamboyant testosterone-infected *New Masses* editor Mike Gold. While I cannot exonerate Mike Gold, I must point out that, though he certainly played an important role in the party press, he was not a central policy-maker; Trachtenberg was. At the same time, I note that while much "masculine" prose appeared in the *New Masses* so did Dorothy Day's account of birth-giving, several front page stories on the Gastonia Strike victim, Ella May Wiggins, and countless articles on working girls. It is easier to draw from this evidence that Le Sueur's equation between "strong" women and the proletariat was more rather than less in keeping with CP parameters than was the strictly one-sided equation between masculine and proletariat. Weakness and effeminacy were, to be sure, equated with "bourgeois" writing, but that equation is made in Le Sueur's writing as well, as we shall see.

To address the situation in *Salute to Spring* as a unified volume, I would like to start with one of the last stories in the book, "Farewell My Wife and Child and All My Friends," quoted from Nicolo Sacco's last words. The time of the story is Monday, August 22, 1927, the morning before the execution of Sacco and Vanzetti. (Josephine Herbst will treat of this same evening and event from the retrospective vision of her memoirs in *Starched Blue Sky of Spain*, to be discussed later.) The locale is mid-California and the characters are a radical worker-activist and his pregnant wife. Le Sueur herself had spent some time in California before that time, working as a stunt woman in the early motion pictures until the studio heads said she would have to have her nose fixed if she wanted to continue in film, and she refused. (Interview.) Jump cut into the story of how this young working class couple prepares to join their comrades to express their outrage at the Sacco-Vanzetti execution are the actual words of Sacco and Vanzetti themselves, addressing their families in a final explication of self and a final farewell.

The portrait gives us a good if not adequate picture of the young communist relationship in the mid-twenties. Ruth, the wife, is well aware of her pregnancy. She knows her husband, Tony, has been issued orders to make for the Imperial Valley and organize lettuce workers. He will do it, of course. He is a determined, stalwart, and loyal comrade. Yet, for Ruth, there is something forbidding: Before he wakes up,

> She reached over and touched lightly, with her fingertips, the warm
> breast of Tony beside her. He clenched his fist in his sleep and she
> saw the way his breast looked like a shield, divided by the black
> curls, setting sharp into the taut belly and the lean ribbons of thigh.
> His dark face on the pillow was like a dirk. (141)

This last line, indeed, the whole portrait of Tony, is rather shattering,
fierce, warrior-like. The passage establishes the relationship between the two--
one of the typical gender relationships little discussed in the CP by its major
female leadership figures such as Elizabeth Gurley Flynn and Dorothy Healey
and perhaps only vaguely suggested by the more traditional helpmate role of
Peggy Dennis and the women Elsa Dixler described in her dissertation.

What is not clear is whether Ruth is herself convinced of her own
commitment to the cause. She is fully aware that she is seven months'
pregnant. "She couldn't stand the deep pain in her breast." (142) She is as
noncommittal about the pregnancy as she is about the movement. She is well
aware of the bother of both:

> She got up and tiptoed to the kitchen and stacked up the dishes from
> the refreshments at the Sacco and Vanzetti meeting the night before.
> If there was no reprieve before nightfall, this would be the last
> meeting. She made sure there were six eggs for breakfast and then
> a fear came into her that the comrades had eaten all the bread last
> night, there were so many people to feed. No, there was that loaf she
> had hidden in the laundry bag. (142)

Ruth, then, is a dutiful movement leader's wife, her own commitment
not an issue. What seems a rather banal concern for household items becomes
an assertion of the private. In this sense Ruth comes to represent the
continuation of the human, more than Tony does for all his organizing. The
interspliced, rather pathetic, notes from both Sacco and Vanzetti set into the
story in italics seem to come from nowhere. The author has created rather a
sophisticated collage to indicate that Sacco's and Vanzetti's personal pathos
is very much present in the household, like a miasma in the air, and it is those
speeches as much as any particular action that bring about the shift in the
subsoil that amounts to a change in Ruth's attitude toward the movement and
toward her husband, perhaps as well to her unborn child. What we see from
the cut-in speeches of the two anarchists is that they are men much like Tony

with wives much like Ruth, bewildered by their actions, to whom they must explain the meaning of their actions. The speeches hang then like a cloud over Tony and Ruth--reminding them, there could we go next. Ruth thinks, "Sacco had a wife and a boy and a girl. His wife, too, had to wake up this morning. . . ."(144)

As the household stirs, Ruth expresses anxiety about what she will do on this infamous day, whether the two will indeed be executed. But in true feminine fashion, concern about the mundane kitchen affairs of breakfast preparations looms as large. She begs to be allowed to go to the demonstration in San Francisco. Tony answers: "No, I told you you can't go, honey. It's too near your time." (146)

Ruth answers by retreating to her own thoughts:

> She wanted to be near him, she didn't even want him to go in the other room to wake up Hal. She wished they had some bacon with the eggs. They wouldn't have had the eggs only some comrade from Sacramento brought them up and said they were for the new baby. (146)

A fellow roomer, Mrs. Clark, then mutters, "Honey, I can't remember very well if the sun was shining, or it was a gray day at Ludlow. . . ." (146)

This reference to the Ludlow Massacre in an early union situation in the Colorado mines links the participants, including Ruth and her unborn child, in a chain of radical event. Ludlow was an IWW situation; Sacco and Vanzetti were anarchists. We can assume that Tony and Ruth, at least Tony, are young Communists.

As the time of the execution draws nearer, so do Ruth's doubts about the unborn child. In the course of reassuring her, Mrs. Clark provides the author's rationale, as I see it, for including the baby in the first place. As a counterpoint to Sacco and Vanzetti, life will go on, radical life will go on, the tradition will continue; the torch will be passed.

A minor anti-feminist point is made in the page that indicates Mrs. Clark's reassurance of the importance of the child. Margo, a young prostitute in the boarding house is picking the cherries that figure for all the characters as the abundance of natural life, the promise of the utopian plenitude. Margo questions whether Sacco and Vanzetti will be killed. She says, "O the bastards . . . the law, the lousy bastards. . . . The bastards, that's the law for you, that's it, a shoemaker and a fish peddler, for Christ's sake. I seen it too. I know it. God knows, the lousy bastards. . . ." (152)

Mrs. Clark, mother superior to the radical commune, then says, "Is it men she's swearing at?. . . Does she think it's just men?" The implication clearly is that it's a class war they're engaged in, not a gender action. But Tony and the others' attitude toward Ruth and the baby does not make this argument entirely convincing. Mrs. Clark goes on to soothe Ruth: "You're sweet and the things you'll see, and the grand things the child will be seeing. Don't fret. Take a sleep, darling."

"That's it," Ruth says. "That's it, maybe we shouldn't be having a child. Maybe Tony will go away. Maybe no one should be having children nowadays what with everything happening like it's happening."

"Nonsense," says Mrs. Clark. "It's the very time for it, of such blood as yours and Tony's. It's the very time to be having children, knowing how it is to fight. . . ." (152) This may well be the touchstone scene from which vantage point to view not only this story but much of Le Sueur's later work.

The final tableau, a streetcorner in San Francisco, immediately following the interspliced speeches of the two doomed men: "The taking of our lives--lives of a good shoemaker and a poor fish peddler--all! That last moment belong to us . . . that agony is our triumph." (156)

Cut to Tony on a soapbox "saying in a clear voice, 'They can kill the bodies of Sacco and Vanzetti but they can't kill what they stand for--the working class. It is bound to live. As certainly as this system of things, this exploitation of man by man will remain there will always be this fight, today and always until . . .'"

The speech is drowned out by a group of children playing around "the black clot of listening men."

Ruth has ventured onto the scene in the company of Mrs. Clark. The image that follows will be a signal of her life with Tony now and in the future. "She edged up closer, skimming the edge of the pool of men. Mrs. Clark came with her. Tony saw her and raised his hand and she raised her hand and he smiled down on her. The chairman took out his watch. There was a silence as he held the tiny timepiece up. She couldn't think anything was happening now, were they killing two men in Massachusetts? She stood with her hand over the kicking child." (156)

That Ruth is not even as strong a figure as Dos Passos's Mary French in a similar scene in the *U.S.A.* trilogy will concern many feminists who judge the feminism of a writer by the role-model quality of her characters. Ruth is none the less similar to many young women characters in Le Sueur's political fiction. Elsa Dixler, in her dissertation on "Women in the Communist Party," points out that the wife-as-helpmate and auxiliary was more common in the CP than the figure of woman as leader and soap-box orator in her own right such as Elizabeth Gurley Flynn. The factor of child-bearing figures very large with Le Sueur. She herself had two children by Communist activist Yakov Rabin (Harry Rice), a Jewish communist organizer who agreed to marry her to give the children a birth certificate (though they grew up using Meridel's name). Although there is evidence from Le Sueur's journals that her relationship with Rabin figured importantly for her emotionally, and was not just a matter of convenience, Rabin was effectively out of the picture soon after the children were born. Le Sueur undertook their support on her own through writing, working at odd jobs, and giving writing lessons to "bourgeois" women.

Her main romantic attachment was to the difficult non-Communist artist Bob Brown, a relationship she is reluctant to discuss. Contributing as much to Brown's support as he to hers, Le Sueur definitely did not play the little woman, auxiliary comrade role herself, although the evidence of her journals suggests she may have subordinated herself to Brown's talent and placed her own needs, from time to time, in second place. Be that as it may, Le Sueur frequently wrote about such wives and women as Ruth in the Sacco-Vanzetti story, who subordinated their own interests to those of their mates. In this case, although not unusual in communist fiction of the period, the baby is a special mark of Le Sueur's particular point of view. The evidence of Dorothy Healey and Peggy Dennis, if not of Elsa Dixler, suggests that children among CP women (perhaps only CP leadership women) were discouraged. Against that tradition Le Sueur invoked the image of the new child almost as a substitute for the revolution itself. The proletarian story formula suggests that the piece end on a note of solidarity, comradeship and the envisioning of the socialist future. Here, Ruth, uncertain of her own place in the revolutionary scheme of things, overwhelmed by the power of Tony, places her hands on the kicking child as a substitute for the revolutionary vision. The child will bear the legacy of Ludlow and Sacco and Vanzetti and the lettuce workers. This will be Ruth's contribution.

This theme may strike some readers as regressive, and perhaps it is. I will discuss Le Sueur and the charge of "essentialism" in greater detail when I consider the Feminist Press collection and *The Girl*. For now, let me just note in Le Sueur's defense that considering the difficulties she faced having her own children and raising them on her own during the most sectarian of the Party's ultra-left Third Period, Le Sueur's special take on the upbeat revolutionary ending--the substitution of a child for the red flag waving and the singing of "The Internationale"--stands as an emblem of her unique individualism within the context of a highly conformist movement.

Although I have invoked the work of Jean Bethke Elshtain in the context of Le Sueur's work, it is clear that the insufficiencies in Elshtain's theory that Judith Stacey points out restrict its usefulness here. The point is, as Le Sueur herself might indicate, if one confines oneself to the private sphere, one has no input into the public. It takes a public action--in this case a streetcorner rally--to attempt to change that aspect of public policy that affects private life. The two are interconnected and cannot be viewed entirely separately each from the other. At the same time, to the degree that Elshtain's emphasis on the primacy of the private sphere is reflected in Ruth's concerns in this story and in Le Sueur's substitution of pregnancy for sloganeering as the hope to change the world, the feminine here is once again aligned with the working class as the "outsiders" who offer hope for change in the public sphere that may yet well up from the private.

To say this is to extend the range of the public and private dichotomy beyond the scope perhaps Elshtain suggests. By redefining the public as the realm of political and economic power and the private as the domain of all those excluded from that power we begin to draw the lines of demarcation more closely in keeping with the terms of Marxist definitions of class struggle. If this is not satisfactory to a strict feminist interpretation, it has the advantage of allowing to the private sector access to an agency of social change that will overturn the fundamental dichotomy of oppression. In Le Sueur's case, the private sector is decidedly feminized. She redraws the standard proletarian conversion story that typically features a working-class male won over to a strike action and from there to commitment to the general movement by placing in center stage a young woman, frequently with child. The conversion of this young woman is frequently more a matter of subtle psychodynamic than raw action and her conversion carries the extra importance of the impact it will have on the genealogical continuum through the child. Nonetheless the point of interest is still the fateful step (as in "I Was Marching") at which point the character steps out of the private realm and into the public to enter the scene of the political/economic nexus as a force for change to a new alignment of the relationship of forces between public and private.

The Sacco-Vanzetti story, with its central nexus of a child-nurturing woman, her movement-oriented mate and a denouement occurring at a public rally to which they both go, serves as the basis for two more stories in the *Salute to Spring* edition, the title story and "Tonight Is Part of the Struggle." The archetypal problem in miniature for all three of these stories is contained in the 1934 essay on the Minneapolis Strike, "I Was Marching." Here we have the author's own voice elaborating on the problem of consciousness, attempting to capture the moment of shift of consciousness, from a volunteer helping out to committed action. This is the theme as well of the other three stories I have mentioned. While this is not an unusual theme in the "proletarian" fiction practiced among the Communist writers of the period, Le Sueur handles the problem of consciousness, primarily a woman's consciousness with exceptional deftness.

In the essay "I Was Marching" Le Sueur identifies herself as a middle-class observer who is "likely to think about a thing, and the happening will be the size of a pin point and the words around the happening very large, distorting it queerly. . . . When you are in the event, you are likely to have a distinctly individualistic attitude, to be only partly there, and to care more for the happening afterwards than when it is happening. That is why it is hard for a person like myself and others to be in a strike." (*Ripening* 158). This, then, constitutes one of Le Sueur's most concerted efforts to depict the act of belonging, of shedding what she will later call her "maggotty individualism." From the vantage point of a middle-class intellectual, accustomed as a woman to confining herself to the making of coffee for the "real" participants, Le Sueur finally asks if she can join the marching demonstrators. Welcomed, she becomes aware of her body. Struggling vainly to get out of her intellectuality, she ends by immersing her prose in the act of joining the demonstration as a living, breathing organic body.

Similarly, for the characters in the three stories I have mentioned, the act of fusion, of organic union, for one with a farmers meeting where she gets the courage to speak up, for another at a Communist workers rally where she brings her baby, and for Ruth at the Sacco-Vanzetti streetcorner rally, brings them out of the isolated bickering of their marriages, out of their dissatisfaction with their lots as women, and allows them to find communion with a larger entity, the fused proletarian/feminist mass.

This aspect of Le Sueur's transcendent vision is transmuted in other work in more directly feminist terms as a distinctly womanist organicism. I, frankly, find it more convincing here than I do in some of the more myth-derived work of the Feminist Press edition. At least in these stories, if the conversion through mass meeting is not entirely convincing, the problem of individualism is, and Le Sueur is never heavy-handed or didactic about her moments of transcendence.

Granville Hicks made a point in the first weekly edition of the *New Masses* of including intellectuals who wanted to come over to the side of the working class as subjects for consideration and publication. This was in 1935, and Hicks's statement can be seen as a foreshadowing of the switch from the class-based unity of the early period of the CPUSA to the popular-front period calling for a multi-class opposition to fascism. Le Sueur has several crossing-class-lines stories, in all three collections. The most notable one in *Salute to Spring* is "The Hungry Intellectual." Here the haunting figure of a down-and-out advertising copywriter caught by the Depression into conditions of poverty is placed into counterpoint to the working-class milieu of the movement protagonists and the ubiquitous fecundity of the first-person narrator, a working-class movement worker's wife and the mother of two. More than that, there is once again an opposition between the title figure and the family who take him in, betraying perhaps a solipsistic anxiety on the part of the writer herself. The narrator is definitely confident about her fecundity, in a way that goes beyond Elsa Dixler's evidence from the women's pages of CP publications of the party's commitment to motherhood as the appropriate role for women. When the down-and-out intellectual expresses the social-democratic point of view that, "Change must come from the intellect with understanding and non-violence, non-resistance," the narrator, proud mother of two, replies, not with Marxist dogma, but with Le Sueur's own feminine organicism: "I don't think it's that way, . . . From having a baby I think it's different. It comes out violently." (55)

Much as the working class characters are sympathetic to the hungry intellectual, he remains stubbornly enigmatically aloof. He refuses to join the movement men when they march on the State Capitol demanding bread and milk for their children (a demand which Dixler treats as strictly, from the CP's point of view, a women's issue.) He is disdainful of a pregnant woman who joins the movement workers on a picnic on the banks of the Mississippi. The narrator refers to the woman's burgeoning belly as "beautiful." The reaction of the intellectual, Hobbs, is to say, "A woman shouldn't come out like that." The narrator grows angry. Hobbs's further self-defining speech at the picnic is to utter the warning, "The masses won't stand together. . . . They won't stick together. . . . You can't make a silk purse out of a sow's ear." (60). Finally, at the end of the story, Hobbs leaves, saying he is getting a boat, he writes in a farewell note, to have an adventure on the river.

If Le Sueur is speaking in some respects through her female narrator, her attitude is curiously, helplessly sympathetic to the intellectual. She feeds him and invites him to partake of family activities even though he is avowedly not a revolutionary. She tries to understand him. By contrast her husband Karl is rather brutish and boorishly unsympathetic. In the end it is Hobbs who turns his back on those who would help him because it is he who is incapable of "standing together." It is a mark of Le Sueur's writing, the mark that may give it lasting value, that she is sympathetic to nearly all her characters, exploring the reasons for their consciousness and their situations in compassionate terms, even when she does not agree with them. This mark differentiates Le Sueur's fiction from the more typical CP-dominated literature.

As to the feminist issue, Le Sueur does not hesitate to promote nurturing and fecundity. However, in this story, not only is it women's role; it is men's as well. The picket line the narrator's husband organizes is for "milk and bread for our children." The fact that Hobbs cannot join in, stays on the sidelines, helping the narrator with her two little girls, could suggest the "effeminacy" of the intellectual that frequently appeared as a motif in the Communist press. It seems likely, moreover, that Le Sueur intended to show the conflict, perhaps unconscious, within the character himself. He wants to belong to the working-class radical family; he just does not want to undertake radical commitment or action. Clearly, Le Sueur is posing the Marxist-Leninist dilemma in relation to the intellectual. Hobbs's belly should tell him to join the workers; his previous consciousness gives him a dimension that supersedes economic determinism--he imagines himself still to be an advertising executive. He sees himself as the silk purse that the others cannot be made into.

The final parting message left by Hobbs when he has disappeared is a note stuck with a butcher knife to the table: "Am going down the river. Save all my letters. Will write my adventures and we will publish them. It will be the only record of the trip. Save all." (63) But, as the narrator notes, "We never heard of him again."

The "say" in this story, the every utterance of the intellectual, is a lie, a fantasy, including most especially the final note, which may cover a suicide. The "true" speech is that of the workers, of Karl and the narrator. Further, the outlook expressed in the story represents a Marxist view of the relationship between mind and belly: namely in the case of the hungry working class, consciousness will express the economic condition of the class. One is left with a concern, however, for the writer herself. If all story-telling is fantasy intellectualizing, what is she doing here? The only answer to that from the context of this story might be that Hobbs was in advertising; the story he would avowedly tell at the end is a romp for the purposes of entertainment. There is, Le Sueur might well suggest, a difference between writing to express a point of view or a thematic expression and writing to turn a buck.

If we take the two stories together, we might view the fantasies of the hungry intellectual in counterpoint to the jump-cut testimony of Sacco and Vanzetti. The conclusion is not that words are of no use. The words of the two anarchists have moved the protagonists to action. The words of the hungry intellectual, on the other hand lead to dismay and possible suicide. If we take up the Elshtain dilemma and pose the question where is the agency for social change if one relegates all energy to the private domain and treats the public with suspicion and disdain, we see a pattern that Le Sueur is presenting of the unification of the woman and the working class. The kicking of the baby in Ruth's womb, the nurturing of the two little girls, these become in Le Sueur's lexicon, agencies of social change, especially, importantly, when united with the rather dubious champions of the communist cause the husbands represent.

The third story I will look at from the *Salute to Spring* collection is also a crossing-class-lines story, this time examining the consciousness and emotions of a working-class girl who has married "up" at her parents' insistence. This story reveals the important influence the work of D.H. Lawrence had on Le Sueur's fiction as well as her "organic" view of the proletariat. On consideration, it seems curiously anti-Marxist but perhaps not out of line with some contemporary feminist thought.

In her journal c. 1920, the young pre-CP Meridel wrote:

I almost went flying off with a whirl of autumn gypsies, who never read books or comb their hair or speak to relatives and I almost did. Why didn't I? They were so brown, so tumbled, so happy all with red berries in their hair.

The theme of the sexual potency of the underclass, both peasantry and working class, works as a leitmotif in the story "No Wine in His Cart." In point of fact, the "effeminacy" or impotence of her husband's manner is the young captive wife's chief complaint. In the story Le Sueur examines closely the consciousness of a young wife from the working class who has married the factory owner.

The denouement of the story is a shift in consciousness in the young wife herself, not a matter of events in the "public" world. Stella, the young wife, realizes that although her husband collects relics of European peasant culture, he himself has no affinity with the robust peasant stock they derive from. The wine cart sits in the garden, where Stella loves to visit it. Her husband Arnold's father brought it back from Sicily. Stella loves to contemplate the bodies of the robust workmen painted on its sides. They lead her to memories of her father, himself a rough workman. The sexuality of the cart is doubly potent. The cart stands as an emblem of Arnold's collectible peasantry, of which Stella herself is one. For Stella, she sees her father's sexuality in contrast to her husband:

> Why had Arnold's body been distasteful to her, his white hands, his white narrow chest, self-conscious, without use. Making money never made use of a man's body, the smell of it got on him. Perhaps a woman never really could love the body of a money-making man. (30)

Whereas Mary McCarthy and Tess Slesinger treat the theme of the bored upper-class wife with ironic disdain, clearly Le Sueur's heart goes out to her character. By making Stella a child of the working class who has been forced to make "a' good match," Le Sueur forges a fundamental link in the situation of the upper-class wife (whom CP presses mocked as well) and the working class.

A strike is in progress in Arnold's factory. Stella identifies completely with the strikers. Arnold announces his intention to organize the "decent citizens" of the town to forcibly break the strike. Stella rebels: "That's dastardly, where's all your fine words, the right of free speech and assemblage, the right to unionize, what's come of it all? You know they don't get much. I know how much they get. I've known it all my life. . . ."

> "He looked at her coldly, 'You'd better go to your room,' he said.
> "'I won't,' she cried.
> "Then he said in a low cutting voice, 'You'd be in that mess yourself if I hadn't married you.''(35)

The identification of women with the working class is most pronounced in Stella's consciousness when Arnold reports on the progress of the strike:

> He told about a street full of men standing side by side like a tide and cracking the bulls over the head, driving them back, stopping trucking completely and the women stood side by side with them. . . .
> "'The women?' Stella cried. 'Were there women there?' Her poor mother had wanted her to marry above her.
> 'Many women,' Arnold reports. 'Even young girls. It was disgusting.'"

Stella reflects on her own condition. "'The women were there,' she said, 'then they weren't marrying above them anymore.'"

Clearly, the place Stella most wants to be is on the picket line. As it is, the best she can do is come to realize herself that she wishes Arnold would die in the melee tomorrow.

In her early 1935 journal, as Le Sueur begins to reflect more than she has previously on middle-class life as opposed to proletariat life and on the meaning of communism, at least to her, Le Sueur speculates:

> Communism of course wouldn't give people a subtle knowing just as such--but relieved again of the money value who can tell what would happen, surely it is a good adventure . . . a marvelous trying at least . . . Remov[e] the money value which is mixed up with mentality mechanization, and the ideal all have produced each other and you could begin to know what 'human nature is. . . . No one thinks that communism is a panacea . . . I think they are more realistic about it than prophets have ever been--but to be rid of the horrible smell of money--to be rid of the stench of the seller and the buyer--Oh Lord . . .' (1935)

This exhortation would seem to indicate that Le Sueur sees communism as beneficial for all people--of equal value to the seller as to the buyer. The "stench of money" pervades all we do.

That women can be especially insidious when affected by the "vapor" can be seen in three of Le Sueur's stories from the *Harvest Song* collection.

"Fudge," (1933), "The Trap" (1933) and the story "The Girl," from *Salute to Spring* all have in common the examination of the consciousnesses of effete middle-class women confronted with male sexuality. In "Fudge" and "The Girl," each protagonist is a spinster, dried-up and barren, confronted either in the past or in an ongoing narrative with the vital sexuality of a proletarian male. In "The Trap" the protagonist is the wife of a doctor. A counterpoint is established between his nest-building for small birds and her refusal of pregnancy, her living in the past, and her exhibition of the small delicacies of the middle-class tea-drinker.

In all three stories the locus of vitality and fecundity is, as with Lawrence and Whitman, with the male figures, especially the proletarian ones. The women, representing middle class women and perhaps intellectual women, are unsympathetic, barren, and sexless.

If we take these two groups of stories together--the political stories set among the working class and the equally class delimiting stories set among the middle class, we can see that in both cases Le Sueur is engaging in a project that is more in keeping with the editorial policy of the *New Masses* than opposed to it. In both cases she is attempting to situate the locus of social change in an agent and to investigate the relationship of the written word to the consciousness of that agent and the relationship of consciousness to action. It may be arguable whether my reading of Elshtain works to shed light on Le Sueur's identification of an amalgam of sexually productive women and virile, sexually charged proletarian men as the necessary agent. It is my contention that Le Sueur sees both as excluded from the oppositional power of the ruling class, and therefore both as arising in unison from the realm of the private. In any event, it is clear that in her gender stance, Le Sueur distinguishes the mode or the idea of gender from the reality of sex. Fundamentally she accepts the CP male leaders' identification of the metaphors of masculinity with the proletariat, the metaphors of effeminacy with the bourgeoisie, and the metaphors of fecundity with "essentialist" women. Sexuality, in true Lawrentian terms, one might say, rather than, or along with, economics, is the decisive determinant.

That this serves merely as an introduction to Le Sueur's work, not an exhaustion of the question either of sexuality or of language, of agency of social change or of determinants relevant to that change, will be seen more clearly in the next chapter.

Chapter Four

Meridel Le Sueur's Feminist Sentence

When I interviewed Meridel Le Sueur in the summer of 1991, she was reading Julia Kristeva. We did not talk much about what Le Sueur thought of Kristeva, but it was clear that Le Sueur felt that through the French feminists she had found an updated means of connecting her work with the theorizing of a new generation.

Le Sueur's feminist--or perhaps I should say "womanist"--work seems remarkable to us now in part for its prescience, in part for its resistance to the dictates of a proletarian writing deliberately gendered as male. Let me deal with one factor at a time.

In the first place to define Le Sueur's feminist--or womanist--prose, we must first attempt to delineate it. Since 1927 Le Sueur has been composing what she terms her "organic" vision out of several elements. For one thing, in search of a sentence suited to woman's experience, she opposes linearity, attempting a mellifluousness of prosaic development that stops short of stream of consciousness. It stops short deliberately: Le Sueur's organicism connects to a vision of the mass or the archetype, deliberately eschewing the individualism prevalent in her generation. To the negativism of the "lost generation" she counterposes a positive outlook that relies on a trust in the beneficence of such natural forces as a nurturing land and the fecundity of woman's reproductive cycle.

When one remembers that the women writing in her generation who received prominence, including Mary McCarthy, Dorothy Parker, Josephine Herbst, and Martha Gellhorn, deliberately set out to compose "like men" in a sentence pared down and packed with irony, Le Sueur's personal determination to craft a sentence based not only on woman's experience but on woman's essence seems remarkably prescient and even courageous.

To be sure, Le Sueur had precursors. Olive Schreiner's *Story of an African Farm* (1883) was an early influence, and the midwest woman writer Zona Gale took her under her wing, as did, for a time, Emma Goldman. These were all self-consciously feminist women. As Elaine Showalter has pointed out:

> In its early stages feminist analysis was naive and incoherent, but by the turn of the century Mona Caird, Elizabeth Robins, and Olive Schreiner were producing cogent theories of women's relationship to work and production, to class structure, and to marriage and the family. (*Literature* 32)

As Showalter elaborates, the writings of these feminist writers, like that of D.H. Lawrence, were "mystically and totally polarized by sex." (33) The sexuality of Schreiner's character Lyndall is potent and palpable and undoubtedly made a strong impression on Le Sueur, who read it in the years when she was rebelliously shaping her own sexual destiny out of materials in opposition to the maternal line of puritanism and success-seeking that dominated her upbringing.

Also during those years, when she was shaping her own writer's sensibility, Le Sueur fell under the influence of the successful novelist Zona Gale. Perhaps Gale's most remarkable novel was a semi-science-fictional approach to women's community, *Friendship Village* (1908). Set in a small Wisconsin town, this novel graphically portrays a community of women, which, although it has its pecking orders, is closely knit. The notable thing is that there are virtually no men. The women all relate to each other directly, primarily as homemakers for absent patriarchs, whose existence is reflected only in the names of the women. The high point of the novel comes when one of the poorer members, Calliope Marsh, throws a party in behalf of some orphan children, getting them together with doddering old women from the nursing home who might like a child to love. The whole village of women turns out to make toys and clothes for the children and serve cake and punch at the party. To be sure, there is a distinction between rich and poor, but, located exclusively in the "private sector," the novel is convincingly built around women's "chatter" and "trivial" doings.

The impression I get from Elaine Hedges and Linda Ray Pratt is that Le Sueur deliberately broke from Gale before joining the Communist Party. This may have been because Gale was not self-consciously working class. While her novel *Preface to a Life* (1926) explores an anti-commercialist sexuality in the person of a secondary woman figure, the focus is on a decidedly small-time capitalist and how he veers between this woman and a more conventional wife and family. Gale does aver in this novel that the choice of pursuing capital in this society forces one to turn away from love and sensuality. Nonetheless, this statement may not have been strong enough to hold Le Sueur to Gale's mentorship. Le Sueur was exploring right from the beginning, as I have indicated, a connection between the oppression of men in the working class and the oppression of the women they ostensibly supported. This was an equation she could more happily develop in the company of Emma Goldman and Alexander Berkman with whom she stayed in New York during her late teens while studying theater. Even so, Gale's concern with the positive aspects of women's communality was to reinforce Le Sueur's own positive feelings about women's lives at a time when she was inclined to turn much of her hostility on her own maternally dominated upbringing.

The one "lyrical" story included in the International Publishers edition *Salute to Spring* is "Corn Village," written in 1930, several times reprinted, and often seen as the archetype for what Le Sueur was to develop as her "organic" mode. Without linear beginning, middle, and end format, "Corn Village" is a memoir, a portrait, suggesting in circular sweeps the author's own ties to the land. The figures, immigrant farmers, the grandmother, the house, are more archetypal than individuated. Rather than a story, "Corn Village" is a lyrical meditation ending on a vaguely anti-capitalist note:

> I have come from you mysteriously wounded. I have waked from my adolescence to find a wound inflicted on the deep heart. And have seen it in others too, in disabled men and sour women made ugly by ambition, mortified in the flesh and wounded in love. (25)

This story, in a spiraling rather than linear prose, using the Whitmanesque apostrophic "you," whirls around in a lyrical spinning out of agrarianism, social consciousness, celebration of the return of the repressed, and an experimental unfolding of personal voice. It is the archetype on which other stories in the *Ripening* Feminist Press edition are based and as such allows us to make a transition in our discussion from Marxism to feminism.

This piece, too, was the first to arouse official CP opprobrium. As Linda Ray Pratt notes in her article "Woman Writer in the CP: The case of Meridel Le Sueur":

> Le Sueur has remarked on numerous occasions that the Party criticized her work for being too lyrical. . . . Hedges quotes her as saying that the Party criticized her work as being "undisciplined" and that the Party "tried to beat the lyrical and emotional out of women." (257)

That the party was even more vicious in its attack on James Joyce and Marcel Proust on similar grounds raises the question whether the party leadership actually made the lyrical/feminine equation or, in contradistinction to its own version of proletarian writing saw such lyricism as Le Sueur's as petty-bourgeois and decadent. It is clear that Le Sueur herself saw lyrical, non-linear writing as related to women's natural voice. In her interview with me in 1991 she castigated linear beginning-middle-end writing as "patriarchal and bourgeois." That she could make such a determination and still remain a loyal communist in a male-dominated organizational structure suggests the tenacity of her socialist vision within or without the construct of her organicist view.

To grasp the dimensions of Le Sueur's feminist/organicism, the source of the "lyricism" Alexander Trachtenberg grudgingly included in his edition, one must find explanations in bits and pieces. First, on non-linearity: in her interview with Neala Schleuning published in 1983, Le Sueur, then in her eighties, explained:

> I belong to the global age of plenitude! Where prose, poetry, everything must be about relatedness and expansion instead of contraction and alienation. Young people now have this. They really can expand and include, rather than exclude. We are moving into becoming related *to*, rather than alienated *from*. All dynamics comes from relationship, dialectics of change.
>
> Women can really express this because they're on the round, not on the linear. Getting into the global world means there's no longer the linear world--no time, no progress. You can only progress along a straight line. Our ecological problems are a result of being on a straight line. We imagine we'll never return, because a straight line

doesn't return (146-7).

Le Sueur's vision of the physicality of this counter-linear revolution explores a little more succinctly how she links up the circle image with a lyrical anti-intellectuality, with her communist vision:

Schleuning asks: The body. In our society today, it has a clinical connotation. The only time we talk about bodies with one another is when we discuss medical things. And touching! We are all so afraid to touch or be close to each other--especially between the sexes. Psychically and physically we deny the reality of the body.

Le Sueur: Yes, many people are this way, alienated from each other, alienated from their own bodies. Perhaps they need more than anything some colossal group belly to give them birth. . . .These people are unconnected and building up mental bulwarks. Never approaching the deep self, they cut off the channels to refreshment and recreation. Maybe they needed some birth more than their mother gave them--and it would have to be a physical birth. . . . no mental births.

Schleuning: You mean non-intellectual?

Le Sueur: Yes. Nothing they could *think* would make any difference at all--nothing they could *know*. A man who knows so much, who makes questionnaires and yet doesn't know the flesh of his wife cannot question her at all about what is in her. Unless a man can take a woman, apprehend her in this tender, living way, he kills her. It would be better not to have anything to do with sex until one can feel and bloom and flare out physically and tenderly towards another.
      We can't have dead people. They have to be struck to fire in the bodies of others, in struggle. This is the only fire that is left alive, under the ash. This passionate identity must be felt by all . . . and made by all. Not intellectually or merely commitment to a "cause," jumping from one cause to another, but in the body, in the passions, in the deepest identity, the true relationship. This is the true image rising out of the carnage. (148-9)

In some late entries (vol. 43) in Le Sueur's copious journals, she introduces the theme of oneness with the land into the system of the equation of roundness, woman, birth, nurturing, the liberation of the unconscious, and the future vision of community. As she says:

> To be human is precisely to be responsible, responsible a little for the destiny of mankind in the measure of his work.
>
> I believe [if] a writer stays within his time and region he will stay within himself and find himself communicating the deeper images of his time and his people. He must conceive of himself in relationship. [A]nything else will land him beached on alien and surrealist shores-- he must be related to all of his time place and people but keeping bringing up the deeper images, unknown the pressures of the deepest waters and undersea nightmares and realities of the submerged--and in our society much is unconscious and submerged while much that is called culture is merely advertised, expected, imposed.

"Corn Village," then, Le Sueur's first major lyrical piece allowed in the communist press, is perhaps her most deeply felt creation in this volume, and foreshadows the organicist concerns that appear in the Feminist Press stories. Some brief excerpts will indicate the tone Le Sueur establishes.

> What does an American think about the land, what dreams come from the sight of it, what painful dreaming? Are they only money dreams, power dreams? Is that why the land lies desolate like a loved woman who has been forgotten? Has she been misused through dreams of power and conquest? (11)
>
>   You look and look and you cannot see life anywhere apparent, only in bitterness, and spareness sold out for that neat, hygienic and sterile success that we all must have. (17)
>
>   The Puritans used the body like the land as a commodity, and the land and the body resent. [My grandmother] never took a bath except under her shift. Hearing her move about her room alone I always wondered what she was doing, so bodyless, with that acrid odor as if she had buried her body, murdered and buried it, and it gave off this secret odor revealing the place where it lay. (20)

If Le Sueur's most cherished mode, a lyricism which she identified with her femininity, was denigrated by the party leadership, if her view of the land of nature was in opposition to Engels's utilitarian materialism (as was, I maintain, Tillie Olsen's and Josephine Herbst's) how was she able to survive the twists and turns of party life over a full lifetime? The answer from her point of view may be complicated, as Linda Ray Pratt suggests. I have already indicated some essential reasons. From the Party's point of view, I conjecture that the reason was twofold. Although quixotic, Le Sueur was compliant. She honestly made effort after effort to curb her natural lyricism, down to putting out leaflets so she would be infused with party "style." (Pratt). Richard Wright and James T. Farrell--and Josephine Herbst--were to challenge the leadership's right to make essential decisions, even to lead. Le Sueur remained complacently in the often overlooked precincts of the Midwest, where she even became for a while state committeewoman. Just as important, Le Sueur remained fanatically loyal to her adopted proletarianism. At the 1935 American Writers Congress session in which Farrell, Philip Rahv, William Phillips and Herbst attacked the party for anti-intellectualism, Le Sueur spoke against the opposition, defending proletarian writing even more eloquently than could Browder or Foster, or Trachtenberg himself. In point of fact, in her 1935 journal, she placed herself to the left of Mike Gold and Joseph Freeman, who "have lost their contact with the back wards america. They are attached and possibly want to be to the advanced revolutionary worker. But do they convey anything. . . ." The sincerity of her commitment to the proletariat guaranteed Le Sueur the support--and publishing services--of the party leadership at a time when that proletarian policy was under attack.

It must be borne in mind, as the party leadership did bear in mind, that if Le Sueur had several idiosyncratic items on her personal agenda that did not correspond to the party's repertoire, the main brunt of her attack was against the enemies she had in common with the party--including "bourgeois" feminists and intellectuals, Lenin's repudiated "anarchistic individualists," and the whole capitalistic value system. Even her tendency to type-cast and archetype-cast her characters in accordance with class-struggle molds was not out of harmony with the party's priorities. I surmise that for all these reasons she was forgiven for being a woman.

It is nonetheless worth noting that the emphasis or overall impression one gets is quite different, depending on whether one reads only the communist press editions of Le Sueur's work or whether one sticks to the major revived source, the Feminist Press edition of *Ripening* edited by Elaine Hedges. While the Feminist Press edition remains an excellent introduction to Le Sueur's work, it tends to emphasize the more overtly feminist aspects of Le Sueur's writing and minimize the "anti-bourgeois" or movement-oriented aspects of her concerns.

  After a good sampling of Le Sueur's autobiographical writing in which she presents both her Midwest agrarian background and her politically progressive family heritage, *Ripening* presents a selection from Le Sueur's early work which is more feminist, or womanist, in its outlook than it is political.

  "Persephone" (1927) is an important formative work of Le Sueur's, standing as a story she was working on all through the twenties, when she felt the domination of her mother and grandmother to be a particularly excruciating oppression. Pratt indicates that the source of the falling out was that Marian Le Sueur wanted Meridel to do something remunerative and sustaining with her life, while Meridel placed her artistic endeavors in first priority. The oppression was more than that, of course. The young Meridel, discovering sexuality in D.H. Lawrence and in her own body, resisted the strangulating atmosphere of her mother's and grandmother's radical puritanism. Putting the two factors together, along with Meridel's faith in the regenerative and nurturing qualities of the land, it is not surprising to find that at the outset of her writing career, the young Meridel was most enamored of the mythology of Demeter and Persephone, the mother and daughter goddesses of the earth and fertility. In updating the story to a contemporary setting, Le Sueur expressed a wish-fulfilling mother-daughter closeness while at the same time developing the archetypal fertility nurturers she was to find central to the "organic" themes she would continue to employ for her whole writing life.

  The story, as indicated by the title, is a retelling of the Demeter/Persephone myth in modern dress. Demeter, of course, was the earth goddess responsible for the fertility of the crops. Her daughter Persephone was raped by Pluto, god of the underworld, and abducted to Hades where she became goddess of dead souls. Through a treaty with Zeus, Demeter won her back for two-thirds of the year. The other one-third, the time of the death of fecundity, Persephone was to spend with her husband Pluto in the underworld. This story's reliance upon ancient species mythology of the interplay between fecundity and mortality seems to collapse the time element in a way that is more postmodern than derivative of such orthodox Marxist historicists as Georg Lukacs. In true Jungian fashion, the myth-ethos exists within the consciousness of the author and the narrator as a species "trace." It is simultaneously of the past and of the present. Le Sueur's narrative strategy, the intertwined time sense which jumpcuts the narrator's account of a train trip accompanying the daughter figure with background narrative of the story of the mother, Freda, and the account of the rape of the daughter by the stockman

March, further accentuates the subversion of the historical march of time-before followed by time-after that Lukacs calls for. Also timeless is the essential duality of the story--the fecundity and fertility of the larger-than-life mother figure Freda who does more to contribute to than to prevent the rape of her daughter by the traveling breeder. Freda contains an ages-old mystery of being:

> Probably because (the country people) were, in a manner of speaking, without a God, when in their dream, in a kind of blind ecstasy over the earth, within the heat, they attributed dimly to the figure of Freda, and with her the other two, an alliance and an intimacy with the virtue and the mystery, along with something sinister, of the natural things of which their lives were made. (80)

The mystery, the sinister force, not to sum it up, becomes, with the girl's abduction, the knowledge of mortality in all that that means, beyond even its definition by Pluto's land of the dead. The narrator says of the girl:

> She among us all had known that living was a kind of dying. When in these realms, she had refused to partake of our fruits and so become enamored, but had closed herself in the dream which is real and from which we die when we are born. (83)

Thus the train trip which encloses this narrative, revealing the double-edged aspect of mortality, the fertility which gives birth to death, which in turn produces life, becomes a timeless excursion into mortality in the midst of fecundity, and the hopeless travel from here to there, onward to an unknown destination, which is the journey we all must travel through life, takes on a cyclical dimension. If there is no telos, there is at least a purpose: life is its own validity. If this vision seems to mitigate against a more Lukacsian sense of progress, as Le Sueur has indicated, it is still not the nihilistic purposelessness that was the mark of the writers who were publishing at the time Le Sueur was undertaking this work.

What we see in this work and some of the other stories I will discuss is a feminism pegged more to an extolling of woman's benevolent "essence" than to a championing of woman's potentially productive place in society. If this story, with its archetypal approach to theme and character, exists outside society, it exists as well outside the "public/private" dichotomy we have been discussing. To be sure, Le Sueur is here depicting an agrarian economy which

most theorists agree conflated the public and private realms.   Even so, the
universe of the "Persephone" stories is decidedly gendered female. And the
mother Freda's virtues consist in assisting with births, breeding and bread-
making, elements in the private domain. It would certainly seem to be clear
from this story that Le Sueur is postulating an "essence," whether feminine or
generally human, that is not constructed, or in this case, much affected by,
external social contexts.

In "Annunciation" (1935), perhaps Le Sueur's most beautifully written
and most admired story, Le Sueur develops her sense of woman's essence
against the backdrop of publicly induced poverty and masculine life. The story,
dedicated to Le Sueur's older daughter, Rachel, who was born in 1928, is a
paean to pregnancy as well as to nature and to the writing which both inspire.
The narrator is in the last stages of pregnancy when she decides to write things
down "on little slips of paper." Since we are to assume Rachel is the child in
question, we note that the poverty of the couple in the story must not be so
much a matter of the Depression, which hasn't yet ensued, as an endemic
large-city crisis complicated by the choice of movement people to endure a
sort of *nouveau pauvre* state beyond what conditions require. In any event,
due to advancing pregnancy, the narrator can no longer work. She is in a
constant state of quarrelling with her husband, Karl, who keeps urging her to
"take something to get rid of it." The only one who wants this baby is the
narrator and her persistence is quiet, personal, and determined. In several
lovely, lyrical passages, the narrator identifies herself with an overhanging pear
tree: she is full and ripe and beautiful, much in the way of Zora Neale
Hurston's Janie in *Their Eyes Were Watching God*, written close to the same
time. The pear tree becomes a life-giving force, standing in its fecundity in
contradistinction to the thwarting force of Karl and the pervasive poverty. It
becomes, in Le Sueur's work, as in Hurston's, a projection of the female force,
the female essence. As in the other stories in this section, "Spring Song," "Our
Fathers," and "Wind," the tension that is created is not so much a matter of the
personal versus the political or the private versus the public as it is the natural
versus the social. It is only to the extent that Le Sueur genders the natural as
feminine that we can see the more modern oppositions. In "Annunciation" the
opposition is more clearly between the feminine natural essence and the
masculine societal context. True to her own writing philosophy, there is not
so much a beginning, middle, and end, as there is an expositional cycle. The
ending is much like the beginning, but in the intervening space the entire
conflict has been delimited. The last two paragraphs indicate Le Sueur's basic
counterposition:

I am writing on a piece of wrapping paper now. It is about ten o'clock. Karl didn't come home and I had no supper. I walked through the streets with their heavy, heavy trees bending over the walks and the lights shining from the houses and over the river the mist rising.

Before I came into this room I went out and saw the pear tree standing motionless, its leaves curled in the dark, its radiating body falling darkly, like a stream far below the earth. (132)

The question of Le Sueur's concept of "essence" is nowhere so beautifully delineated as in the novella "The Horse," written in the 1930s and 1940s and published recently in the West End Press edition *I Hear Men Talking*. In the story, a young woman, Mercedes, is on the verge of being married off, reluctanctly, to a successful engineer whom she does not love. She and her typically bourgeois mother and grandmother take a trip to the father's horse ranch. There, Mercedes witnesses the birth of a colt and persuades her father to let her stay while she is ostensibly making up her mind about the marriage. In a Lawrentian move, Le Sueur has Mercedes identify completely with the young horse (named simply Horse). He is the physical embodiment of her essence, and she overtly protests at having him groomed as a commodity--either race horse or breeder. She breaks him in herself to the extent that when the trainer, one of Le Sueur's erotically cruel proletarian men, Mallard, attempts to ride Horse, the young animal rears up and kills him. This act frees Mercedes to get closer to her suitor and he is the one who finally kills Horse when the animal turns on Mercedes.

What is clear is that the bond between Mercedes and the horse is a sensual, essential bond. What defeats them are the powers that force them to conform to a commodity world. Le Sueur herself says of her mission in this story:

Mercedes rebels against her role as a commodity, being sold off for profit by her family. I could see how important her rebellion might have been. But her relation to the Horse is hardly a solution. It is the flight from the dangerous reality of her family and class into this phantasmagorical unreality that kills her. She is driven to fear, terror, and death, killed by the contradictions. . . .The shadow of the oppressor is over and in us. (240)

In considering the question of "essence" for a moment, I note it is more often the Anglo-American feminists than the Marxists who rely upon a mechanistically deterministic view of human nature. Nancy Chodorow, in the article from her thesis included in the anthology edited by Zillah Eisenstein, delimits the circumstances under which contemporary capitalist society determines the home, the home life, and the product of that environment, the child. The underlying presumption of the argument is that the sole determinant is the societal factor and the man, woman, and child are completely malleable. At the same time, the French feminists, Irigaray, Cixous, and Kristeva, with whom Le Sueur is more in keeping, would seem to suggest that woman's sexuality is a quality essential to her being. Le Sueur comprises her sense of human or feminine "essence" out of both points of view. Clearly in a story such as "The Horse" essential nature can be so resistant to commodification that it will even seek death.

Similarly, in a different vein, in the story from the *Salute to Spring* collection, "The Dead in Steel," the grandmother relinquishes her tax money which she has been saving to keep title to a house she and her family built, but which she can no longer inhabit. She gives that tax money--her essence, in a manner of speaking--to the cause of a steel strike in behalf of her son who was killed in a similar strike. With this action, she resists the commodifying act of having her life's blood transformed into meat for the mortgage.

To locate human "essence" in female characters in Le Sueur's work is not always so easy a task. As Hedges points out in her notes, it is frequently the male proletarian figure who is the locus of eroticism in the story--Bac in "I Hear Men Talking," Mallard in "The Horse," the young hitchhiker in the story "The Girl," and Butch in the novel *The Girl.* Standing in contradistinction to the sumptuous feast of feminine essentialism evinced in the earlier stories, especially "Annunciation," the masculine sexuality in these stories is predatory, evanescent, passionate and at the same time self-centered. Women are straitlaced young girls, schoolteachers, neophytes. They are drawn like moths to light, and yet resist--or in some cases yield. Their only avenue of expressing their own sexuality is through that of the other--the male. As we shall see in discussing *The Girl,* this can lead back to the eroticism of pregnancy and the sumptuous company of women.

For the moment, I turn my focus on the story "Our Fathers," the excerpt from "I Hear Men Talking" which appears in *The Girl.* This story raises questions of historicity and the interaction between essential factors and factors of historical/social context in the shaping of the consciousness of a young girl that allow us to explore the question of essentialism more fully.

In consideration of "Our Fathers," three factors stand out that we have not already discussed in relation to Le Sueur's work but that bring into focus several important considerations. As Le Sueur herself has explained, she was from a very early age fond of collecting "found" speech, the poetry of working-class dialect spoken by mill hands, railroad workers, farmers, and the like. Le Sueur would make notes containing this "found poetry." She was to go on to build whole stories around these snippets continuing into her odysseys by bus across America during the McCarthy period when blacklisting made it difficult for her to support herself. Some of this "found" material she was to record on cassette and some take down to use in a variety of ways. One early way she made use of this found proletarian prose was in "I Hear Men Talking" and the shortened version, "Our Fathers."

In the story "Our Fathers," which starts with the death of the father whom the girl Penelope has hardly known, the exchanges between working men come to stand for the locus of masculinity that stands in contradistinction to the feminine world of Penelope's mother Mona and her rigid puritanical grandmother (much like Le Sueur's own), who is referred to as Gee. Curiously, the counterposition of the masculine dialect to the feminine sophistication tends to undercut Le Sueur's own stated reasons for her interest in working class dialect in the first place. In the opening scene, after Penelope has viewed the corpse, she overhears workmen talking, presumably with some connection to the death of her father:

> "We've got a right to be living, see?"
> "Sure, you said it."
> "It was us made this country, it was us, the bones of my people lie along Hill's railroad and there was a man dead for every tie laid and that's a fact. . . ."
> "That's a fact all right . . . that sure is true."
> "My fathers dug in the earth, threw up bridges, that's what they done, tilled the god-damned soil, that's what, froze on the prairies. We've been buckers and loggers and made nothing while those that held the land became wheat, lumber, coal kings and us lean to the guts."
> "Yes sir, that's right, Tim. . . ."
> "Stand together. Be together. I got brothers to my fathers who joined up with John Brown, stormed Harpers Ferry. Lie now face up in Kansas dirt but they done something, showed us something. . . ." (114)

In Le Sueur's lexicon this is an element of "lost" history that she has made it her mission to recapture. Specifically, in the workings of the story, it serves to identify the dead father as among these men.

The important consideration, however, is the fact of the effect of these events on the impressionable young Penelope. Much as I might suggest that the narrator is the measure of effect in "Persephone," I here propose to show the significance of the utilization of Penelope as measure of effect in this work. This is to employ the concept of feminine historicity as that term has been coined by Ellen Messer-Davidow. [1] The point is that whereas traditional, and most significantly, traditional Marxist historicity presupposes the importance of events in their own right as focal points on a grid of historical development that can be graphed in ascending fluxes, Le Sueur is here postulating a historicity that is peculiarly feminine in three dimensions. First, is what is known as the child as measure of effect. The fact that the child is a girl-child and potential heir to the place of her mother and grandmother in the chain of history is of special importance. In other words, the dialogue we have just seen among the men outside the funeral home exists not only in its own sake as contextually important "found" speech but is important because Penelope is passing by, hearing it, and letting it shape her vision of her father, her environs, and her place within that context. To the extent that Penelope will have a public role to play as an aide in the farmers' mortgage action later in the main novella this eavesdropping on the masculine private domain will contribute to the shaping of Penelope's public existence.

The second area of feminine historicity also depends upon Penelope as measure of effect. This is in the context of her relationship to her mother and grandmother as they reluctantly add to the telling of the story of the father's death. The story of Penelope's heritage is told to her by her grandmother in two ways. First is the recounting itself. Second is the two sets of artifacts: the box of photographs which Gee takes out to show her and the box of quilt pieces, both peculiarly feminine repositories of family and species heritage, both of which will eventually devolve upon Penelope.

Going through the photographs with her acerbic grandmother, in an attempt to fix her own identity, Penelope picks up the photograph of an ancestor:

> "Who is she?" Penelope asked, for in her hand was a picture of a grim woman rising out of her full skirts and sleeves and curving bodice, a baby who was to die curved in her arm, looking at nothing, its bald head between embryo and death. The woman did not look at the child, let it fall loosely in her lap as if it could not have been the

Christ child, or any child worth much, giving it over to death more than to life, and looking out, her mouth grimly set, blighted already by the spirit's longing. . . .

The grandmother explains: "Some woman of the men folks probably--some wench." (119)

In other words, women have been collecting these "found" snippets of generational history for eons. The photographs, like the quilting scraps, like her relationships with her mother and grandmother themselves and the bits of dialogue of working men who may have been men like her father will become the stuff of history, a history carried and savored from womb to womb rather than from spear to gun.

At the end of the story, the event of the day takes shape in Penelope's consciousness:

She heard the great steps of her grandmother in the next room and knew she was buried in the long accretion of her desires and had been thrown forward deep into the flesh by a cursing, striding race, thrust from powerful women and men who were in fear and terror of a flight they had to take across unknown prairies having no myth and no speech, upon which they were forced into endless action without word, fighting, brawling, conceiving without song. (121).

In the act of passing this legacy on to her own children, Penelope will participate in a movement of history that, like a silent current, can be stronger than the upheavals marked on the seismographs of masculine and historical materialist record.

When we look at historicity in those terms, we see that Marxism is in agreement with the fundamental patriarchal determination of what is important among world events. Marxism's contribution is to offer an explanation for the reasons for upheavals and shifts in terms of determinations of means of production. Marxism postulates materialism whereas Enlightenment liberalism and the patriarchal tradition offer idealism and great men's ideas as explanation. The locus of action, however, is the same, the "public" world of production, war, senates, and upheaval. Many authors, including Marx himself, have pointed out that this phallocentric site of historical action misses the force of those not in power--peasants and workers in Marx's notation. A gynocentric history would pay attention to women and children as the scene of history. While this is most in keeping with psychoanalytic theory, including that which valorizes the mother as instrumental to the development of the all-important son, the true reverberation can be felt in the absurdist school of Beckett and to an extent Joyce. While theirs are not feminist texts, they do suggest that the large patriarchal sweep of events is deceptive. Given the existentialist concept of mortality, those events will become like Ozymandias, buried under the sands of time. What is consistent to the species, what lasts, is its DNA, and although we do not know exactly how that is affected by historical-social-psychological circumstance, we do know that it is carried through the reproductive line.

Joan Kelly-Gadol in "The Social Relations of the Sexes: Methodological Implications of Women's History," discusses women's history:

> But women's history also opens up the other half of history, viewing women as agents and the family as a productive and social force. The most novel and exciting task of the study of the social relation of the sexes is still before us: to appreciate how we are all, women and men, initially humanized, turned into social creatures by the work of that domestic order to which women have been primarily attached. Its character and the structure of its relations order our consciousness, and it is through this consciousness that we first view and construe our world. To understand the historical impact of women, family, and the relation of the sexes upon society serves a less evident political end, but perhaps a more strictly feminist one. For if the historical conception of civilization can be shown to include the psychosocial functions of the family, then with that understanding we can insist that any reconstruction of society along just lines incorporate reconstruction of the family--all kinds of collective and private families, and all of them functioning, not as property relations, but as personal relations among freely associating people. (24-25).

To some degree this argument serves to reduce the charge of essentialism against Le Sueur. Her sense of nurturing, more metaphor than commandment, is a socially constructed sense. To understand how Le Sueur reconciles the gynocentric historicism of a story like "Our Fathers" with the phallocentrism of Marxist historical materialism as expressed in literary terms most eloquently by Lukacs, one needs to make a bridge by means of the communality and social responsibility that Marx envisioned for his utopia and the communist movement proposed to replace the angst of the individual it condemned in the modernist and postmodernist literary tradition.

While a gynocentric historicity such as I have been discussing can be seen in the work of Tillie Olsen and Josephine Herbst in some ways similar to that of Meridel Le Sueur, in none of the work I am discussing is the social awareness of the need for communality as important as it is in Le Sueur's work. That Le Sueur felt strongly the need to identify with a communality she saw located within the Communist Party can be seen in her 1935 answer to Horace Gregory in *New Masses*, called "The Fetish of Being Outside." In this piece Le Sueur castigates "bourgeois individualism" in the person of the alienated poet. The communist ideal is for Le Sueur the answer to this anxiety.

> For myself I do not feel any subtle equivocation between the individual and the new disciplined groups of the Communist party. I do not care for the bourgeois 'individual' that I am. I never have cared for it. I want to be integrated in a new and different way as an individual and this I feel can come only from a communal participation which reverses the feeling of a bourgeois writer. What will happen to him will not be special and precious, but will be the communal beginning, what happens at all. I can no longer live without communal sensibility. I can no longer breathe in this maggoty individualism of a merchant society. I have never been able to breathe in it. That is why I hope to "belong" to a communal society, to be a cellular part of that and able to grow and function with others in a living whole. (*Harvest Song* 200).

That Le Sueur did not come easily to this position can be seen in an entry in her 1934 journal:

> The creativeness of my mind cannot go away now. I must hold to it. I feel a terror and then I feel the social love and the new social growth of that tip of green that is like a love . . . people welcoming that from the frustrated evil loves. . . . These scenes are a blunting of sensibility in me this violence is not an expression it is something sickening, something you cannot stand. . . .

This sense of communality and connectedness not only with the feminine reproductive experience but with the life cycle, the proletariat, and the communist utopia come together in especially profound ways in Le Sueur's most accomplished novel, *The Girl*. In this work, written during the thirties but not published until 1978, the culminating vision shifts the emphasis from the primarily socially connected stories of *Salute to Spring* or the predominantly feminist writings of *Ripening*. The triple strands of reproductive nurturance and organic fecundity in a kind of present-tense imperative, combined with a gynocentric historicity that I have discussed, that connected to a social vision of communality is plaited together in what has come to be recognized as a major literary contribution to the heritage of the Depression era.

The Girl does not offer an especially prime example of Le Sueur's feminist lyricism, but is nonetheless an important stylistic tour de force. Taken from the "found" speech of the narratives of her students and members of the collective she conducted at the Workers Alliance in St. Paul during the Depression, the narrative is a patchwork Le Sueur has stitched together from bits of individuals' stories that turns out to work remarkably well. In its own way *The Girl* is a conversion novel of the type favored under the heading proletarian realism--but with a not-so-popular feminist twist. In the narrative, rich with authentic discourse, if not with lyrical circularity, we follow the unnamed Girl from one pole or realm to another. The first seems gendered masculine, and consists of the speakeasy, the Girl's inamorato, Butch, the proto-Fascist Ganz and, importantly, the women, Clara and Belle, tough but loving, who turn tricks when they can't make enough waitressing and generally service the men. Into this realm the Girl is a neophyte, a tabula rasa. Although she is rather brutally initiated into sexuality by Butch, they have at least one good time, too, when, as Paula Rabinowitz notes, desire is etched on their bodies. They share their dreams, dreams of living with nature, of living easy, of living with love. These dreams are not to be. Butch scabs on a picket line where his brother Bill is killed, and when that still doesn't work to get him a job, he agrees to pull a holdup with Ganz and Hoinck. The scene is borderline lumpen, and in Butch Le Sueur draws a portrait of a working-class type who could as easily follow the Fascist Ganz as his own dreams of utopia and communality.

The Girl does take those dreams to heart. Pregnant by Butch, she returns home to her father's funeral. There her mother's historicity, as well as her own hopes and dreams and profound sense of loyalty, become inscribed on the Girl as well. This will be one of the factors that will effect the Girl's maturation. When Butch is killed in the heist, the Girl leaves the male-dominated world of the speakeasy and enters a female domain, along with Clara, now tubercular and syphilitic, and Belle, who has commandeered a warehouse. The Girl has refused the men's suggestion that she have an abortion. The child--the child of the communal love of her and Butch, the child embodying Butch's dreams, her mother's and her own--is becoming a presence in her womb. In terms of the polarity I am suggesting, the character of Amelia, the communist activist of the Workers Alliance, stands opposite to the force of Fascism Ganz represented. Amelia, herself with six children, helps the Girl and Clara out of the detention home where the Girl has been threatened with sterilization. It is worth noting that in the home the Girl has befriended a deaf and dumb girl with whom she communicates by notes. What I make of this is yet another manifestation of the mistrust of "the say" we saw in "The Hungry Intellectual," and the faith in the truth of working class "speech." This point is further made in the duplicitous friendship of the social worker on the Girl's case who then puts in a report terming the Girl "maladjusted" and recommending sterilization.

If Amelia is a worker-intellectual or worker-Bolshevik as Trotsky and Lenin would have termed her, she is also plain-spoken and does not elevate herself above those she is trying to help. Specifically, Clara is dying, and Amelia organizes a mass protest demonstration to get her milk and iron. Clara dies too soon. But just as she does so the Girl goes into labor and produces a baby girl, amid the "humming" of a room full of women. The Girl will name the baby Clara, and the baby's birth is seen as the harbinger of the birth of a new communal world organized by women.

I personally marvel at the tenderness and feistiness, as well as the continuity Le Sueur has stitched into her patchwork of other women's stories, though I understand one editor rejected it because it lacked "authenticity." In terms of the question of essentialism, it would seem that Le Sueur is definitely postulating a women's essence, composed of birth-giving and solidarity, as well as shared sexuality, that is more powerful and sustaining than the individualistic socially-constructed beings of the men's existence. I maintain, however, that with the defeat of the men in the bank hold-up, and especially of the Fascist Ganz, Le Sueur is still extolling the values of communality and solidarity, albeit in feminine form. The birth does not substitute for the mass action; they come together in a unified finale. To be sure, the way of the men, scabbing, hold-ups, abortion, even beatings, has been nihilistic, and it is the actions of the women which are communistic. While this might not have proved attractive to the CPUSA leadership, it makes for a novel which any classroom of the period could profitably study as one of the most authentic, if not most typical, statements of the Depression and of the hunger for community that it has always been Le Sueur's mission to express.

Notes

1. See especially, Ellen Messer-Davidow, "The Philosophical Bases of Feminist Literary Criticisms." *New Literary History.* Vol. 19. Autumn 1987. No. 1. 65-103.

Chapter Five

Tillie Olsen's

Yonnondio: From the Thirties

Tillie Olsen's work poses several important challenges. To take a strictly chronological approach, in the order of publishing, we would have to look at the stories in *Tell Me a Riddle* first, for those, published together in 1960, established Olsen's reputation as a modern writer of exceptionally high caliber, of interest to a contemporary generation, and, in turn made the rediscovery and first-time publication of *Yonnondio: A Novel of the Thirties* possible. Those two works of fiction, along with a memoir and collection of essays, *Silences*, have established Olsen's reputation as a writer of significance in our time and an exquisite stylist. To facilitate examination of this body of work, I will divide my inquiry into two segments: the first on *Yonnondio,* the second on *Tell Me a Riddle.*

Tillie Olsen's career, spanning five decades, is something of an enigma, especially as it has been presented by herself in *Silences,* and by such biographers as Mickey Pearlman and Abby Werlock, Deborah Rosenfelt, Erika Duncan, and others. Born in 1912 or 1914 (the exact date has been lost) to Russian socialist immigrant parents in Nebraska, Olsen was the second of six children, an avid reader and participant in her parents' socialist discussions. Yet she dropped out of high school before completing twelfth grade. Although her father sometimes farmed, frequently held working-class jobs, he was, by all accounts, a conscious socialist working-class intellectual in a tradition that was to be hailed by both Lenin and Trotsky as "worker-Bolshevik." He himself was at the forefront of several mid-west strike actions and found himself, and his daughter Tillie along with him, in the company of IWW leader Big Bill Haywood and Eugene V. Debs. I do not want to minimize this radical-worker-intellectual tradition, especially among the immigrant socialist community in the period in America just before and after the Russian Revolution, because I think it can contribute much to our understanding of Olsen's writing career, if not to *Yonnondio* itself.

The important thing to bear in mind is that *Yonnondio* is not strictly speaking an autobiographical work. The parallel is that it is set in the midwest before the Depression and takes a working-class family, on the edge of poverty, as protagonists, and a daughter, Mazie, who would be about Olsen's age, as focal point. At the same time, the family in its entirety lacks the class or socialist consciousness that played such an important part in Olsen's own home situation. As a matter of fact, precisely the point of *Yonnondio* in its original intention, as indicated in the manuscript in the archives in the Berg Collection, is that Mazie comes to radical consciousness as a young woman after several drastic setbacks in her home situation and becomes a communist organizer. As originally intended, the novel would be a conversion novel, a genre familiar in the thirties, tracing the path of the radicalization of a young worker-intellectual, in this case female. The difference between Olsen's conversion story, as originally outlined, and many of the conversion stories of Le Sueur that I have previously discussed is that Mazie's conversion occurs not by, with or through a male who is already committed, but strictly through her own experiences by means of exposure to communist ideology. That Olsen, retrieving and refurbishing the novel for publication in the 1970s, did not see fit to carry the story out as originally indicated in her notes to the point of Mazie's conversion, is probably responsible for the novel's sense of validity for a modern post-Stalinist generation.[1] As it is now, the novel ends, as has been often noted, with a mark of assertion of the human will and spirit through the self-proclaiming action of the infant Bess in the face of the extremely discouraging experiences that have beset the entire Holbrook family.

In point of fact, the Holbrook family experience--and Mazie's own-- was different from Olsen's own childhood in a significant respect. As I have noted, Tillie Lerner was an avid reader, wrote her first story, which I will discuss, at age seventeen, and the result of her readings was frequent exposure to the socialist journals and literature that came regularly to her parents' household. Making the step to joining the Young Communist League when it played a paramount role in the radical movement following the Russian Revolution was a natural outcome, one both in keeping with and accepted by her family situation. Furthermore, Olsen continues in *Silences* to discuss the priority she always gave to political activism over developing her talents as a writer, even after she left organized Communist Party affiliation in the mid 1930s, testimony to the strong hold the "worker-Bolshevik" tradition had on her entire life. This is not to minimize the role played in her life by the need to raise four children in straitened financial circumstances, but surely that was in part a matter of decision rather than happenstance.

None of the factors indicated in *Silences* or developed in the most useful biographical writings on Olsen seem sufficient to explain her rather enigmatic writing career. Tillie Lerner began her career, as might be expected, as a writer of promise in the Communist movement in the early thirties. Her early poem, "I Want You Women Up North To Know," published in *The Partisan 1* (journal of the John Reed Clubs, precursor to the *Partisan Review*) in 1934, indicated a profound identification with the untutored over-exploited women sewing dresses in Southern Texas. At the same time the poet expresses an anti-bourgeois antipathy that may provide a key to the enigma which she herself does not discuss. Two articles on her strike experiences were widely hailed, and when the first chapter of what was to be *Yonnondio*, "The Iron Throat," appeared in *Partisan Review* the entire left-intelligentsia greeted her stellar debut. Olsen (then Lerner) was then nineteen and had just given birth to what the editor, in the contributors' notes hailed as "a new citizen of future Soviet America." The piece itself was greeted by Robert Cantwell, writing in *The New Republic,* as "a work of early genius." On the strength of this first chapter, Lerner was avidly sought by Bennett Cerf of Random House and offered a monthly stipend to complete the work. Settling her infant daughter with relatives, Lerner went to Los Angeles to seek isolation and complete the manuscript. She enjoyed the company of novelist Tess Slesinger, who by then had left the Trotskyist milieu to join the more family-oriented Communist Party and was writing film scripts for the Hollywood studios as well as notes for her own fiction. The young Lerner was further lionized by Lincoln Steffens and his coterie of important intellectual socialists in Carmel. All this seems to have done more to harm than to further young Lerner's progress. In an interview with Werlock, Olsen named as the most significant people in her life in that period not the radical literary superstars who sought her out but the "worker-Bolshevik" maritime men she knew from the Young Communist League. (Pearlman & Werlock 22) Olsen soon bundled up her unfinished manuscript, retrieved her young child, and settled in San Francisco with maritime activist Jack Olsen, to whom she bore three more children. The Olsens persisted in left-wing union and political activity, through the Cold-

War period. Tillie Olsen's own testimony as to the importance to her life of radical activism indicates the degree to which the Olsens' commitment to socialist activist politics continued through the intervening years. When considering the factor of personal choice, it must be remembered that radical activists in this period were excluded from academic and "career" positions and probably would have rejected them as "bourgeois" if they could have had them. These factors plus the decision to carry three additional pregnancies to term in a milieu where abortion would have been more the norm, may well have been factors silencing Olsen's writing in a crucial period of her life, but that conjecture may well be problematic. Clearly, she had early on been given the opportunities many young writers cried for. The left's approval can be seen in Granville Hicks's 1935 summation of the start of her career:

> The new sensibility expresses itself in the way scenes are built up, in the subtle inflections that make dialogue reveal character, in the figures of speech that are used. It creates a different tone and atmosphere out of thousands of delicately shaded perceptions, recorded, selected, and arranged in ways that the writer can never explain. It is particularly apparent in writers who are capable of a high poetic intensity. Tillie Lerner's first short story, "The Iron Throat," which catapulted her into prominence when it appeared in the *Partisan Review,* has this intensity. Through the feelings and thoughts and reveries of a child, one is shown the fear-ridden lives of a miner's family. Nothing could accomplish this but the awareness of the implications of apparently insignificant things that is the mark of a poetic mind, and to know the significance of these particular things one would have had to live with workers, as Tillie Lerner has done, and fought in their battles.
>
> It is yet to be demonstrated whether Tillie Lerner can sustain the burden of unifying, through an entire novel, what her extraordinary insight gives her. (319)

Surely the world, or at least the left-intellectual world that played a prominent role in the literary life of the thirties, was waiting for more work from this extraordinary young writer. That none was forthcoming for another twenty-five years may have been due to the circumstantial factors Olsen herself indicates in *Silences.* I myself raised a psychological question that may not be worth pursuing when I read over the young Lerner's first unpublished short story, "Not You I Weep For," in the Berg Collection. The story is preserved in two different versions, but both have similar constructs, the relationship between a poor girl who likes to read and a rich girl who likes her company. Pearlman and Werlock have discussed this story at length so I won't give all the details. One version opens with the funeral of the poor girl, nicknamed Fuzzie, and recounts her life in high school struggling for an education; the other opens with the rich girl, Ruth, reading Fuzzie's obituary and recounting her appreciation of her less fortunate companion. Ruth is verbally proficient, compared to Fuzzie's stammering gracelessness. Fuzzie has been identified by critics as the Tillie Lerner character, but when we note that it is Ruth who has the grace of speech and self-consciousness--if not radicalized--that surely even the adolescent Lerner must have had (she herself created Ruth as well as Fuzzie) we can see in this story more of a *Doppelganger* effect. Ruth and Fuzzie are one person and may well indicate a personality conflict that troubled the more mature Olsen. What is clear from the conflict is that it is a life-and-death struggle. Fuzzie loses out, succumbing to the diseases concomitant with poverty in both versions, and Ruth goes on to a more glamorous world without her. If one examines the story in the light of Olsen's later work, it is clear that the young Lerner's powers of insight and poetry depend upon the survival of the more inward-looking, more self-directed character--Fuzzie. It was the successful rich girl who would have to be sacrificed if Fuzzie was to go on in future incarnations. This is strictly a matter of conjecture, based, perhaps on evidence that may prove flimsy. Still, given the overwhelming importance of Olsen's class-conscious background, one can more easily see her character Mazie ultimately abandoning the working class for more lucrative prospects than Olsen herself as a young woman abandoning the beliefs and the life commitments she held to so passionately for the sake of the seduction of "bourgeois" success.

There are many useful strategies available that could facilitate a fruitful reading of *Yonnondio*. I am tempted to pursue the question I have previously raised about the relationship of the family to situations of social duress. Michael Staub has presented a helpful understanding pursuing the contrast between speech and silence in the construction of Mazie's sense of self. An investigation of family relations in a social context might better illuminate the effect of the novel as it was written and as it is now given. Surely, social concerns reflected the prevailing ideology of the period when it was written. However, I prefer to examine the process of the development of the individuation of the touchstone character, Mazie, since for a modern generation character seems more important than social concern.

In point of fact, there are two strands I hope to isolate from the narrative with the intention of weaving them together in a portrait of a self emerging from the thirties experience, continuing into present time. One of these strands, the major locus of my investigation, is the development of Mazie herself in several key episodes in which she is prime actor on her own. A minor subject of inquiry will be the authorial interventions, which several critics have noted represent a highly charged intrusion of the author's own voice into the narrative construction. These two strands seem to merge, or intertwine, culminating in a final crucial but often overlooked scene in the existing text in which Mazie makes her first overt revolutionary gesture.

The first authorial intervention occurs early in the first chapter (the one that was published in *Partisan Review* under the title "The Iron Throat"). The situation is the opening sequence when the Holbrooks are in the mining community in Wyoming. A neighbor boy of about thirteen has been inducted into the mines and the author intervenes to offer him a paean. The author offers him, as he goes into the mines, a direct apostrophe, expressing an attitude which, as we shall see, she is to develop in fuller form in her approach to Mazie herself. That may be the only justification we can think of to explain so impassioned an address to a character who has no role to play in the ensuing drama. A key passage in that address reads as follows:

> Earth sucks you in, to spew out the coal, to make a few fat bellies fatter. Earth takes your dreams that a few may languidly lie on couches and trill "How exquisite" to paid dreamers.
>
> Someday the bowels will grow monstrous and swollen with these old tired dreams, swell and break, and strong fists batter the fat bellies, and skeletons of starved children batter them, and perhaps you will be slugged by a thug hired by the fat bellies, Andy Kvaternick, or death will take you to bed at last, or you will strangle with that old crony of miners, the asthma. (14)

Several things can be noted about this passage. For one thing, the fact that the young miner is of little significance to the narrative yet receives the bounty of the author's impassioned apostrophe suggests a reduction of all the characters to typology. They are being regarded--regarded as individuals to be sure--precisely because of the role they might conceivably play in the suggested forthcoming revolution. They are workers before they are people. Furthermore, we note the gender-bias indications. As with her first published poem, "I Want You Women Up North To Know," Olsen clearly suggests that the class division supersedes the gender one. While it might be argued that in the poem, working-class women are appealing to upper-class women not strictly out of the hatred that is manifest in the lyric but also with a desire, a hope, to convince those upper-class women to listen more attentively to their plight, here, the reference to those lying on their couches trilling "how exquisite" to (significantly) paid dreamers is corrosive in its contempt. (Not to mention the standard communist derision of "fat bellies.")

The second authorial intervention, following Mazie's abduction by the deranged Sheen McEvoy (which I will discuss further) reiterates this contempt for establishment artists and their patrons.

> And could you not make a cameo of this and pin it onto your aesthetic hearts? So sharp it is, so clear, so classic. The shattered dusk, the mountain of culm, the tipple; clean lines, bare beauty--and carved against them, dwarfed by the vastness of night and the towering tipple, these black figures with bowed heads, waiting, waiting.
>
> Surely it is classical enough for you--the Greek marble of the women, the simple, flowing lines of sorrow, carved so rigid and eternal. Surely it is original enough--these grotesques, this thing with the foot missing, this gargoyle with half the face gone and the arm [Sheen McEvoy]. In the War to Live, the artist, Coal, sculptured them. It was his Master hand that wrought the intricate mosaic on this face--splintered coal inlaid with patches of skin and threads of rock. . . . You will have the cameo? (30)

Again we note, without belaboring the point, that while "cameo" has come to have many metaphoric meanings, its root (and use here) is as a wealthy woman's ornament. We further note in passing that this juxtaposition of high or classic art to the setting of the arduous work in the mines is the theme of Rebecca Harding Davis's *Life in the Iron Mills,* which the young Lerner came upon by happenstance and made it her mission later in life to revive.

The contempt Olsen exhibits toward art and artists and even toward writing about her own subject matter is so palpable and pungent in this passage that it is a wonder not that Olsen was silent for so many years but that she was able to write at all. One wonders, considering her reneging on Bennett Cerf's offer, whether she didn't in some way see Random House as the proposed recipient of her "cameo."

So compressed, so artistic--in Granville Hicks's perhaps more welcome reception--is this passage that I will quote the conclusion:

> *(Dear Company. Your men are imprisoned in a tomb of hunger, of death wages. Your men are strangling for breath--the walls of your company town have clamped out the air of freedom. Please issue a statement; quick, or they start to batter through with the fist of strike, with the pickax of revolution.)*
>
> A cameo of this, then. Blood clot of the dying sunset and the hush.   No sobs, no word spoken.   Sorrow is tongueless. Apprehension tore it out long ago. No sound, only the whimpering of children, blending so beautifully with the far cry of blown birds. And in the smothered light, carved hard, distinct, against the tipple, they all wait. The wind, pitying, flings coal dust into their eyes, so almost they could imagine releasing tears are stinging. (31)

In order to situate Mazie in this cartoon of a cameo of striking workers served up to languid patrons, I want to recall Olsen's first story, unpublished, "Not for You I Weep." Here, as I have indicated, we see a similar counterposition of a poor, unaffected, unbecoming girl, Fuzzie, and her high school counterpart, Ruth, whose very affect, whose very life, is an aesthetic creation. That Olsen (Lerner) identified with Fuzzie is clear. It might also be noted that Fuzzie is given to melancholy, is rather sickly, and--twice--her funeral is imagined in depressive detail. At the same time, Ruth is seen not with contempt, but with an appreciation for her compassion. Ruth has gone to New York and is living on her own when she gets the news of Fuzzie's demise (we note the name Fuzzie, a nickname for the character Nena Ashrach, is a denigrating reference to Nena's kinky hair bestowed upon her by Ruth as a perhaps misplaced affectionate tease--it is a name the author adopts without apparent irony throughout both versions of the story). It is perhaps a little out of the field to speculate whether Ruth leads the life the young Lerner imagined a writer might lead, saw the juxtaposition of the death of her soul-character and the continuation of the rather upper-class-minded Ruth, and contributed that anxiety to her own situation. Certainly, to conclude the point, it is difficult to write if you have contempt for your prospective audience and for the person you are likely to become if your writing succeeds.

It is a matter of further speculation to guess that perhaps what saved *Yonnondio* from complete annihilation if not from more than thirty years in an attic crate, is that Mazie is in some ways a continuation of Fuzzie as Lerner/Olsen might have liked her to develop had she let her live.

Mazie is six when we first meet her in the Holbrook household in the mine community in Wyoming sometime in the early 1920s. She is a precocious child, sensitive and unaffected--much like Fuzzie but not so melancholy. As a matter of fact she is hopeful and proud of the things she can already do:

> "Pop, I can make the bacon when I stand up on the box, and I can wash the baby, honest. Pop, momma says I'm gonna get an edjication, and my hands white. Is that a story, Pop?"(18)

Her father's tone in his reply is ambiguous--has he contempt for the future he projects for her? Ironic misgivings as to its possibilities? Or is he merely hopeful:

> Fillin the kid's head with fool ideas, he thought wrathfully. But she could become a teacher. Aloud--"Sure you are. You'll go to highschool and read books and marry a--" his stomach revolted at the thought of a mine boss--"a doctor. And," he finished, "eat on white tablecloths." (18)

While this answer does not satisfy Mazie, she accompanies Jim into town and it is there that the first crucial scene takes place--Mazie's abduction by Sheen McEvoy and near destruction at his hands. McEvoy is an ex-miner who was disfigured, maimed, and deranged by a mining accident. He sees Mazie in the dark where she is waiting while her father is in the saloon. McEvoy seizes upon Mazie, sweeps her up, chants an incantation to the effect that the mine is a great mother who must accept the sacrifice of a child (Mazie) in order to quench her thirst for more men. He is stopped from throwing Mazie into the maw of the mine shaft by a passing night watchman. In an apostrophic passage, the author seems to exonerate McEvoy because he is the victim of social forces. She sees in him the result of a life of mining and mine accidents rather than a crazed lunatic responsible in some way for his own actions. Mazie, feeling the gelatinous mush of McEvoy's face and lips hot against her own face--a sensation that will haunt her memories through the rest of the narrative--is too terrified to cry out. Her deliverance is almost sacred. If, in her guise as sacrifice that others might live, she has been likened to a Christ figure, she becomes through this catharsis the crucible that will result in the deliverance of all her kind from the hell of mine and industrial labor. Mazie's final conversion to revolutionary action, which would bear this interpretation out, takes place only in the unpublished version of the final notes, but is prefigured in a final scene of action when she is angered to the point of throwing a corncob at a rich woman in a car in Kansas City toward the end of the novel. I will, in the meantime, try to trace how she gets to that point.

The near-disaster wreaked by McEvoy may well be the catalyst as well that propels the Holbrooks into the decision to leave the Wyoming mine and head for a farm in South Dakota. The farm sequence is an idyllic time for the family, a pleasant sojourn in nature and family togetherness they will utilize in the future to dispel the harsh feelings they will have in response to the brutalizing life of Kansas City stockyard existence in the final sequence, after foreclosure and poverty undermine the possibility of continuing on the farm.

For Mazie, the key configuration of her farm experience is her encounter with the old man, a neighboring farmer, Mr. Caldwell. Rich in natural and astronomical lore, gifted with natural poesy and generous with both his wisdom and books, Caldwell befriends Mazie. As we can imagine Olsen's father passing on to her a radical heritage originating in revolutionary (1905) opposition to Tsarism and continuing in the American midwestern labor struggles of the early decades of the century, so Caldwell becomes Mazie's mentor in a quest for knowledge and artistic sensibility. So important to her is this relationship that Mazie risks slashing her bare feet on corn stubble to go to him when he is sick. When he dies, Caldwell bequeaths to Mazie a set of books, classics she should read if she is to develop her aesthetic intellect, but Jim sells them for fifty cents before she can get to them. No matter, Mazie will read them herself in due time, if we can see in Mazie the young Fuzzie and the developing Lerner devouring a library full of books in alphabetical order. That Jim callously sells Mazie's inheritance for a pittance may suggest the disrespect of the working class (male--Anna champions "edjication") for "book-learning." This is a counterposition we have seen in some of the work of Meridel Le Sueur previously. At the same time Caldwell, despite his death, despite the loss of his books, has become the main counterweight to the languid ladies and their "paid dreamers" of the apostrophe cited above. Caldwell is an unpaid dreamer; his aestheticism is the natural sensitivity of the worker of the land that Le Sueur was to extol, and for the duration of the development of her consciousness in this unfolding his words will echo in Mazie's mind as a form of sigil of the aesthetic and intellectual sensibility that will be Mazie's salvation and the source of her culminating power.

To be sure it is economic circumstance not Caldwell's death (a minor incident as far as the total farm experience is concerned) that determines the Holbrooks' decision to abandon the farm and move on to Kansas City. However, if we are to avoid viewing the farm sequence as an isolated episode, we can place it in the context of the psychological knitting up of Mazie's private intellectual/aesthetic skein. For Mazie, Caldwell's death is of a piece with the failure of the farm experiment as a whole. The combined experience, both the intellectual enrichment of Caldwell's friendship and the physically reviving plenitude of outdoor life, stand as a foreshadowing of the goodness that Olsen will continue to indicate she sees as the possibility for life in general and the working class in particular. Mazie, exposed both to physical benevolence and to Caldwell's natural aesthetic intellectuality, will always know that life can be good, that humankind can be beneficent and nurturing, and this knowledge will inform the outrage she is to develop at circumstances (such as those that force her family to leave the farm) that mitigate against benevolent human community. From the point of view of the structuring of Mazie's psycho-intellectual development and of the subliminal structuring of the novel as a whole, Caldwell's death, as much as the mortgage default, is indeed the reason the family must move on.

Once in Kansas City, the author again intervenes with her prejudices about art and artists:

> Yes, it is here Jim and Anna Holbrook have come to live. . . . past the two blocks of dump and straggling grass, past the human dumpheap where the nameless FrankLloydWrights of the proletariat have wrought their wondrous futuristic structures of flat battered tin cans, fruit boxes and gunny sacks, cardboard and mother earth. . . . (And Beauty? Until the mammoth stone beauty of the city has carved itself into their blood, the children can lie on their bellies near the edge of the cliff and watch the trains and freights, the glittering railroad tracks, the broken bottles dumped below, the rubbish moving on the littered belly of the river.) (61-62)

Again, in the sardonic jab at Wright and accepted standards of beauty, we see the young artist, Lerner, rejecting the terms of the very community she had been invited to join.

Regarding Mazie, however, it is clear from the text, both in Caldwell's company and at the outset of her sojourn in Kansas City, that she starts out innocent of such ironic contempt and even sweet in her disposition and optimistic in her outlook.   How she is transformed into a potential revolutionary is foreshadowed in the remainder of the existing text as much as in the remaining unpublished notes. Indeed, the transformation seems to take place in a moment's prefiguration in an early Kansas City scene:

> Clutching a pail of lard, dreaming a sweet dream of twilight on the farm and darkening over a fragrant world, her face not shadowed by the buildings above, her nostrils not twitching with the stink in the air, her eyes not bewildered by the seething of people about her, dreaming the sweet dream unutterable, a hard body crashed into her and a voice thundered: "Whynt you look where you're going, stinking little bitch," and she was pushed in the stomach, punched down sprawling, a drunken breath in her nostrils. (84)

Mazie remembers this stench as a revisioning of Sheen McEvoy's dangerous nearness, and, pushed roughly into a gob of spit, she feels a pang of memory:

> (Fear remembered such a breath. It seemed a mass pressed itself into her face, wet earth, or something she did not remember. In a minute she would be lifted and carried through a blackness of terror.) (84)

It is hard to tell whether the association with McEvoy includes the man--apparently working class--who shoved Mazie in the same mood of forgiveness due to social circumstance that was granted to the miner. Certainly the working class world Mazie at that point enters is Brechtian in its harshness, with Mazie herself, in her innocent sweetness, as virtually its only redemption.
     In the next scene vital to Mazie's development--that of her father's rape of her mother--we are once again torn between a sociological and an individuated characterological method of interpretation. From the family point of view, Jim has been working hard, drinking hard (there is a snatch of Sandburg in the air) and is in the mood for sex. Anna, unknowingly pregnant, and overworked herself, is not in the mood.   Jim takes her by force, aggravating a near-fatal miscarriage. Mazie, huddling in the next room, awake and alert, takes it all in. But the ending of the scene and the chapter focuses in on Jim, compassionately, as he sits

with Mazie against his heart, and dawn beat up like a drum, the things in his mind so vast and formless, so terrible and bitter, [that they] cannot be spoken, will never be spoken--till the day that hands will find a way to speak this: hands. (95)

We might consider from this quote that the effect on Jim of his act of rape of his wife is for him to turn the blame on society and himself become hardened in his revolutionary resolve. (Indeed in the unpublished notes he does become involved in a militant if unsuccessful strike.) This revolutionary zeal will be foreshadowed in the Fourth of July fireworks celebration Jim engineers--but I will not be able to develop that point further. The effect on Mazie is more complex.

Crucial to the revitalization of Mazie's sense of womanhood after the shattering blow of her mother's rape and miscarriage, is the scene in the vacant lot where Anna takes the children so that she can gather the greens the doctor has ordered as necessary to the regeneration of her damaged body. It turns out to be a psychological revitalization as well, and Mazie once again is in the position of passive witness or measure of effect.

Anna has found a catalpa tree with its rather vaginal blossoms and the act of sucking their sweet juice transports her into what seems to Mazie to be a utopian sense of womanhood:

> In between gathering [the greens Anna] sucked the blooms, and Mazie saw that each time before, she drew her breath in deep to smell, deep as if she had to blow off dandelion heads or pop a paper bag. A remote, shining look was on her face, as if she had forgotten them, as if she had become someone else, was not their mother any more. "Ma, come back," Mazie felt like yelling, in rancor, in fear; jumping up, snapping her fingers into that dreaming face to bring attention, consciousness of them back, make it the old known face again. (117-118)

Mazie's discomfort is not to last, for just as her father's taking her to his bosom in his guilt prefigures a forthcoming uprising, so her mother now cradles Mazie in a femininity born of the nature Catherine Stimpson has seen as beneficent. In this act, Mazie avowedly develops a sense of self, strengthens her resolve to unite with her femininity and lays aside for a moment questions of more typological sociological concern:

[Anna's] fingers stroked, spun a web, cocooned Mazie into happiness and intactness and selfness. Soft wove the bliss round hurt and fear and want and shame--the old worn fragile bliss, a new frail selfness bliss, healing, transforming. Up from the grasses, from the earth, from the broad tree trunk at their back, latent life streamed and seeded. The air and self shone boundless. Absently, her mother stroked; stroked unfolding, wingedness, boundlessness. (119)

To continue my investigation of the author's relationship to art, I note that in this passage are several snippets of American folk song and English folk song, which, like the Sandburg that inspired Jim's lust, suggest a positive attitude toward the "people's" art we have seen garnered and extolled by Le Sueur, which was supported by the *New Masses* and the entire communist milieu. Considering the author's plight as I have indicated it, it is perhaps a relief to see that some artistic norms can be emulated with no cost to the young artist's integrity.

From a feminist point of view, while many critics have noted the restrictive gender-shaping statements Mazie is subjected to--boys don't have to do dishes; girls don't get fireworks--it seems to me that this scene between Mazie and Anna is stronger in its positive sense of closeness and mother-daughter continuation than any externalized gender injunction could be. That these injunctions don't much faze Mazie, and that her identification with her mother's naturalness as a source of generation and regeneration of self are stronger determinants can be seen in the protracted and important scene in which Mazie plays on the dump with other children.

Mazie is now nine years old, and on her own, at a crucial time in her development. In the midst of what seems a rather problematic heat wave, a triangle develops--Mazie is caught between twelve-year-old Jinella, the dump princess, and Erina, a disfigured retarded girl, whom Mazie also befriends while playing on the dump. Without making too much of the association with the early unpublished story, I might invoke in this triad something of the split self seen in the uneasy friendship between Lerner's Fuzzie and Ruth. Jinella is very much the feminine princess with expensive (correcting for the circumstances) tastes. Further, there is a contrast between inner space and outer space between the two apexes of the triangle--Jinella and Erina--that recalls Erik Erikson's experiments with children of this age of both sexes.

To foreshorten the report on Erikson's University of California experiment a bit, the results of setting children to construct play scenes seem to be: "the girls emphasized *inner* and the boys *outer* space." (Italics orig.)

(270). Erikson goes on to draw conclusions from this that may be questionable. The point that pertains to Mazie in the dump scene is the summation of the experiment:

> The male and female spaces, then, were dominated, respectively, by height and downfall and by strong motion and its channeling or arrest; and by static interiors which were open or simply enclosed, and peaceful or intruded upon. It may come as a surprise to some and seem a matter of course to others that here sexual differences in the organization of a play space seem to parallel the morphology of genital differentiation itself: in the male, an external organ, erectable and intrusive in character, serving the channelization of mobile sperm cells; in the female, internal organs, with vestibular access, leading to statically expectant ova. The question is: what is really surprising about this, and what only too obvious, and in either case, what does it tell us about the two sexes? (271)

While I personally find this argument to be a possible challenge to the anti-essentialists in the women's movement, I will not discuss that notion at this point. I have invoked this passage to suggest that Jinella, in her gunnysack enclosure with her accumulation of scavenged decorations and trinkets, is the quintessential female, and that Erina, with her dead bird (appendage) that won't stay buried and her stump of an arm that ends in a little knob, and who is always to be found outside, is the male figure or as masculine as a female can be, and that Mazie vacillates between the two.

Clearly, Will has more the run of the dump in truly masculine fashion, but his physical difference, alongside the privileges his social-minded parents have foisted upon the situation, put him out of the realm of becoming a vector in Mazie's personal equation of self. (We might note that even the conversions of the two in the unpublished version are different: Will becomes an active organizer; Mazie listens to a speech as a typically passive bystander.)

Mazie goes from "shame and self consciousness" in roughhouse play that reveals her underwear ("No more for her that lithe joy, that sense of power" (127)), that is to say from a pre-sexual childhood "sense of power" tarnished by sexual awareness, into a sexuality with Jinella that is virtually carnal.

In this play, Jinella is the quintessential female in her "inner-directed" lair, and Mazie, though still basically passive, is virtually carnal in her acting out of Jinella's romanticized fantasies--again, fantasies derived from popular culture (movies) and art. What is important for Mazie, what she learns from

Jinella, is not so much the exposure to hyper-feminine sexuality and her own somewhat masculine (if passive) role in the games the two play, but the power of imagination Jinella, like Ruth before her, exhibits, an imagination that constructs a whole play-world out of the bits and pieces of found cultural effluvia. That Mazie (and Olsen) admires this quality is obvious:

> On the dump there is Jinella's tent, Jinella's mansion, Jinella's roadhouse, Jinella's pagan island, Jinella's palace, whatever Jinella wills it to be that day. . . . Here sometimes, in humble capacity, Mazie is admitted--*if* she brings something for the gunny sack into which the curtains and tent themselves go when Jinella must go and which is stuffed with "properties":. . . . Anything that dangles, jangles, bangles, spangles. . . . Luxuriously on her rug, pretend silk slinking and slithering on her body, turbanned, puffing her long pretend cigarette: Say vamp me, vamp me. I'm Nazimova. Take me to the roadhouse, I want to make whoopee. Hotcha. Never never never. O my gigolo, my gigolo. A moment of ecstasy, a lifetime of regret. (127-128)

Jinella develops other friends, but Mazie doesn't entirely take in the rejection. She is still hunting for gifts for Jinella's voluminous gunny sack when, in the stifling heat which makes a hell for all the characters--Jim in the packinghouse, Anna doing chores in the shack and Mazie and the children in the dump--Mazie runs into the deformed Erina who intones the damnation of God as the reason for the temperature inversion. Mazie's response to Erina is one of fascinated revulsion with an undertone of personal identification:

> Erina's breath [like McEvoy's] was in Mazie's face; Mazie saw how the pus oozed from her eyes, stuck on her eyelashes; weed stickers-- maybe lice--in her hair. *Go away, Erina; it's so hot and you are wavy like everything else. Last night I was your body, I was you.* (138)

If Jinella is Mazie's introduction to sexuality, femininity and a sense of culture and beauty (such as it is) that transcends mortality, Erina is manifest as the counterpole. Outdoors, her phallic bulbous stump obvious, worrying about a dead bird pet (that recalls the baked baby birds Jim had brought in from the freezing cold on the farm), Erina introduces Mazie dramatically both to a masculinized feminine way of being and to the very notion of mortality itself. As Erina says: "When you die your soul goes to hell or heaven but your body gets et and stinks." (139)

It is perhaps stretching a point beyond the evidence to suggest that the two works together, the early story and this passage of Olsen's first novel, indicate an identification of femininity in the person of Ruth and Jinella with a not entirely acceptable immortality (like the immortality achieved through art) and Erina and Fuzzie with a constant immersion in the facts of mortality and a more masculinized persona. It is not my place to speculate on the relationship between Olsen's own persona and this conflict, but surely it bears some weight on Mazie's development of self.

What comes through as well is the identification of the heat wave-- which, I note, is an authorial not a divine construct--with mortality and the conditions of all the characters' oppression with suprahistorical circumstance rather than sociological determinants. The fact that this seems not to fit with the structure of the novel I have previously indicated, which would seem to lay the characters' problems at the feet of society, may be the fault of the author or of the analyst or may be the redeeming feature of the fragment of the novel as it exists.

Most critics of the work note the final sequence in which Anna finally recovers from her morbid passivity to clean the house, against the advice of her kindly neighbor, and to start the canning in a productive act that links her to Jim's work at the packinghouse, and baby Bess ecstatically bangs the canning jar lid in an announcement of the triumph of self and indeed of the entire human spirit. This seems, to the modern view, an apt ending for the book, and most of us are just as glad Olsen did not go on to work out her plan in accordance with her unpublished notes, although in a new edition she has added details pertaining to Anna's plight if not to Mazie's conversion.

I would just like to close my own reading by noting the intertwining of the themes of mortality with sociology that Olsen introduces in the extant section. If baby Bess's lid banging is a triumph of human spirit, it is as much a triumph over the mortality of the oppressive heat and Anna's variation on the sexual theme which condemns her to illness, slatternliness and morbidity (and ultimately, in the unfinished notes, to death by bungled abortion), as it is a triumph over the sociological conditions of poverty, hunger, both her father and mother's hard work, and despair.

The fact that it is Bess who enjoys the epiphany and not Mazie may be seen by stricter readers than I as a flaw in the construction of the novel as it now stands, since it is, if anything, eminently Mazie's story. We might prefer to see Mazie take some action on her own rather than to be once again a passive recipient of the effects of the joy of the baby sister which will act as harbinger of the "goodness" of the human spirit to which Olsen herself has attested. On the other hand, to close with Mazie listening to a speech about the glories for the working people in the liberation of Soviet Russia (as Olsen actually wrote out in her unfinished notes) and going on from there to become an organizer of oppressed people, might, in the current context, be more depressing than uplifting.

In an interview quoted by Deborah Rosenfelt, Olsen indicates that she still sees her work as laying bare the "circumstances [that] are the primary key and not the personal quest for identity." But perhaps her modern readership is more responsive to--and more convinced by her more totalizing summation: "I want to write what will help change that which is harmful for human beings in our time." (404)

Olsen scholar Elaine Orr recently compared *Yonnondio* with Henry Roth's *Call it Sleep*, published in 1934 during the period that Olsen was writing her preliminary draft. Orr calls the reader's attention to the mother-child relationship as the central focus of both works, noting the difference between Roth's avowedly Oedipal mother-son connection and the often overlooked centrality of the mother-daughter link in Olsen's work. What Orr fails to incorporate into her reading is a most important difference in the significant ideology underlying the two works and lying at the heart of the figuring of the mother-child relationship. Briefly, as Alfred Kazin notes in his introduction to the 1991 edition of *Call it Sleep*, for Roth it is character that is the guiding impulse, not socially constructed factors; for Olsen, as she herself has stated, the intention, if not didactically executed, was to present social forces as the shaping determinants of individual action and even of character. At the same time, it must be remembered that Olsen in her interviews has always been at great pains to assert her belief in the possibilities inherent in the human will--the resources and "resilience" available even to a beset segment of the species. As Mickey Pearlman reports her conversation with Olsen:

> Olsen has spent over 50 years investigating the wellsprings of strength and "human resilience," ideas often reflected in her stories, and she believes that it is "one of the great characteristics of the human race" that "we do not remain forever in degrading circumstances, circumstances that are harmful, circumstances that are unpleasant, if we can find a way out." What, she asks, is "the source of that in human beings? What does it feed on when there seems to be little for it to feed on, and what does it have to do with what a human being

is, the nature of being human? What's the relationship of human caring in all that?" (2)

For a feminist reading closer than Orr's to both Olsen's stated ambition and to the commentary of the period of initial reception, I draw upon Catharine R. Stimpson's review of *Yonnondio* in *The Nation* at the time that the book was published in its present form in 1974. Stimpson notes Olsen's commitment to a presentation of her characters--the entire Holbrook family--as victims of social, economic, and natural factors. At the same time, as she alerts us, "Olsen believes that human nature, if permitted to express itself freely and spontaneously, will be good." Significantly, Stimpson calls our attention to the factor of nature in the narrative as contributing to this goodness: "Physical nature is the most fertile setting for such expression, although moments of human community, a family singing or a picnic, can suggest a harmonious balance among people, animals, plants, earth, water, fire, air" (565).

Factors of nature as significant forces in the text have already been discussed in this chapter, but it is interesting to note that Stimpson's early analysis of *Yonnondio* is as a social document more than a modernistic psychological inquiry. Stimpson indicates that this is not a strict deterministic or naturalism: "Olsen's compelling gift is her ability to render lyrically the rhythms of consciousness on victims. Imaginative, affectionate, they are also alert to the sensual promise of their surroundings." (565)

It may well be to Orr's credit that she introduces, surely not uniquely, the importance of the focus of attention on the sensual relationship between mother and daughter in Olsen's novel. At the same time it seems misleading to view her reading of Olsen against Roth outside of the social content of the two works and the general critical consensus of the import of the underlying ideologies from which each is conceived.

The benefit of contemplating Elaine Orr's juxtaposition of Olsen and Roth is that what is seen to emerge from both is the importance of the process of individuation, universally agreed to be the significance of Roth, too often underplayed in the case of Olsen. In both cases, as Orr notes, our attention is focused on the emergence of a child from a social-familial nexus and the emphasis is on the shaping of the consciousness of that child or adult-to-be-- Mazie in *Yonnondio*, David in *Call it Sleep*.

A follower of radical intellectual discussions, if not of the entire range of the Marxist debate, Olsen and her work seem to explore the dialectical question of the relationship between the individual and her consciousness and social forces in terms more sophisticated than those of the classical Marxists themselves. As Olsen told critic Michael Staub in a telephone interview in 1986 with reference to *Yonnondio*: "I was writing about great human beings, and the circumstances in which they find themselves. I was writing about how circumstances shape people and how children are formed and deformed. My writing came out of what I knew and saw in other human beings."

Even in *Yonnondio*, as we have seen, and as Orr suggests, a psychological dynamic is more apparently at work than it is in many of the products of the "proletarian" era of the thirties that have not survived into this generation.

Of course, one wants to raise the question of feminism and gender determinations, a question which has figured largely, as might be expected, in the feminist discussions of Olsen's life and work.

As both the Holbrook son, Will, along with Mazie have been projected in Olsen's unfinished notes into similar outcomes--communist organizers both, both gaining revolutionary consciousness where only, in the published version, the problem of mere survival counted, we might hold off our discussion of gender considerations to take a closer look at the Marxists' view of consciousness. The Leninist--and Trotskyist--view of human nature was to prove as utilitarian as any capitalist subordination of human instinct to industrial demand. Just as an example: In 1923, while still at the height of his power, and enjoying Lenin's approval, Trotsky published an article in *Pravda* on what the university should produce by way of a graduating student body. There was apparently some debate that the goal should be to produce "the new socialist man." Admittedly in a state of siege, surrounded by capitalist countries on all sides, Trotsky argued that the goal of the university should be to produce "soldiers for the revolution." (*Problems* 107-120). Obviously it never occurred to anyone on either side of the debate to raise the question that is only now being posed among some left-wing academics in the West, namely, how do we find ways to let the students themselves set their own goals and make use of the university as a site for the development of the individuated "truly human" self?

Olsen herself surely feels that such a self must be socially responsible as well as happy and productive. That view seems integral to Olsen's vision. But especially as her stories show, she never regarded the individuated self as a creature useful to the social project in the strictly utilitarian way that the Marxist politicians did. For this reason, no doubt, her work transcended proletarian realism, as Hicks promised.

The gender question, in its opposition of essentialism to social construct, poses the question of the relationship of individual consciousness to social ideology in terms potentially even more dynamic than the mere survivalism of "vulgar" Marxism. I have already indicated how obstinately obtuse the male-dominated thinkers of the Marxist movement were on this question. Let me make that point one more time in a slightly different way by once again quoting Trotsky. Now the time is 1936; Trotsky is in exile in Norway, mobilizing his dwindling collection of followers to call attention to the perils of bureaucratization under Stalin. Prime target of this article, entitled "Thermidor in the Family," intended as an excerpt from *Revolution Betrayed,* is the question of community kitchens, in the bureaucratized Soviet state, child-care centers and the emancipation of women from the home into the labor force. Facilities are closing, poorly organized and under-utilized. The thickening layer of government officials and those growing rich at the expense of the disorganized masses have such facilities as they need.

Trotsky's concern is that when he was in charge of the Soviets, all these operations were put into effect for the purpose of the emancipation of women. He still ardently supports such measures and bemoans the fate of the revolution evidenced by their erosion. The women's victory is nearly lost. He also makes the case that abortions, won by the early Soviets, are now, with new edicts on the need for a workforce, outlawed; family enclaves, discouraged as citadels of bourgeois authoritarianism (in a point that foreshadows Max Horkheimer's argument in *Critical Theory*) are now being reinstituted to bolster the authority of the new bureaucracy. (*Problems* 80-93) Considering the time, the circumstance, the argument has interest. At the same time, I would like to introduce a point here that I hope to develop more fully, namely, that nobody, not even Trotsky, apparently found an effective way to ask the women what they themselves wanted.

Olsen, to be sure, does not concern herself with the problem of establishing mechanisms for determining social decision in the future utopia or any other state, but her primary emphasis on individuation and the development of consciousness in a very human way in the context of a milieu of writers generating pragmatic didacticism merits further investigation.

As the major significant response to *Yonnondio* since its publication in 1974 has come from feminist critics, the question asserts itself whether the most important factor to be considered in reading the novel effectively is a social/economic determinant or a gendered bias. Olsen herself would surely be most inclined to accept Paula Rabinowitz's synthetic view:

Leftist women's fiction of the 1930s rewrites women into the history of labor and workers into the history of feminism.   By encoding classed gender and gendered class in narrative, it presents alternative sites for theorizing the interrelationship of class and gender. Narrative itself then becomes both the form and the content of new histories and new theories about women, literature, and politics in 1930s America.(4)

Given this context, there are at least two ways to read *Yonnondio*. One is as a sociologically/gendered determined discourse on the family under conditions of capitalist oppression; the other as the shaping of the individual self--Mazie--as the resultant vector determined by similar forces.   As Rabinowitz points out: "The complex evocation of Mazie's consciousness through a fractured narrative style locates this construction in the family." (127) Incidentally, since Will figures in the unfinished outcome in ways similar to Mazie, it is not entirely just to suggest, as Rabinowitz does, that Olsen's focus on the girl-child indicates an entirely feminine determination of the result of family situation.

As far as that family situation is concerned, the distinction one can make between the Holbrooks as a family and the Schearls of Roth's novel is that the former are in Stimpson's words "victims" of circumstances of poverty and shaped by that poverty as a mutable social condition, whereas the Schearls' are, each and all, victims of perhaps immutable passions. The Olsen family is determined by poverty; for Roth poverty is merely a prevailing condition, a given, like the weather or mortality. The point is that the father, Jim Holbrook, is oppressed by working conditions, as a miner, as a tenant farmer, as a city worker in the sewers and packinghouses in the pre-Depression era while Mazie is coming of age.   He in turn takes out the rage and frustration of his condition in brutal assaults and verbal abuse against his wife and family.   In the proverbial chain reaction, Anna responds, alternating defensiveness with like-minded abuse, to the children--and the sequence in turn determines both Mazie's inward-looking affect in the present and her predisposition to accept a socialist alternative and the coming to radical consciousness in the unfinished projected notes. Against this chain of abuse, several factors emerge to indicate the "goodness" of inherent nature that will ultimately assert itself, that Stimpson indicates, the "hope" for humankind that Olsen herself discusses in the context of this work.[2]

I might note that while this chain-reaction theory makes for appropriate Marxism of the period, it does not necessarily correspond to the sociology of the family in the Depression.   In several studies of the family in the Depression, notably that of Cavan and Ranck, conditions among families were found to vary both with regard to gender roles and frequently with regard to the responsiveness of the family as a supportive organism sometimes superseding gender determinants. What was generally found was that patterns of supportive behavior that manifested themselves before the onset of the poverty-making circumstances tended to continue. Families in crisis found those crises exacerbated by the Depression, while families with productive networks for mutual support tended to remain intact and to see the Depression as an external circumstance against which supportive joint effort must be mobilized. This sociological information suggests that while the Holbrooks may have been typical of a certain segment of the working-class population, even in their gender relations, they may not necessarily have been universally normative.

What does come through in a reading of *Yonnondio* is that the family nexus provides what Olsen herself has called a "network" within which the individual can find such sustenance as may be available and, as Orr, Rabinowitz and other feminist critics have noted, key to this nurturance is the maternal figure, in this case, Anna, and the maternal site, the house or shack, such as it is. Whether or not nature is a gendered force, it certainly figures in this equation.

Thus, we see that Olsen's view of the family as the site of the nurturance of the "hope" in Olsen's words, or the prevision of the socialist individual, is in contradistinction to the prevailing Leninist, Trotskyist and even Frankfurt theorist figuration of the family as the site for the transmission of bourgeois authority in general and the oppression of women in particular. Certainly, in the farm sequence, all the Holbrooks are pulling together to attempt to achieve success. And even in the final scenes, when Anna has recovered from her husband's brutal assault and her own disorganization, the juxtaposition of scenes with Jim working in the packing plant and Anna both canning and taking in laundry and tending the rather self-assertive children under a unifying July heat wave, suggests a virtual cooperation of effort. The work is the same, the natural conditions are the same; only the site is different.[3]

While Jim, in a temper tantrum, and his boss opportunistically, may denigrate women's work, clearly the author--and the children--do not. As Rabinowitz points out, this positive view of the family as site of nurturing in opposition to oppressive social conditions, is prevalent in the women's fiction of the time, from Clara Weatherwax to Mary Heaton Vorse to Fielding Burke to Josephine Herbst, and was not necessarily out of favor, Leninism notwithstanding.   As can be seen in both Trotsky's complaint and Elsa Dixler's documentation, the prevailing winds had shifted by the early 1930s to reinstate family values as a concomitant part of the communist tenet-- whether as a reassertion of authoritarianism as Trotsky and Horkheimer suggest or because there really is something supportive and nurturing of the human spirit in the family "network" as Olsen and her friend Slesinger indicate remains for future generations to determine.

Let me at this point note the curious effect the weather conditions have on shaping the relationships within the Holbrook family. Stimpson has noted the positive festival atmosphere when the weather is propitious, the picnicking, and, I add, the important sensual transcendence Anna achieves when she takes the children on an outing to gather greens. I note, however, that the weather is not always benign, indeed, becomes itself a major oppressive force. Since Olsen, not God, has invented these weather conditions in this context, one must give to them some import. Rosenfelt's view that the July heat wave that closes the book suggests a force that unifies Jim's and Anna's working conditions only begs the question. As a natural condition, both the cold in the farm sequence, and the heat in the Kansas City[4] stockyard episode suggest an immutable force in the firmament, inhuman, intransigent, and ultimately beyond the capacity of the human species to control.   The conditions of oppression become, in the meantime then, not societal, but suprahistorical, natural, as natural and immutable as mortality itself.

It may well be this reckoning with immutable law, mortality and natural forces that gives to *Yonnondio* the capacity to emerge from the social determinism of the thirties when other good works have vanished from the shelves. In the guise of weather conditions, I frankly find the question of immutable mortality as it presents itself here to be a little unconvincing. Olsen could just as easily have invented a balmy breeze in from the river.

Notes

1. I have consulted the Berg Collection archives in the New York Public Library with reference to the outline for the unfinished remainder of *Yonnondio.* I was struck, at a cursory glance by a passage in which the young woman Mazie has grown to be is converted to radical activism by listening to an outdoor organizer speak about the marvels taking place for the benefit of working people in the humanitarian Soviet state. At the same time I am indebted to Deborah Rosenfelt's article (p. 390) for a capsulated account of Olsen's original intentions.

2. For a full expression of this positive outlook, see the quotes from Rosenfelt.

3. Rosenfelt discusses the unifying effect of the oppressive heat wave on page 403 of her article.

4. Various readings place this last episode at various places. On the evidence of the Armours reference, one might well assume the city is Omaha, Nebraska. I have scanned the section several times, and, since the reference to a river is to the Mississippi River, not the Missouri, I have assumed the city to be Kansas City. I was unable to corroborate this with Olsen herself.

Chapter Six

Tillie Olsen's Riddle

Almost unique in her generation, from her background, Tillie Olsen has made the connection with the new generation without a special attempt to revive her "lost" work. *Yonnondio* might have been republished just on the strength of the interest in Olsen's stories, collected in *Tell Me a Riddle,* even without the renewed interest in women writers of the thirties, largely sponsored by the Feminist Press (with which Olsen has had some relationship).

The reasons for the interest in her work in its own terms, not necessarily as historical artifact, may be many and varied. I would like to concentrate on two important considerations in her work, one stylistic, the other thematic.

Essentially, both aspects of Olsen's work that I want to look at are unified by a single concept: the dialectical interrelationship between the individual and the social--a subject that seriously occupied the Frankfurt school and Antonio Gramsci, writers of Olsen's generation, if not of her ken. Specifically, as a thematic interest, I am concentrating on Olsen's view of the relationship of the individual to the family and the family to the social as that has been discussed by Max Horkheimer in his important essay "Authority and the Family." While it is true that the subject matter of her stories relates to social questions, her stylistic treatment suggests an individualistic, inner-directed method. The thematic intent of Olsen's stories may still be to investigate the effects of social factors on individual characters located in the nexus of the family. Nonetheless the effect of her highly idiosyncratic prose style is to individualize the characters and focus the reader's concern within individual consciousness rather than within society. While, as we have seen, this is true of her first major effort, *Yonnondio,* it is the guiding determinant, in my opinion, to a reading of the stories in *Tell Me a Riddle.*

According to Olsen, although she had put the manuscript of *Yonnondio* in the attic and had given up all hope of taking time out of her busy schedule that included raising four daughters, taking menial jobs to augment the family income, and participating with her husband Jack Olsen in local political activity, she never stopped thinking about possible stories and jotting down ideas on (frequently lost) bits of paper. When her children were well on their way to becoming self-sufficient, and the pressure of political activism subsided in the early fifties, Olsen, at her daughter's urging, took a class with Arthur Foff at San Francisco State (Burkom and Williams 74). She brought him a rough draft of the story that was to become known as "I Stand Here Ironing." Foff was greatly impressed with Olsen's talent, said he had no more to teach her than she already knew, and strongly encouraged her to go on with her writing. The result was four terse, compact stories about family life produced within four years, published as they came out in important quarterlies, and collected by Dell under the title *Tell Me a Riddle,* the title of the final story in the volume. One more story came out of that period, although it may have originated in the thirties, "Requa-I" the beginning of a novel, which has never been made popularly available, though it exists in several sources. I will discuss that story in a later chapter.

Since I utilize Horkheimer's thesis on authority and the family as my main underpinning for my analysis of Olsen's stories' thematic manifestation, let me sketch out that thesis here in brief. Horkheimer suggests that the family serves a two-fold or three-fold purpose, at one and the same time mutually contradictory. On the one hand, in the figure of the Oedipal father figure, the family transmits the authoritarian values and conservatizing influences that bind society together and help to preserve and maintain the status quo. At the same time the family is an enclave, in Elshtain's terms the realm of private retreat from the slings and arrows of outrageous fortune--the "network" of nurturing Olsen herself discusses. Within that construct the individual is simultaneously the recipient of the nurturing and the self-aware rebel against authority. In this way Horkheimer amends traditional Marxist theory which postulates the clash as being between social forces at odds in Elshtain's "public" sphere.

Horkheimer analyzes the dual nature of the family and of the individual within that family, which combines both the familiar Oedipal overturn of the individual against familial authority, and the strengthening factor of the family which enables the individual to break free. This seems a useful tool for understanding Olsen's thematic development. We note that Horkheimer's view does not restrict itself to the patriarchal and Oedipal relationship of son to father, in the authoritarian paradigm, but investigates as well the role of women and nurturing and the conservatizing character of mothers' as well as fathers' roles.

It is interesting to note that Horkheimer's thesis is borne out not only in Olsen's stories, but in more up-dated sociological terms in Richard Sennett and Jonathan Cobb's *The Hidden Injuries of Class*. Perhaps what this latter sociological investigation adds to our inquiry is a question that Horkheimer does not raise as to how authoritarianism, nurturing and individualism interact with the forces of class consciousness that were determinants in Olsen's own thinking. I note that this interactive or dialectical line of thought, especially as it relates to the role of women or mothers in transmitting authority and conservatism as well as nurturance tends to overthrow much prevailing feminist thought on the "mother question," especially as that has been expressed by Chodorow and Sara Ruddick. Furthermore, it adds a more dialectical equation to Elshtain's rather simple, if attractive dichotomy.

Since this question of mothering is nowhere more eloquently expressed than in Olsen's first revitalized story "I Stand Here Ironing," I will look at it from the point of view of Horkheimer's paradigm. Let me say first that I confess to having a difficult time for personal reasons reading this story as it reflects too closely in almost excruciating detail my own experience, taking the daughter's point of view. However, I will try to confine my remarks on this story to a look at why it has been so effective in generating discussion and reader interest.

First of all, as Robert Coles has noted, the instigating voice, urging the mother to ruminate about the plight of her daughter as she stands and irons her dress is the voice of the guidance counselor at the school--the voice of authority. I note, perhaps out of personal bias, that it is to that voice that the mother directs her guilt-ridden rationalizations, not to the daughter. As Helen Pike Bauer has noted, the daughter herself, when she does appear on the scene is light-hearted and joking, less "troubled" by her troubles than her mother is. The mother's self-recriminations read as an internalized view, in negative, of what "society" expects of a mother. This view is as much reflected in the idea of mother as nurturer indicated by Ruddick as it is in the work of Dr. Spock.

Abandoned with the child at the age of nineteen, the young narrator left the child with relatives and paid caretakers who did not find her "a miracle," as she herself would have liked to have done had she been able to stay home with her. Embedded in this complaint, and the further incident in

which the mother and new stepfather have first left the young child long
before she was ready, then brought new "bright," beloved children into the
household, is the portrait of how class expectations affect a working-class
mother.

As we saw in *Yonnondio* the traditional social realist view was that
society works on the father in the family (as Sennett and Cobb show
continuing into the sixties) who in turn works his authority resentment out on
the wife, who in turn mistreats the children. Here, a more complex pattern
pertains. The mother has internalized standard bourgeois family ideology in
the form of guilt that she cannot match up to it. To be sure, the father of the
girl left during the Depression because he could not bear not to be able to play
the manly role and hold down a job. The narrator is both guilt-ridden and
pleading for exoneration (in the eyes of the unnamed guidance counselor at the
school) because she herself has had to play the masculine role and support
herself and the child. Why she left the child home alone at night is not
explained (for political meetings--as my parents did?). Further, why the
mother 'did not intervene more effectively when a new brood of half-siblings,
"golden- and curly-haired . . . quick and articulate," (9)challenged the first-
born's dark, quiet and "good," is likewise not explained. In point of fact, the
narrator discusses the daughter's problems almost solely in terms of social
factors and time-limitations. The result, it seems to me, is a notable lack, for
the daughter of what Ruddick calls "maternal thinking," and a substitution of
what Sennett and Cobb see as a more masculine injury of class, the failure to
meet authoritarian expectations both as a parent and as a provider.

If we want to consider that a much-beset working-class mother might
have other options in her own thinking and attitude toward her disadvantaged
child, we have only to look at other working-class women's work, from
Olsen's contemporaries in the thirties to such new African American writers
as Ann Petry and Terry McMillan.

Horkheimer's thesis that an individual will yet emerge from the
authority-bound family network, imbued with strength through nurturing that
enables him or her to seek an independent relationship with the world allows
us to see Olsen's daughter figure in a new light. Surely the "troubled" daughter
has some potential for self-development. Blessed with the wit to entertain
with her comedy despite her "goodness" and "adaptability" (features my
mother said allowed her to farm me out wherever she had to without my
visibly complaining), with a clear indication of a need to love this avowedly
seemingly rejecting mother, the self of Emily emerges in little snippets in the
end that indicate some desire and capacity to survive beyond the self-pitying

complaint about benefits she never received according to accepted standards of maternal nurturing.   It is this hope for the emergence of a self in Horkheimer's thesis that links it to what we have already seen in Olsen's own words and in the words of her more notable discussants, of a hope for the goodness of humankind and a belief in human progress.

As we shall see, all four stories in the *Tell Me a Riddle* collection are unified as variations on the theme of a family that has been conservatized or at least is subject to the conservatizing influences of "bourgeois" social and moral codes challenged in its value-determinations by what I shall call a "loose cannon," an individual who stands outside the family values, though in ways nurtured by them.   It almost seems as if Olsen has taken Horkheimer's paradigm and put it in an effective setting.   Horkheimer's thesis formulates how the family operates to transmit the authoritarianism of the dominant society.   Olsen combines, perhaps unintentionally, this theory of family development with elements of the working-class voice of Sennett and Cobb, and something of the "maternal thinking" of Ruddick and Chodorow.

In the first story, "I Stand Here Ironing," all those forces are at play within the consciousness of the narrator-mother.   As we have seen, as Robert Coles discusses, the dominant voice to which the mother is answering is that of the guidance counselor in the school, who seems to be, in Coles's terms, condescending and presumptuous as well as maternal herself in her concern. Having eloquently established the social and personal nexus within which the girl Emily has come into her teens, we then see Emily herself as an independent spirit. Perhaps the nurturing mechanism with regard to her has broken down in her case. Perhaps her "troubles" are the manifestation of an inner war with the duality of a household that is socially conscious yet individually negligent.   In any event, there is a subtle switch in the tenor of the mother's thinking that makes for a dynamic of change within the story itself, without which the story might not be technically viable. In this reading, we see the mother resisting the guidance counselor's demand at the beginning: "Even if I came," she says, "what good would it do? You think because I am her mother I have a key, or that in some way you could use me as a key? She has lived for nineteen years. There is all that life that has happened outside of me, beyond her."(1) Here, in a mood only transitorily pursued, the mother takes up an aspect of her complaint she will never entirely jettison, never entirely adopt--that of social determination leading to personal exoneration. ("She is a child of her age, of depression, of war, of fear.")

While at times the narrator seems infuriatingly (to me) self-involved, that is, concerned more with her own impression in the eyes of the guidance counselor than she is with how she herself can help her daughter in an immediate sense, given the misfortunes of the girl's childhood situation, the mother concludes with a note of uneasy acquiescence in the guidance counselor's intrusive insistence on being of help: "Let her be. So all that is in her will not bloom--but in how many does it? There is still enough left to live by. Only help her to know--help make it so there is cause for her to know--that she is more than this dress on the ironing board, helpless before the iron." (12)

We note that the dress on the ironing board, which, as Midge McKenzie's film of the story graphically makes clear, is the centerpiece of the narrative, is an article of the shaping of an affect, the show of personality before an outside world rather than the substance of that personality. Further, in her struggle for health and good humor, the girl takes up mime and comedy, both studies in the interaction between affect and self. It may be useful to read that observation back into the narrator's own ruminations to see them as creating tension between what the world expects, what she expects of the world and what she herself can make of this independent "loose cannon," the girl in her quest for a selfhood, despite its being poorly nurtured, has become. We cannot say that the family has not been nurturing in this piece, in Horkheimer's terms, but certainly the world, if the narrator's jeremiad is to be accepted on its own terms, has not been.

It is marginally interesting to note that the form of the girl's struggle for independent remove from the family is a linguistic strategy--comedic mime--a point of interest to be pursued more fully in discussing the other stories. At this juncture let me summarize by saying that in terms of the dynamic of this story, the fact that it is an outside force--the guidance counselor--who triggers the mother/narrator's very act of self-consciousness tends to bolster Horkheimer's thesis. If we can see the dress on the ironing table as the article of clothing to be worn in a context including the guidance counselor, then the action recapitulates the reaction. From a feminist point of view, just as it is the "womanly thing" to be standing and ironing--a task Olsen has, with this story, indelibly etched into the feminist consciousness as a woman's way of thinking--so it is the "womanly thing" to take upon oneself sole responsibility and sole concern for one's offspring. The narrator might have been discussing the girl's "troubles" with her husband, the girl's stepfather. By locating the nexus of the spinning out of the girl's development solely within the mother's consciousness, Olsen locates "maternal thinking," precisely at Sara Ruddick's starting point--within the psyche of the isolated, guilt-plagued mother. As Olsen herself indicates, in a quote employed by Burkom and Williams: "Cultural programming--to 'place others' needs first, to feel these needs as their own' robs most women of the totality of selfhood necessary for artistic creativity." (78) Here we see Olsen's variation as indicated in *Silences* of Virginia Woolf's "angel in the house." At the same time, considering Olsen's background, I raise the question whether the fact that Olsen's narrator cannot take the leap that Ruddick herself does to extend "maternal thinking" into the political realm may have been to her--and her daughter's--detriment. I, for one, wind up feeling frustrated with the belief that surely the unhappy pair are not so entirely victims of circumstance. Surely, there was something they could do to show each other more love, understanding and willingness to help. Yet, this story stands, despite my hesitancy to embrace it, as part of the continuing legacy of the important discussion of the relationship of woman to society and of family to independent self.

* * *

I have a less vital but still affecting private response to the next story, "Hey Sailor, What Ship?" Both of my stepfathers and many of the comrades I knew while I was growing up were merchant sailors before the 1950s blacklisting. Olsen's story, dedicated to "Jack Eggan, Seaman," killed in the Spanish Civil War in 1938, attests to the exceptional qualities the men of the merchant marine displayed. As Melville suggests, merchant sailors, perhaps because of the logistics, tend to read and think more, and more independently than do shoreside workers. This may be because they are freed of the conservatizing influence of family life combined with the fact that they have free time when there seems to be nothing better to do than to read.

As "loose cannon" in this context, Whitey is an alcoholic sailor in off a ship in San Francisco visiting his old friend Lennie and his wife Helen and their daughters. Whitey and Lennie hail back to the Longshore strike of 1934, and Lennie and Helen and their three daughters are virtually Whitey's only experience of "family." Whitey buys presents, cleans the house, and talks dirty. He cannot seem to fit in as a natural member of the household. His diction is coarse and working-class, he drinks heavily and there is a subliminal sexuality to his free play with the little girls that all concerned try not to notice. In terms of plot, Whitey has been demoted on the ship, replaced as union representative, an act which makes him aware of his age, his vulnerability and his impending retirement. He turns to Lennie and Helen's family as a source of continuity in his life. This does not entirely work out for him, as the oldest daughter, Jeannie, is appalled by his manners and his speech. Lennie and Helen display too much pity for his condition to allow him to rest easy, and the whole visit to the household has been a holiday rather than a way of life--shore leave.

One way to look at Whitey is to see him as Mike Gold's itinerant worker updated by twenty years. Whitey is the super-macho proletarian when there are no longer proletarian uprisings. Furthermore, he is seen, as Le Sueur has seen her proletarian males, from the vantage point of a sympathetic woman. If Olsen's voice is not strictly Helen's, it is at least within the circle of the family that we view Whitey, and the super-macho proletarianism he represents. As an outsider, Whitey serves to show, by contrast, what the family can and cannot do. The question is posed as Whitey enters the household: "Who is real and who is not?" (16) Whitey clearly experiences the family as what Olsen herself has referred to as a nurturing "network," and at the same time as an imprisoning web. For their part, the family is uneasy in Whitey's presence. He challenges not so much their basic internal structure as their fundamental relationship with the world at large.

The battleground in this story is not so much consciousness as behavior. Whitey never seems to do the right thing. Drunk, sleeping it off, Whitey's very patterns of life do not synchronize with the family's. His lavish gifts of food and cleaning labor cause embarrassment. The oldest daughter protests against Whitey's cursing: "Listen, Whitey, says Jeannie, I've got some friends coming over and . . . Whitey, please, they're not used to your kind of language." (29) Whitey offers Jeannie ten dollars which her father makes her return. She is angry and distressed, not because of losing the money, but because she will be embarrassed in front of her friends by Whitey's stubborn refusal to curb his language. This refusal, then, becomes Whitey's linguistic strategy of refusal of the family's terms of "civilization."

In this story, as in the next one, it is through the children that society imposes its social norms on the family. Rebellion comes in shunning, as Whitey does, ties, however attractive, to wife and children and household.

Keeping this point in mind, we can see in Whitey's descent into drunken slovenliness the demise of the radicalized working class itself. As Sandy Boucher noted in her interview piece in *Ms.*, Whitey is "most of all damaged by the loss of that belief in brotherhood among workingmen that had made his life worth living." (27). The unnamed narrator seems to be speaking for a generation when she says:

> Understand. The death of the brotherhood. Once, once an injury to one is an injury to all. Once, once they had to live for each other.

And whoever came off the ship fat shared, because that was the only way of survival for all of them, the easy sharing, the knowing that when you needed, waiting for a trip card to come up, you'd be staked.

Now it was a dwindling few, and more and more of them winos, who shipped sometimes or had long ago irrevocably lost their book for nonpayment of dues (35-36).

This is not to say that Olsen has betrayed her own dream of conveying a sense of hope in the face of great despair. Whitey has a humanizing influence on the family which will remain after him, and, as Burkom and Williams observe:

The dream of brotherhood is tempered by the sense of betrayal and loss, the knowledge that while the ideals of freedom and brotherhood can never be fully realized they do not vanish but continue to live on informing daily existence. Understanding that the human condition is thus paradoxical--riddling--becomes central. (75).

If the narrator of "I Stand Here Ironing" is the conscience of womankind, embodied in a distressed mother, Whitey seems to be the conscience of the working class or at least of its radicalized wing. In the context of the unwittingly conservatized family, Whitey's sense of lost camaraderie is exhibited in shopping and cleaning. A genuine sailor, not a "scenery bum," Whitey cannot survive on shore. He is, almost literally, a fish out of water. The interspliced consciousness must be in a narrator's voice, not Whitey's own, because Whitey can not really experience his own consciousness. The narrator knows him better than he knows himself.

In this way, Whitey serves for the family as a source both of independence and of independent heritage they themselves do not have to experience. If written by a modern-day Mike Gold, Whitey might have been seen as a figure of attractiveness and potential adventure. Now, to the female-dominant household, Whitey seems, with his booze and his cathouses, pathetic and repulsive. Willy-nilly Whitey in his unattractiveness serves to confirm the conservatizing influences of the family. As much as they seem to rally around him, they are in reality rallying against him. He expresses, badly, independence and rebellion from conformity that the rest of the family can now themselves refrain from.

If the language of "I Stand Here Ironing" introduced the taut compressed voice of consciousness that has become Olsen's trademark, the narrative of "Hey Sailor, What Ship?" is, if no less poetic, broken by the diction of dialogue. The effect of the poetic aspects of this tale--the authorial interventions, the refrain of the title, the condensed expression--is to make of this piece almost as much of an interior depiction as is the first one. The framing is the framing of the household, like the framing of a mind, insufficient to hold Whitey, as "loose cannon" for long. He must break free on his own terms. And when he does, the family will be confined as before, aware of the terms of its own confinement--and of its benefits. In this way, as I will discuss further, Olsen fuses, almost uniquely, a sense of social consciousness, based on a thirties realism, with a formalistic taut, complex, ambiguous diction that situates her within modernist poetics. In this story she expresses the working class, if she does not directly address the working class in its own terms.

* * *

I admit to a personal response to the next story, "O Yes," as well. I attended an inner-city San Francisco junior high school at about the same time as the story's protagonist, Carol, and confess to having had a similar ambivalence, perhaps for similar reasons, on the race question. While the social life of my school and the teen sub-grouping was strictly racially segregated, my parents' own lives, my upbringing, led me to believe in full integration both in the personal and political sphere. My stepfather helped a group of co-workers in the construction workers' union mobilize a black caucus, which in turn put through a motion to send a one thousand dollar donation to the Rev. Martin Luther King's bus boycott in Montgomery, Alabama (eventually enabling us to spend an evening with the Kings as we moved to New York). I was simultaneously proud of my stepfather and mortified lest my friends in the neighborhood take note of the many African Americans who frequented my parents' house--only communists talked to Negroes, they might think. Further, even after we moved to a slightly more liberal climate in New York, as I entered high school and I had one or two black friends in school, I did not even tell them about my trip over the Thanksgiving holiday to Monroe, North Carolina, to make arrangements with NAACP leader Robert F. Williams to connect with civil rights lawyer Conrad Lynn to get two little black boys, aged seven and nine, out of jail where they had been put for kissing a white girl in a game of house. The two aspects of my life were completely separate. For all of those reasons, I find Tillie Olsen's story on one family's attempt to address the race question to be exceptionally courageous.

On one hand, Olsen avoids the unrealistic cant of communist rhetoric, as expressed most recently by Angela Davis, which minimizes the effects of race prejudice on the working class. On the other hand Olsen attempts the rather awesome task of locating the source of racism within the family and individual nexus. Again, we have the sense in which the family is the conservatizing yet nurturing network, challenged by a "loose cannon," in the person of the African American school friend, Parialee.

The radical tradition on the race question that undoubtedly informed Olsen's consciousness, going back to fiction and articles in *The Masses* (Jones) suggested that it was possible in these times under these circumstances for two people of unlike races to unite; it was a matter of changing individual thinking. Angela Davis makes much of the friendship of (white) Elizabeth Gurley Flynn and (black) Claudia Jones. As Davis says:

> As many Black women had argued before her, Claudia Jones claimed that white women in the progressive movement--and especially white women Communists--bore a special responsibility toward Black women. (169)

The sentiment was not new. The prototypical story on race relations appeared in the March 1911 *Masses*, entitled "The Classmates," written by Inez Haynes Gillmore. This story, starting from mutual racial mistrust and prejudice among the middle classes of both races, works its way toward reconciliation and awakened awareness of the wrong-headedness of prejudicial teachings. The two girls in college together, one white, the other black, become fast friends. All that is missing is what Olsen adds, a sense of awareness of the social pressures each must overcome in order to make this friendship work. If an ending of racial cooperation and friendship is the norm in these radical stories, we can see what strength Tillie Olsen has had to muster to counter the teachings of her native milieu, in order to leave us with the rather disappointing news that racial harmony, at least at the time of her writing, cannot so easily be achieved.

Integration and interracial cooperation was typically the radical norm: "Black and white, unite and fight," the standard slogan. In my opinion, Olsen, undertaking to delimit the very real pressures placed on a working-class family to bend to the prevailing racist norms, in the context of Olsen's own radical upbringing and personal ideology, is little short of heroic. Like photographer Dorothea Lange's single-handed venture into the World War II Japanese internment camps to expose inhumane treatment at a time when the entire nation was mobilized to eradicate the "yellow peril," Olsen's story, by not adopting anybody's acceptable line on the race question, by honestly and forthrightly examining the serpent within her own bosom displays a courage I can only marvel at. All I did by spending the weekend in Monroe, North Carolina, with the precocious black leader Williams and his family was jeopardize my life (and possibly his); my peer group support was not in danger--if anything it was enhanced.

At first reading, the story is about a baptism. Ostensibly it is the baptism of Carol's friend Parialee, which Carol and her mother attend; Carol becomes overwhelmed with emotion, and faints. But it is also Carol's baptism into adulthood, and her mother Helen's baptism into a feeling of helplessness at the recognition that conditions--conditions that affect her own children--are beyond her capacity to alter or intervene in.

Carol and Parialee have been friends and classmates for several years as young children growing up near each other. The mother, Helen, has encouraged this friendship. Now, entering junior high school, the two are subjected to the divisive powers of a racist society. Carol is being "tracked" into the college prep program; Parialee into the non-achievers. Furthermore, both are subject to the peer pressures of their outside groups. Parialee adopts the diction of her peer group; Carol the fears that her friends will discover she has a black pal. While the conflict comes to a head as Carol faints at the singing in the African-American church during Parialee's baptism, the rest of the story shows how the split intensifies and becomes irrevocable. Social norms of racism prove stronger than one household's attempt to defy them. The well-meaning mother is powerless to prevent this process.

As Annette Bennington McElhiney put it:

> Helen tries to find words to help her daughter understand herself and her relationship to others. She realizes that Carol is growing up and has been baptized or reborn into a state of awareness of social conventions and the human misery that they sometimes cause. (80)

The locus of this multiple baptism is the racial situation. Friends as children, as their mothers are friends, Carol and Parry are growing apart, primarily due to societal pressures which inscribe and reinforce racism on each generation virtually as a puberty rite. That this is especially true in the working class is made clear in the older daughter Jeannie's diatribe, which includes the claim that they could move to a more expensive neighborhood and find black children who were offspring of doctors and professionals with whom there would not be this rift.

In an amendment to Horkheimer's paradigm, it is the older daughter,

Jeannie, who acts as the primary conservatizing force. The mother does not until the end relinquish her efforts to see the two younger girls continue their friendship. Helen is baffled and mystified by the working out of racism within her own family against her will. Jeannie understands only too well why the separation must occur, and in the course of spelling it out, seems to condone the racist system, or at least to reinforce it:

> "They're in junior high, Mother. Don't you know about junior high? How they sort? And it's all where you're going. Yes and Parry's colored and Carrie's white. And you have to watch everything, what you wear and how you wear it and who you eat lunch with and how much homework you do and how you act to the teacher and what you laugh at. . . . And run with your crowd." (54)

The first obvious factor in the odd mix of the relationship between the two ethnically divergent families is the name of the girls. Carol is markedly conservative as a name, while Parialee is marked with the "sheer verve" that Karen De Witt, writing in the *New York Times* notes as the distinctive quality of "black Americans . . . naming themselves." Obviously the meaning of pariah is embedded in the girl's name, but it may, given the context, be a flaunting as much as a self-denigration. As De Witt develops the point:

> Rhythmic and melodious, idiosyncratically spelled [the] names are uniquely black. . . . E. Ethelbert Miller, director of the African-American Resource Center at Howard University, said he sees the newly invented names as "a form of black style."
>
> "It's like not tucking in a shirt or wearing a hat backwards," Mr. Miller said. "It makes your child appear unique by giving it a name that stands out." (E3)

As the distinguished African American critic Houston A. Baker, Jr., notes:

> The simple English word *name* has an awesome significance for black American culture that it can never possess for another culture; the quest for being and identity that begins in a nameless and uncertain void exerts a pressure on the word *name* that can be understood only when one understands black American culture. . . . and, paradoxically, one of the surest ways of understanding the culture is through its

linguistic artifacts.(120)

From that point of view, the story "O Yes" is almost entirely linguistically constructed. Having been introduced to Parialee as the "loose cannon" in our Horkheimer-based paradigm, we are plunged into the church scene itself.

Two factors coalesce at the baptism scene to contribute to Carol's catharsis. The first, if we follow Baker, is the implicit hatred of white culture embedded in the African American ritual. The second is Carol's own mortal fear of being found out as a "nigger-lover" by her schoolmates.

While N.M. Jacobs is persuasive in her argument for consideration of the birth imagery in the Jesus scene, especially for understanding Alva's recapitulation of the birth of the Infant in the birth of Parialee when she herself was fifteen, I choose to regard Baker's analysis of Negro ritual as more to the point. The church scene inundates Carol and Helen, the only two whites in the audience, not only with the ripe imagery of birth and rebirth, but with, in Baker's terms, the images of slavery and emancipation through God which

> speak of the vitality, literalness, and closeness to the soil of the people who produced them; they speak moreover, of a people who believed in the nearness of God, in his personal nature, in his graciousness and his power. Black sermons, in short, constitute some of the finest poetry of belief ever written, and their fusion of the earthly and the abstract makes them pulsate with meaning. (30)

To make overmuch out of the sensuality of the baptism as a factor causing the outsider, the pariah, the white girl, to faint, is perhaps to place one in jeopardy of the cliche. It is a mark of Olsen's versatility that she is able to convey the full impact of the ritual and the responsiveness of the audience, and at the same time maintain some sympathy for Carol as she worries what will happen

> If Eddie [Parialee's school friend] said something to her about being there . . . if he talked to her right in front of somebody at school. (41)

The rift between the two girls widens, between the two families. It is as if they have made choices rather than having had their respective disparate cultures foisted upon them. Carol's family and school relations--notably her subtly racist teacher--keeps her clearly in the mold in which she can enjoy the privileges of white supremacy. She is "tracked" on the road to achieving educational success.

For her part, Parry seems to have decided for herself as much as having become a victim of cultural decision in her adoption of an affect in keeping with black teenage culture. Bringing homework to Carol, who is home with the mumps, during one of the last afternoons the two girls spend in each other's company, Parry already seems lost to ghetto culture--or perhaps "lost" is a white imposition. Perhaps her baptism was her birth into her own people's culture as much as it was the expulsion of Carol from the African American community. In any event, while Parry's turn back to the ghetto is primarily linguistically rendered, there is an undercurrent of hard-edged "reality." She will not be placed in the college preparatory track; she will not be advantageously situated for purposes of developing a career; she will have less money for the necessities, and the pleasures, of life. Whereas a mere matter of months before the two girls had done their homework together, Parry now banters:

> You really gonna mess with that book stuff? Sign on *mine* says do-not-open-until-eX-mas. . . . Flicking the old read books on the shelf but not opening to mock-declaim as once she used to . . . Vicky, Eddie's g.f. in Rockface office, she's on suspended for sure, yellin to Rockface: you bitchkitty don't you give me no more bad shit. That Vicky she can sure sling-ating-ring it. . . . NEXT mumps is your [white] buddybud Melanie's turn to tote your stuff. *I'm* gettin the hoovus goovus. (58)

Thus the friendship ends, as much the victim of an elected as an imposed cultural dictate. Rose Kamel sees in this imposition the victimization of Olsen's typical female character due to immutable social law. As she notes, Helen, Carol's mother mourns, *"It is a long baptism into the seas of humankind, my daughter. Better immersion than to live untouched....Yet how will you sustain?"* (61) To this Kamel notes,

> *The seas of humankind,* reminiscent of Anna's sailing song in *Yonnondio,* remind us as well how landlocked, trapped are the Annas and Parrys whose youth will erode under an exploitative system offering them little bread and no roses. (65)

If there is little hope for racial harmony in this story--if circumstances seem too oppressive to be controlled--there is yet Parry's feisty racial pride and Carol's abiding, if guilty, concern to offer the suggestion that they may yet meet again--perhaps on a march to Washington listening to Martin Luther King.

* * *

In a revision of Horkheimer's view of the relationship between women and the family, the mother in the final story, "Tell Me a Riddle," (unnamed until near the end; then called Eva) is not only the conservatizing influence but the "loose cannon" it has been the business of the family structure to control. While assuredly, the story is more than the sum of its thematic gestures, I will look at the familial and political notations before going on to address Olsen's unique stylistic achievement.

The structure of the story is simple. Eva and David are aging. He has the offer of a "haven" from his organization (which may be something like the Jewish socialist group Workmen's Circle) or union.

This "haven" is a retirement colony. It would require selling the house in which Eva is comfortable and where she wants to remain. Told that Eva has rampant cancer, David, quarreling as she quarrels every minute of the way, takes his wife on a tour of children and grandchildren for a final visit. They wind up in Los Angeles, with the granddaughter Jeannie, who nurses Eva to the end, an end which sees a gesture of reconciliation between the aging, quarreling grandparents, and the final conclusion to the vitality of their lifelong spat.

From the point of view of a woman's interest, it is the house and the children that have been confining, restricting and conservatizing. Eva has had to stay home with many children while David went outside the home to work. While she very much wants to stay in her own house now that the children have gone and she can experience it for the first time as truly her own, she projects onto her daughter's house the closed-in feeling she had known all her adult life:

> For it seemed to her the crowded noisy house was listening to her, listening for her. She could feel it like a great ear pressed under her heart. And everything knocked: quick constant raps: let me in, let me in.

> *How was it that soft reaching tendrils also became blows that knocked?* (86)

From a woman's point of view, this really is the touchstone riddle-- how is it that soft reaching tendrils also become blows that knock? Because Eva can ask this question, experience both the tendrils and the knocking, the trip to her children and grandchildren seems to backfire. In an affecting scene, her daughter Vivi holds out the grandchild that she says she had just to please her mother. Eva cannot respond. She cannot hold her own new grandchild. She cannot cluck and coo with supposedly typical grandmotherly warmth. She has had enough of domesticity. One senses that she would rather be sitting in her own house reading her beloved Chekhov. Perhaps a loving family man like David, who has had access all his life to relations to the "outside" world, to Elshtain's public domain, can never understand the depths of longing a woman who has spent all her life in childbearing and child-rearing can feel for a moment of quiet by herself in her own domain away from the clamor of offspring. As some women have said to me under similar circumstances, perhaps Eva is just "tired of being a mother." Certainly Eva's resistance rankles David and forms, together with his insistence and obtuse refusal to understand her circumstance, the strange antiphonal cacophonous duet the two sing to each other throughout the story.

This duet is what gives to this story its special flavor. David's constant invented epithets "Mrs. Inahurry," and so on, Eva's Yiddish curses-- "You should plant your head in the ground and grow like an onion; you should hang like a chandelier and burn" suggest that even in old age the couple are, as always, long on the front of a useless war. The fact that the war does not subside, even in the face of Eva's cancer, suggests an optimism, in my determination, rather than the pessimism that has been frequently noted. It is the battle that gives life to this couple. To abandon it now in favor of maudlin sentimentality would be to give way to the forces of death and oblivion. The fact that they both keep up the fight and do not change their ways just because the end is near is encouraging, if also, to their children, dismaying.

By contrast, the chance meeting in Los Angeles of a long-ago neighbor, Mrs. Mays, points up an alternative way for Eva to be, if she chose to be different. Mrs. Mays lives by herself in two rooms. Sitting on a bench in the sun, they catch up easily, "Thirty years are compressed into a dozen sentences; and the present, not even in three." Mrs. Mays, a widow, enjoys the sing hall, a community event Eva has no patience for. She is complacent; waiting for the end. Eva's battle with David, by contrast, can be seen as an outrage not only against her life with him, but with death itself. She will not sit easily in the community sing; she turns off her hearing aid. She has no stomach for the community doings of the Haven, which David has by now abandoned. Surprisingly, however, in the last stages of her cancer, in her delirium Eva begins to speak volumes, even to sing. Her youth comes back to her in a rush. She remembers the girl who was a friend to her who was sentenced to exile in Siberia for revolutionary activity in 1905. "She, who in her life had spoken but seldom and then only when necessary (never having learned the easy, social uses of words), now in dying, spoke incessantly." (103) If the terse, taut quarreling between Eva and David has been an assertion of the maintenance of status quo in the face of death, Eva's sudden outpouring becomes a plea for a validation for all the life pent up in her that was not lived. It is a personal life, a private life, a life that excludes David and the children. Without being a lament, Eva's final "excited laugh, and incessant words" seem to be a barely coherent statement that there was another life locked up within her crying to be released.

It is difficult to separate so feminist a theme from a "political" theme--for surely, in this case above all, the personal *is* political, but since I am discussing these authors in the context of radical politics, that concern seems not out of place here. Surely, the Communist Party, when Olsen was coming to age within its purview, had an attitude toward motherhood, as I have indicated. Lenin and Trotsky may have campaigned for the "liberation" of women from domestic drudgery and child care, but the novels extolled in the radical press, from Gorky to Gold to Abraham Cahan, and most especially the six novels placed in the Gastonia strike, touted the virtues of the super-sacrificial mom who, although she led her family, was killed or saw her sons killed in the fight. These works idealized the standard radical mom, who was supposed to put her family first, stand by her man or her son and become the standard-bearer herself of the radicalized family, fighting for peace, justice, and economic improvement in a communal battle. Eva--and Olsen--adamantly resist and refuse this stereotype.

In that context, I take note of a framing mechanism in the story "Tell Me a Riddle." It may seem a long stretch to interpret David's "haven" of communized cultural and group activity as a prototype of the communist future Olsen as a girl envisioned. However, Eva's rejection of the "haven" is as well a rejection of the communized life, in favor of the very kind of individualized independence of spirit Lenin railed against. Throughout the story, as she travels from family member to old friends, Eva consistently rejects communality and conviviality. What I define as the final term in the framing mechanism is that the flood of memory released at the end, when Eva is in the final stages of cancer, connects her to her girlhood dreams and girlhood vitality and conviviality as a socialist organizer against the Tsar in 1905 Russia. Her memories of herself are of a socially idealistic vivacious young girl infatuated with another young revolutionary girl, who is sent off to Siberia. These memories, seemingly the last time Eva could envision a self that was both idealistic and functional, seem to obliterate the forty years of her life as wife and mother, as David rather caustically asserts. Without going so far as to wonder whether Olsen feels that way to some degree about her own life, whether the mourning for the lost idealistic activist girlhood is the author's own lament, surely it is heartfelt. As Helge Normann Nilsen notes in an article on the political theme of this story:

> The utopian vision, or conviction, belongs to Eva, the ailing grandmother, and it has been a hidden, but essential part of her entire existence. She is brought back to it in spite of the fact that circumstances have prevented her from devoting herself actively to the realization of her youthful ideals. During their long married life together, Eva and her husband David have grown apart in many ways, and their children have become American Jews, assimilated and with little or no awareness of the ideas and the faith which their parents had been committed to in their younger days. (163)

Nilsen goes on to draw "obvious parallels" with Olsen's parents, Samuel and Ida Lerner. I am making the less obvious equation with the life of Tillie Olsen herself. Certainly the ambivalence about radical idealism and communality expressed throughout this work makes for its veracity, its vitality and its riddle.

It is David who sums up the political point as Eva makes her final gesture toward him, which is both a personal reconciliation and a political statement about the regenerative quality of abiding love:

> She was whimpering; her hand crawled across the covers for his. Compassionately he enfolded it . . . Still was there thirst or hunger ravening in him.
>
> That world of their youth--dark, ignorant, terrible with hate and disease--how was it that living in it, in the midst of corruption, filth, treachery, degradation, they had not mistrusted man nor themselves; had believed so beautifully . . . falsely? (113)

To close on this note is to convey the impression that the entire collection has been a quest for belief, an odyssey guided by the question, where is the source for hope for the human species, especially in the context where the light of social determinism seems to have failed. For Tillie Olsen, as Timothy Arthur Dayton[1] seems to indicate in his dissertation linking Olsen to the regeneration of American modernism, language itself, the very diction of her narratives, becomes an assertion of that individualism that her own political tradition and abiding collaborators denigrated. Perhaps the riddle of our time, for a modern author, is that finding one's own voice is as important as finding one's own time. The terse, taut sentences congeal not so much despair at the ineptitude of the individual, but an anger, a compassion, a hope so intense as to be virtually inexpressible. Not following any easy dictates to speak "in a language the masses can understand," Olsen directs her voice not so much to the popular ear but to the poetic listener who yet can respond to a deep-felt need to explore the locales of hope and despair in our time. If this does not make her exactly a modernist, neither does it place her in the camp of slavish social determinists. To summarize: Olsen is a poet with a mission, and the mission, in modern times, is to pose the riddle of the sphinx--What does it mean to be human in the face of mortality?

Notes

1. Dayton, Timothy Arthur. "Recontextualizing U. S. Literary Modernism: Randolph Bourne, F. Scott Fitzgerald, Tillie Olsen, Jim Thompson." Ph.D. dissertation. Duke Univ. 1990.

Chapter Seven

Josephine Herbst: The Major Novels

In a 1931 issue of *The Nation* left-wing critic Isidor Schneider lambasted what he called the "Hemingway" school of fiction writers for their "over-accent on simplicity." By "simplicity," Schneider meant, as he himself indicated: "to suppress literary personality or 'style,' to substitute actual colloquial speech for conventional literary conversation, and to rule out all effects designed to stimulate emotion." (184) Of the writers he included in this "school," Schneider singled out Josephine Herbst for special disapproval. Because Schneider gives such an incisive foreshadowing of the development of Herbst's narrative style--against her own acknowledgment--I will quote the full section on Herbst:

> I will take advantage of a personal friendship to give what I think is a very good example of the unnaturalness of the new technique. One of the better-known novelists of the new school is Josephine Herbst, author of "Nothing Is Sacred" and "Money for Love." Miss Herbst believes that in her writing she is natural and realistic because she avoids literary effects and reproduces what she considers authentic speech. Miss Herbst is a writer with definite narrative gifts. But to know how genuine and abundant are these gifts one should hear her tell a story. It may be a casual meeting with a shopkeeper or a neighbor that she tells about, but at once it becomes an important occasion; it stirs in us that warm glow of acceptance which fine narrative makes us feel for all its characters.

I have always anticipated hearing Miss Herbst talk and I have given her closer attention than she knows. While she was speaking I made an analysis to discover what made the stories she told so effective. I found that in these spontaneous narratives she used a multitude of adjectives, metaphors, and similes, and those gestures, pauses, and facial expressions which in writing have to be conveyed by prose rhythm and the weights and intensities of well-chosen words. In her speech, in short, she is unashamedly rhetorical. However, when she sits down to write, she is overcome by scruples. She avoids the literary effects that she uses naturally in her speech. As a result, her novels have not realized to the full her narrative powers. (185)

Herbst was incensed and fired off an answering salvo to *The Nation* entitled "Counterblast," in which she defended the simplicity of her style, although she all but disowned the poorly-received *Money for Love,* and denied that there was indeed a "Hemingway School," although she and her husband John Herrmann, a novelist also mentioned by Schneider, were spending a good deal of time with Hemingway in Key West in that period.

While Herbst did not point up the obvious dichotomy in Schneider's position--on some occasions he was for proletarian realism, on others for stylistic traditionalism--the fact remains that the trajectory of Herbst's career, from the first novels, through the autobiographical family trilogy known as the Rope of Gold Trilogy, to her final posthumously published memoirs *The Starched Blue Sky of Spain,* shows Herbst at her best when she is at her most personally engaged with her work, developing the talents of the raconteur Schneider indicated she had in private conversation, and fusing the two aspects of her writing talent--journalism and fiction narrative--into a vibrant, socially concerned prose technique.

It is the fusion of journalism and fictive techniques, I maintain, that makes the final volume in the trilogy, *Rope of Gold* (1937), Herbst's most satisfying fiction work. I grant that one of the factors in the success of this volume may be the infusion of the self in the person of the autobiographical heroine Victoria Chance, at last come of age. At the same time, it would seem that the inclusion in the structure of the plot of events with which Herbst had personal experience and about which she had written as a journalist is an important factor contributing to the vitality of the narrative as a whole.

There can be no doubt that Herbst was influenced by Hemingway as well as by fellow midwesterners Sinclair Lewis and Sherwood Anderson. The charge made by many reviewers of her early books is that they seem to have the dry sardonic midwestern tone without heart or compassion. Herbst herself grew up in Sioux City, Iowa, at the turn of the century, but decided early on to become a writer. Her first literary job was working for H.L. Mencken as a reader for one of the magazines affiliated with *Smart Set.* Then she was able to go to Europe, to Berlin, with the help of socialist writer Max Eastman, who interceded in her behalf with the Roger Baldwin fund. My impression, based both on my own research into the Herbst archives at Yale and on Elinor Langer's helpful biography, is that Herbst rather fell into radicalism because it was in the air among the Bohemian literati with whom she traveled both in Greenwich Village and in Europe. It was in Europe that she met the young writer John Herrmann, himself from a well-off business family in the Midwest. They were to marry and maintain a difficult relationship for a period of over ten years. By all accounts, Herrmann did himself join the Communist Party and accept several organizational assignments from the Party leadership. Herbst remained on the periphery, an active supporter of social causes, but retained her independent voice. When she did write for the *New Masses,* for all intents and purposes a Communist organ, she did so not as a hack but as an independent reporter whose views on a given issue may have happened to coincide with those of the Communist Party. When her views diverged, as in the proletarian orientation issue pressed by James T. Farrell and William Phillips in 1935-37, she freely sorted through the issues on her own terms in her own way, refusing to follow either side slavishly. Although she frequently remained silent when her political companions might have wanted her to speak out, she did address the 1935 American Writers Congress which was instrumental in opposing the "romantic" proletarianization of the Midwest writers gathered around *Anvil.* At that convention, Meridel Le Sueur spoke in support of proletarian writing, while the Party leadership supported the move of Phillips and Rahv to subsume *Anvil* under the directorship of the East Coast intellectual crowd they had collected around *Partisan Review.* [1] Since Herbst's speech was not included in the published collection that was produced from that conference, it is not clear what role she played in the public dispute. Even on the basis of her clear public association with Phillips and Farrell, it is only conjecture that she spoke in their behalf or at least on issues sympathetic to their pro-intellectual, anti-proletarian cause. It is clear that Herbst's major public declaration, her letter to *New Masses* chastising Mike Gold for lambasting Farrell's attack on Odets, placed her unequivocally in the camp of the anti-proletarian opposition.

    Although I hope to show that in her later work it was the fact that she was deeply emotionally involved in the events about which she wrote that allowed her to develop from a journalist to a successful fiction writer, I also want to indicate that even in her early work, which was indeed as spare and bloodless as Schneider indicated, Herbst wrote from personal experience, and fused fictive with journalistic technique.

The difference may well be in attitude and emotional response to the facts of her own life and of her surroundings. Placing her first novel, *Nothing Is Sacred* (1929) in her native Iowa, she writes with a sardonic malevolence nothing short of contempt. The situation is that there has been an embezzlement in what had seemed to be a respectable, genteel, middle-class family. Three grown daughters and their mother are affected. Writing of this novel when a later, better-received one appeared, William Troy in the *Nation*[2], said:

> Her characters, placed in a contemporary and painfully humdrum setting, revealed themselves to be so empty of mind and soul as to be wholly lacking in any kind of significance, moral or otherwise; and the futile automatism of their actions probably depressed their creator, as they certainly did the reader, with a pretty acute feeling of spiritual nausea.

The source of Herbst's contempt can be seen in her non-fiction article published in *The American Mercury*, "Iowa Takes to Literature." This is a diatribe against the pretensions of the new middle-class women's clubs who give themselves literary airs out of boredom. Writing of these literary clubs, Herbst says: "At bottom, it is largely a women's activity. The Kiwanians and Lions who now sit solemnly under literary lectures are merely on the fringe of things; the moving spirits are their wives." (466)
Herbst goes on to note:

> What appears on the surface to be a preoccupation with affairs of the mind, turns out on examination to be at its best a pathetic groping toward some sort of light, and at its worst only a silly attempt to escape from boredom. (467)

The attack on the supposedly vapid female mind is so remorseless, one can only assume it to contain an element of misogynism. This may be hindsight, a position taken in light of the current women's movement. Herbst was undoubtedly bolstered in her point of view by the radical bohemianism of her milieu and the popular strains of such writers as Hemingway and Sinclair

Lewis. Nonetheless, Herbst, like any writer, had choices. Ruth Suckow and Willa Cather chose to see in the midwest middle-class woman a source of positive values, or of distinct moral interest. Herbst joined her voice, perhaps for reasons of her own rebellion against her upbringing, with the male-dominated condemnation of the so-called fatuous middle-western middle-class woman. If this was not outright misogynism on Herbst's part, it may well have been on the part of those with whom she joined forces. The communist forces attacked the midwestern middle-class woman, as we have seen in the work of Le Sueur and Olsen, and the diatribes of Mike Gold, and Herbst, for her own reasons, added her voice to the general anti-feminine outcry. To my mind, this seems a bit masochistic, considering that Herbst herself derived from such women, but that may be pressing the point beyond what is warranted. Certainly, if Herbst condemns the women of the milieu in which she grew up it would seem to be little wonder that she has portrayed them so unsympathetically in her first novelistic attempt.

Her second novel, *Money for Love,* which she herself was to disparage in her answer to Schneider, reveals even more of the painfully oblique masochism and anti-womanism. This novel follows on what Herbst's biographer Elinor Langer has shown to be an autobiographical incident--the abortion conceived in a liaison with the married playwright Maxwell Anderson and subsequent attempt to extort money from him. In this novel, the lead character, Harriet Everist, attempts to extort blackmail money from her married ex-lover, Bruce Jones, in order to pay for the career and the affection of a rather diffident young medical student, Joseph Roberts. It is surprising, when one considers how closely the events of the novel parallel events in Herbst's own life, that Herbst is as unsympathetic to her heroine as she is and as unemotional in her style. Writing about her heroine's motivation for her blackmail attempt, Herbst is practically caustic. She shows none of the sympathy one might expect from a woman who has been through a similar experience herself.

> In the end [Joseph's] medical education [in Europe] would cost less than in this country and mean more. Besides, Harriet wanted to see the theaters of Vienna. She might learn the language and get somewhere on the stage there. She had no idea how to go about it but was sure it could be done. It would certainly be a triumph and just show the folks in Indianapolis something.
>
> It would show Bruce Jones. He was taking his time about answering her notes. It looked as if he thought he could treat her any

old way. It took almost a week for him to answer her last note. When the answer came, it was typewritten and without a signature. It just showed how scared and cautious he was and gave Harriet a good deal of confidence in the outcome (108).

In the end, Harriet gets her money, or at least part of it, but she does not get, or experience, love. Her young doctoral student is still in love with his former wife; the wife's sister cautions him against getting involved with Harriet, and he winds up staying in the liaison unabashedly for the money Harriet has to offer rather than as a matter of love.

Herbst's anxiety about women, and about the role of the story-teller was evident in her early published story, "The Elegant Mr. Gason," based, according to Langer, on a true event in Herbst's mother's life--even the name of the old beau, Gason, has not been changed. In this story, published in H. L. Mencken's *Smart Set* under the pseudonym of Carlotta Greet, Herbst quite sympathetically portrays a mother's (Emma Bowen's) remembrance of a past lover. The occasion is the return from England of the two daughters, Maud and Rita, who have run into the son of "the elegant Mr. Gason," about whom they have heard so much all the time they were growing up. While the two daughters are regaling the gathered clan with hilarity at Mr. Gason's expense, the mother, Emma wanders off to ruminate over her lost love affair with Gason, triggered by the chance discovery of certain gifts from him she has cherished all these years. It is a moment of touching, quiet, romantic reflection, standing in sharp contrast to the raucous recounting of the encounter with which the girls are regaling the gathered clan.

For her part, the Herbst character, Rita, "never could resist a good story." The contrast between Mrs. Bowen's private, sensitive, poignant recollections and Rita's boisterous, show-offy telling of the story of the encounter, which takes center stage at the end of the story must give pause for thought. Our heart--Herbst's heart?--is with Emma Bowen and her private loss. Her rather boorish, well-meaning husband, Fred, is enjoying Rita's performance, at the expense of his wife's pain. And Rita--Rita the writer-to-be--is enjoying trading on her mother's poignant life tragedy to make herself the center of attention. The scene is summed up in the ending. The mother, Emma, has just come from a meaningful rumination over her former lover's gifts. Young Rita is recounting vivaciously the tale of running into Gason's son.

Everyone was bursting into laughter--Fred was laughing the loudest of them all.

"By George, Emma--that's a good story."

Emma wiped the tears of laughter from her eyes. She slipped her hand under Fred's arm.

"Oh, isn't it?" she gasped. "And no one could tell it better than Rita."

"You're right," Fred agreed gravely. "No one can beat *that* kid." (39)

If this is indeed an appropriate reading of this story, it indicates, if not the familiar misogyny (for the story is sympathetic to the mother if not to the daughter)--at least an anxiety about the influence of the writer--and her responsibility. It may seem far-fetched to read in the spare, lean "Hemingway" style Schneider and others on the left decried, an anti-sensual, anti-emotional, therefore anti-feminine stance. If this is true, then it is also true in Herbst's case, that her "Hemingway" writing was more closely linked to the "bourgeois" period of her early work than it was to her later work that was more acceptable to the left-wing proponents of "proletarian" writing.

The delineation of what is feminine and what masculine writing in the context of class-defined outlooks is sometimes difficult to determine. The issue is in some way more confusing with Herbst, because Herbst resisted injunctions to write according to class determinations in a way that others of her generation did not. At the same time, as we have seen, she was certainly not above associating middle-class women with empty-headedness and oppressive views, especially in her early work, while she found it easy to connect to the masculinity that various writers from divergent vantage points have agreed constituted the American working class according to the radical outlook of the thirties.

While Herbst apparently made an effort to redefine the terms of the class war according to her own family's experience, it is possible to see a class/gender distinction in her work generally, and specifically, by comparing two unrelated short stories.

The first story, "Pennsylvania Idyl" was written in association with her husband, John Herrmann, published in *The American Mercury* in 1929 and set in a locale near where she and Herrmann had a country cottage. The story, taking place during Prohibition, is about an accident in which a beer-hauling truck crashes off a bridge and spills out for the taking its hoard of kegs of beer. The characters are all given by first name; the diction is working class and the action all hinges on getting the beer out before the state troopers show up. The troopers are obligingly tardy, the beer-heisters are predominantly masculine, and the whole of the action, an anti-authoritarian romp primarily among men, is all in good fun. A brief example shows the leanness at work in the Herbst/Herrmann style:

> As they worked a wrecking crew came up. They were from Easton. They got busy with ropes and got out on the wreckage and everybody thought that now there would be some action. Karl and Andrew and Steve came back and stood around waiting to see the dead man hauled up. The crew got busy, but instead of trying to hoist the trucks they went right after the beer. They had good stout ropes and as there were five of them, they were able to get a lot of good beer out of the water and rolled down the road. Some said they were selling this stuff at five dollars a keg to city guys in cars who didn't have the nerve to step in and get it for themselves. All the people on shore kept a sharp lookout on the road toward Easton and someone yelled,
> "Beat it! The cops are coming!" (55)

By contrast, the characters and setting in "Embalmer's Holiday," published in *Accent* in 1941, are both middle class and predominantly fussy middle-aged women and effeminate widowers. All the characters are referred to as Mr. and Mrs., the prevailing grog is eggnog, the action takes place on Christmas and is a gathering of abandoned spouses who have befriended each other. Even the gentleman, Mr. Dyer, the purveyor of the eggnog recipe, is known for his cooking and for his gentility. The sour note, the conflict, arises when a newcomer, Mr. Spotwood, an embalmer, arrives. Although his demeanor is only slightly more typically masculine than that of Mr. Dyer, he seems intent on picking a quarrel. The result is that a note of mortality darkens the camaraderie and gives us the feeling that the company are making do with each other like stranded souls with nothing left but each other to cling to. As the author notes, with the barest trace of ironic disdain:

> It was inevitable that the three friends should remember with dramatic clearness the Christmas before. At that time they had been united with their respective husbands and wife and together with six other apparently happy pairs had a big Christmas party. Mr. Dyer said that to his knowledge all but two couples were now dissolved. For some reason the news made Mrs. Fleet and Mrs. Greer very

cheerful. . . .

Mr. Dyer thought it was because they [the remaining couples] were peculiarly sensitive. Mrs. Greer said that she had never thought of Flossie Stone as particularly sensitive. Mr. Dyer said that Bill Stone was as sensitive a man as you'd find. Mrs. Fleet said who would have thought that last Christmas was to be the final Christmas she and Jim Fleet would ever spend together (85).

Clearly, the tone of the Pennsylvania story is more convivial, easy-going and even jovial. One might guess that Herbst would have preferred to find herself in that scene to awakening in the Connecticut Christmas party (the story is written after her separation from Herrmann) wondering as Mrs. Fleet does whether her husband is going "to press his face at the window in the back door and stamping off the snow come in calling out, 'Hello baby, here's your boy.'" (91) ("Your boy," I note, is how John Herrmann frequently closed his letters to Herbst when they were together.) While the tone of this story is not so brutally sardonic as had been the tone of the middle-class- and female-dominated narratives of the early novels and stories, one still feels that "Embalmer's Holiday" is for Herbst a cautionary tale. It seems likely that she dreaded winding up with such a collection of discards, and that may well be why she exorcised her grief by seeking out the more far-flung, if solitary, adventures that her reporting assignments led to.

It is my contention that Herbst spent her later efforts working out a renewed relationship to women, to womanly writing and to the relationships she herself had as a writer who was both a creative artist and socially concerned.

It is the fusion of journalism and fictive techniques, I maintain, that makes the final volume in the trilogy, *Rope of Gold* (1937), Herbst's most satisfying fiction work. I grant that one of the factors in the success of this volume may be that the autobiographical heroine, Victoria Chance, is both at her most interesting when she has come of age and is also herself more interesting as a character than the rest of her family, with whom we have been previously concerned. At the same time, it would seem that the inclusion in the structure of the plot of events with which Herbst had personal experience and about which she had written as a journalist is an important factor contributing to the vitality of the narrative as a whole.

Of special importance for this inquiry is the reportage Herbst filed with *New Masses* editor Joseph North on both an important situation among farmers in the Midwest, which she covered, and the 1935 uprising in Cuba which led her to Havana following her breakup with Herrmann. Both of these events figure significantly in *The Rope of Gold,* the final volume in the trilogy, and both contribute to a texture of richness of emotional import and authenticity only intimated by her previous work--and finally brought to fruition in the memoirs.

Herbst embarked on the trilogy shortly after her return from Europe after her marriage to Herrmann. Apparently she saw in her own family story, tracing through the maternal line, an important paradigm of the midwestern middle class in post-bellum America. The first volume, *Pity Is Not Enough,* begins with a character closely modeled on her uncle, a carpetbagger in the south, whose shady business deals undo him. Another uncle fares better in business but fails to help the key figures, Anne and Amos Wendel, stand-ins for Herbst's parents. Modern-day readers are apt to find the writing intriguing as a social document, both from a feminist and an Americana vantage point. However many reviewers at the time, not seeing the trilogy in its entirety, and more accustomed to sweeping portrayals of midwestern life in the work of Sinclair Lewis and Sherwood Anderson, noted a lack of emotional value and stylistic interest, in this edition. The next volume, *The Executioner Waits,* fared better. Here Victoria, youngest daughter of the Wendels, emerges as a stand-in for Herbst herself, meets Jonathan Chance, and joins him in defying his parents in particular and the bourgeoisie in general to take up the radical cause. That cause, and that relationship, form the central dynamic of the final volume, *Rope of Gold.* Perhaps influenced by her friend Dos Passos, Herbst has jump-cut "camera's eye" passages, and introduced ancillary story lines through the character of the farmer organizer Steve Carson and Victoria's sister Nancy. The vibrancy of the detail, the powerful emotive quality of the prose undoubtedly owe much to the fact that Herbst partook of these events directly herself and wrote about them journalistically in both left-wing and mainstream sources.

To elucidate the relationship between Herbst's journalistic reportage and her novelistic treatment of social events, I will focus on two key episodes in *Rope of Gold* and trace their narrative development to the journalistic events on which they were based. Herbst wrote journalistically about many events, both in the left press and in such mainstream journals as *Scribner's*: The Scottsboro Case, Soviet Writers Conference, Spanish Civil War, Berlin under Hitler--all were covered in important ways by Herbst's intrepid reporter's pen. The primary events she fictionalized, however, were the farmers' movement of the early thirties and the Cuban sugar strike of 1935 that brought Batista to power. Both events, which Herbst initially covered as a reporter for various publications, are woven into the web of *Rope of Gold* in a way that enlivens a primarily orally received hand-me-down narrative with the vibrancy of lived adventure. Whereas the main part of the trilogy, especially in the first two novels, derives from material Herbst received second-hand in the form of stories, letters, diaries and hearsay from her mother's family, with some exception, the farmers' strike and the Cuban uprising events resonate with the gaze of the on-the-scenes participant/reporter. Further, whereas the saga of the autobiographically-derived Trexler-Frey family seems at times a dubious vehicle to carry the weight of Herbst's analysis of middle-class America as a whole, the journalistically derived episodes sharply focus the political perspective, placing the characters and the narrative definitively in a social context of meaningful dimension.

Farmers, it seems, were hit hardest and earliest by the onset of the Great Depression. Both Herbst and her husband, Herrmann, were involved in incendiary activity to protest and perhaps ameliorate the situation, Herrmann as a Communist organizer, Herbst as an on-the scenes reporter. Herbst traveled to her native Iowa to cover a farmers' strike in 1933 and in the course of reporting the event for *Scribner's* and *The American Mercury* found herself deeply moved and engaged with the people of her home terrain in ways she had not expected. Her article in *Scribner's*, originally published in 1933 and reprinted in 1937, utilizes dialogue, vernacular and the type of personality portraits Tom Wolfe was to extoll thirty years later in his discussions of "new journalism."

That Herbst was moved beyond the scope of a nostalgic return homeward is evident both in the *Scribner's* article and in the letters she wrote to her close confidante Katherine Anne Porter, which Elinor Langer quotes in her biography. After a stint working to supply the emergency needs of stricken farmers, Herbst wrote to Porter: "My head gets foggy if I hang around the intellectuals but if I go out where the farmers are talking turkey it all gets fairly simple." And further on: "The trouble with us and our kind is that under this system we are such isolated bastards. . . . Once we are grown we have too little contact with real struggling people." (166) Thus, for Herbst, the venture to the front lines where people were struggling, was not only the answer to the call to revolutionary duty--although as her *New Masses* reportage of similar events attests, such a call was included in her mission. For Herbst, more was involved: getting out of the hothouse environment of the Bohemian radical intellectuals of New York, getting away from abstract theorizing, and keeping an open mind and a steady eye alert to the nuances of actual "struggling" peoples' actual behavior, including their talk and their manner.

It seems clear that Herbst's choice of assignment was as much her own as it was that of any party higher-up. She was attracted to the farmers' situation because it was occurring in her native state. She felt a special empathy for these particular farmers, as she has revealed in her letters to Katherine Anne Porter. While some of her later sojourns, such as those to Berlin, Spain and Cuba, may well have been undertaken or agreed to as a means of avoiding the heartache of her various liaisons, most notably that with Herrmann, as Langer suggests, the exchange with Porter would indicate something in the nature of a return of a prodigal to Herbst's Iowa undertaking. Certainly there is never any hint either in the correspondence or in her notes, that Herbst undertook party assignments that she herself had not initiated or at least willingly agreed to.

Resentful of the way the left-wing groups, the Communist Party especially, frequently manipulated people in the front lines of the demonstrations of the day--the farmers especially--Herbst obviously determined to treat her characters, when she came to incorporate them in her fiction, as vibrant human beings rather than as tools or symbolic representations of party dictate. Two farmer characters figure significantly in the trilogy, clearly derived from Herbst's experiences on the front lines of the farmers' struggles in the Midwest. The more important of these two characters is Steve Carson, the young farmer from South Dakota who dreams of getting free and using his powers as an inventor to rise up as per the American Dream. Carson's story does not mesh with the stories of the principal players, Victoria and Jonathan Chance, as that of the other farmer, a Pennsylvanian, Tim Robb, does. However, the narrative of Carson's struggle to get off the farm in a time of rising industrial unemployment, his marriage for love and subsequent inability to get free from his father-in-law's meagre acreage, followed finally by radicalization and participation in a farmers' strike, is told with a pathos that can only be deeply felt. It is as if Herbst had utilized all her newly unleashed empathetic powers--powers garnered and intensified in her own experiences with struggling farmers--and forged in the character of Carson an answer both to the belittling disbelief of middle-class intellectuals and the over-romanticizing of the Communist theorists with whom she associated.

Already an organizer of farmers, Carson as an observer seems as much a stand-in for Herbst herself as is the main autobiographical character, Victoria Chance. Certainly he is etched with the passion and intelligence Herbst conveyed to the readers of her reportage. So passionate was Herbst about even her more conventional report of a farmers' organizational meeting in Chicago in 1933, that she pulled it out of *The New Republic* because the editor threatened to cut itemizations of the farmers' grievances, then subsequently published the intact piece in *New Masses*. The degree of personal identification--possibly the source of her passion--she felt for the farmers she had personally shared quarters with can be seen in her delineation of Steve Carson's consciousness as he boards a boxcar to join up with a group of striking farmers:

> It gave him the feeling that he was going places at last and he felt lighthearted as he modestly leaned against the door and listened to the older men joke about the days when they had their pictures taken in store clothes and stiff new hats. Now their feet were in broken shoes, their workshirts were a faded blue, the overalls patched and frayed at the edges. They looked at one another, puzzled, groping, trying to make out what had happened to the country of their childhood. Once, every hired man saved to buy a little farm and every man who owned a farm figured on selling out and getting to California before he died or sharing with his kids and spending his last days looking at fat cattle and good acres tended and cared for all his life like his own children. Their bewilderment sizzled up at the words "monopolies" and "finance capital." (157)

By personifying the farm situation in the character of Steve Carson, and by creating in him a vibrant figure who transcends the stock strawmen of proletarian realism, Herbst breathes fictional life into what strikes us now as the more or less stale stance of her political journalism. Steve Carson is the living breathing figure Herbst perhaps meant to convey when she wrote in *New Masses*:

> This is a new self-conscious type of farmer meeting at Chicago. Talk to him on any subject relating to his condition and he has a confident, militant answer. . . . Perhaps no other class of people is in such a favorable position as the farmer to see the contradiction in the New Deal surplus production plan. The frugal farmer has raised food all his life, he has been drilled by the government on every device to get the most from the soil. Now he is ordered to turn under crops and to destroy hogs. He also knows there are millions unemployed in the cities and many hungry on the farms. Some of these town men came out to help the farmer on the picket lines. In Sioux City they did not spill milk on the roads during the strike but gave it to the

unemployed.   That the government talks "surplus" under such
conditions makes the farmer feel he is living in a world absolutely
crazy and that officials are proceeding with straight faces does not
restore his confidence. (20)

Viewed from the more personal perspective of Steve Carson, we see
the farmers as people, not as political pawns. Witness Carson's musing before
he gets on the boxcar that will take him to the strike:

> He wanted another chance to look at the farmers close up, as if he
> were examining his own future. The bunch at Yankton was a little
> more grim. They had the look of men who stare too long at the sky
> for weather. . . . It's hailing, god help the corn. Too much sun, the
> wheat is withering up. (156-57)

By contrasting these two modes of viewing the farmers, one as
political type, the other as personified individual, we see that a synergistic
effect takes place in the relationship between Herbst's journalism and her
fiction. The fictionalized account through the passionately drawn figure of
Steve Carson allows Herbst to convey the deep feelings actually being
involved with struggling farmers in her home town aroused within her in a
way that the constraints of political reportage did not allow. Fictionalized, the
situation takes on the dimensions that evade foregone conclusions and easy
answers. Certainly Carson, leaving wife and baby behind and mortgaging his
future on a hope of revolution, is not easy to sum up. We have all the doubts
we might have of a Dos Passos figure; little of the certainty of *New Masses*
critic Granville Hicks.

At the same time the well of lived passion Herbst has drawn on in
these farm episodes brings a vitality to her narrative--even when we doubt the
developmental viability from a plot point of view of the Carson strand--that
should certainly satisfy Isidor Schneider.   Indeed, her most journalistically
derived novel, *Rope of Gold*, has also been the most positively received both
at time of issue and when the trilogy was reissued in separate editions.

Perhaps more intriguing even than the farm struggle episodes is the
penultimate segment of the novel dealing with the Cuban uprising of 1935.
What is interesting from the standpoint of investigating the intermeshing of
journalism and fictive technique is the personal saga Elinor Langer elucidates
and Herbst herself developed in the novel. Compared to the personal drama,
the political coverage conveyed in Herbst's *New Masses* articles, revealing not

a trace of personal angst, creates a puzzling picture of the duality of the two aspects of Herbst as a writer.

The situation that Langer describes is that Herbst and Herrmann were breaking up their marriage. Herrmann had found another woman who became his wife. Herbst had had a couple of passionate liaisons with young women poets, but at the time she was offered the Cuban assignment, was primarily alone, mourning the loss of Herrmann. Langer presents a double column of Herbst's perhaps overly rational diary of the actual events of the uprising alongside excerpts of unanswered letters Herbst wrote to Herrmann, scolding, cajoling and generally pouring out her grief in the lugubrious manner of the lovelorn.

A third piece to the puzzle is presented by the *New Masses* dispatches themselves. Communist editor Joseph North is especially adulatory about Herbst's Realengo account. Realengo was a collective, far up in the mountains of sugar cane country, accessible only by donkey and an implicitly trusting guide. Herbst's account is singular for the portrait she gives of people--women and children especially--living without electricity or running water, but with illimitable hope. Herbst had been admitted because she had a Soviet stamp on her passport left from a previous trip to Moscow to a writers conference. Herbst, to be sure, personalizes her account. Nonetheless, the message is clear. The revolution is about the reorganization of property holdings, and the future is on the side of the poor who have the inspiration to take the initiative to accomplish that reorganization.

Reading this account after reading Langer, one is apt to do a double-take. Was Herbst schizophrenic (in the popular sense of that term) or did she just have a remarkable capacity to rise above her personal troubles or to transmogrify them into social travail that could perhaps be effectively defeated? The closest one can come to a perspective on the problem is to read *Rope of Gold* itself. Here, in the person of Victoria Chance on a reporter's mission to Cuba, Herbst develops the situation of the personal versus the political, though not in quite the same terms Langer does. For one thing, the female lovers, who may well have alienated Herrmann in the first place, are missing. Also, Herbst herself seems to explore the peculiar position she is in as a thoroughly professional reporter in a front-lines situation who is at the same time suffering from overwhelming heartache. In Cuba, amid the fighting, Victoria Chance is composing letters to the husband who has left her back home. The difference in the fictionalized presentation is that Victoria does not seem to be undergoing a case of double-vision to the extent that Langer's presentation of Herbst's Cuban diaries and dispatches would seem to indicate.

In one instance, after composing an especially lugubrious letter to her husband, Jonathan, in her Havana hotel, Victoria walks out into the fresh air, takes in her surroundings, with more visual perspicuity than the depressed are usually capable of, and tries to find some philosophical insight to help her see herself on her own:

> Every morning she rushed out, went about blindly, sniffing the air, her mind catching up this and that, ticketing it, putting it away. For what? . . . Her eyes, shielded from the sun by the brim of her hat, saw the feet of the passersby, in good snappy shoes, in torn rope-soled sandals, bare and scarred. The bare toes scraped and scratched aimlessly in the dust, the roped soles turned their piteous torn fragments to the light of day. On the benches, rest for the weary but for her there was no rest. Not here. Not there. The ceaseless eternal preparations of life must be now coming to some great secret; it would presently be revealed. (335)

The answer to the puzzle of a personal and a political that seem to be pulling in opposite directions seems to reveal itself both in the reportage and in the novelistic episode centering on Cuba. The answer, as Herbst herself steps back from the immediacy of painful feelings and passionate social involvement in both narratives, seems not to be that the political is a substitution for the personal, a deflection, or dehumanizing sublimation--at least not in Herbst's case. Rather she seems to anticipate the healing power of everyday life that many post-revolutionaries, not to mention many abandoned lovers, have found. Knowing the whole situation, we can read between lines in the final summation of her *New Masses* dispatch on Realengo:

> I am writing this many weeks later than the visit yet it is impossible not to write of it as if it were in a continuous present. This is Pennsylvania farming land. On May Day the farmers of this community had May Day in Doylestown. A woman told of the effort to evict her family of eight children. . . . They had to pay her a dollar apiece for five pigeons before she would go and the little humble triumph sounded good to every farmer. The meeting on the courthouse lawn closed with singing the *International* and I remembered one Sunday afternoon in Realengo 18 where it rained hard on the palm roof all day and little boys played a game with beans on the earthen floor. . . . We had been talking about the

problems of Realengo and some of the men had again drawn maps to show the relation of this district to Santiago and Havana where workers had gone on strike in sympathy with Realengo last August. Soon it was too dark to make maps and we began singing, first the *Marseillaise* and then the *International*. . . . Neither jail nor guns can completely silence such singing. (159)

If she ends her reportage on a note of far-reaching optimism, she concludes the Cuban section of *Rope of Gold* in the throes of the split-level problem:

Sometimes she went . . . to the university on the hill and talked with some spirited student, and all the time, every day she left herself standing by the desk in the hotel, patiently waiting for a letter, for a cable, for an old newspaper, folded up with the word "hello" written upon it in Jonathan's hand. There were moments when the sun, the talk, the strange tension in the very air, made her fears childish and stupid. She had only to finish her work, to take the boat, to go home, to find Jonathan and he would catch her up in his arms. . . .(340)

To see the resolution of the personal/political dichotomy in the Cuban episode in the novel in the same terms that it appears in the reportage we must reach for the conclusion that what follows the Cuban/Jonathan passage bears some relationship to the problem. This is a continuation of the Steve Carson weft. Seeming to bear no connection to the Cuban passage and to Victoria's pain, the Carson story appears yet to bear a resemblance to that of the evicted neighbor at the end of the *New Masses* story. This episode would indicate that in the midst of defeat and misery and even heartache there is still reason to hope. The passage describes the birth of Carson's son--considering the poverty and the black ever-present dust, a mixed blessing. A letter from his farmer/comrades, urging him to rejoin the struggle as soon as possible, makes of the Carson passage in relation to the pathos of the Cuban section a note of cautious optimism. The cry of the baby through a shield protecting it from dust echoes the villagers' strains of the *International*.

Precisely because of its dichotomous pathos--a pathos Herbst was clearly experiencing through the adventure itself--the Cuban episode is perhaps the strongest single element of the trilogy. It is true that the passage probes the severity with which political was severed from personal in Herbst's radical milieu and even gives a glimpse at a perhaps extreme coping mechanism--

running into gunfire--to salvage a broken heart. At the same time, however, it is here that Herbst begins to hone the graceful perceptions that make of her later memoirs truly first-rate reading. One hears and sees parrots in the air; cows slosh in the mud outside the huts; macho waiters pour sparkling daiquiris, and even high-level dignitaries stupefy startlingly with their stultifying boredom. Again, this heightened perception, which Herbst is to develop in her Spanish reportage, creates a vivid and vibrant narrative which can only derive from lived experience. Alongside it the financial doings of the Trexler brothers, which comprise much of the early volumes, stories derived from family legend rather than experience, seem at times tedious and plodding. Certainly, to return to Isidor Schneider's complaint about the spareness of the early novels, the desire to relate a cogitated and transmogrified, yet vivid life as it hit the sensual apparatus at the moment, and to transform that into an experience that will inspire similar sensual moments in the reader, has brought Herbst's prose out of the realm of false simplification and into the realm of the lived. At the same time we note that she has finally become more sympathetic both to herself as a character and to the women in the various sequences and has adopted--to the benefit of the pleasurableness of the reading--a prose and narrative style that incorporates the sensual, the emotional, and other qualities that are now under debate as "feminine" writing.

* * *

The point I want to make about Josephine Herbst's *Rope of Gold* trilogy is to call attention to its special significance for contemporary Marxist and feminist debates about what constitutes an agency for social change and the role of history--feminine history importantly included--in constructing and developing that agency.

Josephine Herbst's early stalwart determination to avoid the entertainment values of literature embodied in the sentimentalism, fussiness, prosody, and even gracious good humor that it was her generation's mark to thwart, contrasts with the more interesting nuances of her later work (and I find little of interest in her early work). This work offers the intellectual pleasure of witnessing the unfolding and development of the kind of sociological/economic themes I have indicated. This is not to say that her characters are not fleshed out vibrantly or that they are little more than ciphers in an imagined class-struggle situation, as were many of the characters in the "proletarian" novels she shunned. Quite the contrary. Having studied a considerable amount of Marxism since she and her husband John Herrmann came into the communist milieu, Herbst chose to return to her own family as subject matter and frankly chart the course of a middle-class middle-American road to socialist transformation. Having scanned most of her correspondence in the Yale archives, I am struck by how little she seemed to be aware of the degree to which she was entering into a fray among Marxist theoretical circles, charting her own course, and delimiting answers that would only be pursued productively two generations later.

Although Herbst was a friend and correspondent of James T. Farrell and William Phillips, she did not follow them into the Trotskyist movement and her correspondence with them, while addressing the questions of "socialist realism" and "proletarian realism," was primarily relevant to the period after she had composed most of the trilogy and of little interest in the kind of discussions of free will and determinism and the constitution of agencies of social change and constituency of the proletariat that occupy latter-day academic Marxist theoreticians. The only sign I have found that Herbst had a basis in theory for the line of inquiry she pursued in the trilogy is in her 1966 answer to David Madden's request for a contribution to his compilation *Proletarian Writers of the Thirties,* a request, as has been often noted, she refused. Denying the efficacy of the term "proletarian" and its relevance to her work, Herbst writes, "I thought of the writing as 'revolutionary' in the sense that the whole century was going to be involved, in one way or another, with revolution, and I think this is quite right." (Madden xvii)

Herbst goes on to spell out the relationship she sees between an era she characterizes as "revolutionary" in terms that are decidedly not "proletarian."

> When I was writing my trilogy I never thought of it as 'proletarian'--in fact I hated the term, and thought it never comprehensive enough. . . . We weren't afraid of being didactic and I wasn't afraid of being subversive. In fact, I intended to be. . . . The urgency of the times crumpled much that would have made the works more valid but there was never time or space. The whole business of that kind of world view and type of writing needed room for development which never came. (xxi)

Perhaps the meat of Herbst's position in writing forthrightly about the middle classes in the teeth of a proletarian tempest can be expressed in the quotations from Marx selected by the modern-day theorist Joseph Ferraro. Referring to *The Holy Family,* Ferraro interprets Marx's discussion of "'the sentence that private property pronounces on itself by producing the proletariat,'" to mean "The proletariat therefore has the universal historical mission of emancipating humankind; it does so because in it is found 'the abstraction of all humanity, even of the *semblance* of humanity.'" (80)

I don't know whether Herbst herself would discuss the proletariat in those terms, averse as she was to placing herself in a conspicuous position in the internecine battles over "proletarian" writing, but from her trilogy and memoirs, certainly, it seems clear that it was precisely an "abstraction of all humanity" that could yet perform an emancipatory mission given the right conditions of consciousness that was most nearly the subject of the quest of the better part of her prose. If we take the "Rope of Gold" image as a symbol of her intent, and combine that with the import of her journalistic observations and her later memoirs, we can see that it was clearly Herbst's mission to propose the fusion of class forces rather than the sundering of them. Middle-class intellectuals combined with workers and intellectuality per se has as much validity in her work as does the "honest brogue" of mineworkers. If we follow Herbst's proposals, we might see that the emancipation of humanity will come from the juncture of an amalgam of social forces working in unison rather than by the imposition of the will of the working class alone. In this fashion, Herbst shifts the locus of emancipation from the belly to the head and heart.

Furthermore, to delimit a feminist position on this issue, we can borrow from Elizabeth Fox-Genovese's discussion with Elshtain's division between public and private spheres. Fox-Genovese argues that Elshtain's division of masculine into public and feminine into private domains tends to limit women to an essentialist position and exclude them from the political world where the important decisions are made that affect their own welfare. Clearly in the trilogy, if not in the early work, Herbst develops a trio of siblings who represent the difference between males who are monetarily defined in capitalist terms and women, who, remaining outside the sphere of capital, can prefigure the path to revolutionary commitment. Let us see how that develops.

Herbst's commitment to a study of the American middle class dates to the beginning of her commitment to writing in the first place. Starting out as a reader and sometime writer for H.L. Mencken, Herbst developed the supercilious half-mocking tone with which her generation--from Sinclair Lewis to Dorothy Parker--tweezed open the wounds of monetarily-oriented America at the beginning of the century. In Herbst's early fiction, men and women are equally afflicted by the bug of capital.

In her early prose, Herbst quickly adopted her characteristic anti-sentimental style. Her sentences are short and direct, devoid of decoration and emotion. Her first novel, *Nothing Is Sacred* (1928) is set in her native Iowa, where it caused quite a commotion. It has a Sinclair Lewis plot told in a Gertrude Stein flatness of narration. The central characters are members of a middle-class family who seem comfortable enough, except that one member, Harry, has embezzled $3,000 in dues money from his lodge. The plot is then focussed on the relationship of Harry's crime and need of money in relation to three sisters (including his wife) and their mother. For our purposes, what seems important to consider is that all elements of the characterizations and plot elements are monetarily constructed. Harry's wife's coldness and diffidence--even her affairs--and the mother's concern for her old age, along with a younger sister's husband's misbegotten affair and the girl's abortion are all motivated by desires for money and the warping of the personality that can be brought on by viewing people as pawns in a game to accumulate more of it . There is, in the novel, very little in the way of humanly assertive stuff of life that is not economically determined. Of course, this economic determination is not, and in Herbst's work, never would be, a matter of Marxist dogma translated into fiction, anymore than is the work of Sinclair Lewis, Sherwood Anderson or F. Scott Fitzgerald. Herbst, though already a Greenwich Village radical of sorts when she wrote this novel, was not following any set "line." She was, rather, in keeping with the mainstream writers of her time. She explores the psychological dimensions of the mother's domination as well as the import of the lives of the daughters, isolated from the working world and financially dependent upon their husbands. As a result of their dependence, they seem to become all the more bitter and caustic, allowing their frustration to take the form of monetary concern.

It is difficult to determine from Herbst's notes and correspondence the degree to which she herself saw the money motive as inescapable in capitalist society and the resultant heartless greed of her characters as unavoidable, a point of view that would seem to be indicated by her early work. As Daniel Aaron notes, in a proto-postmodernist note, Herbst rejected emancipatory narratives either of the right or of the left, and confined herself, in that period, to meticulous, uninflected dissections of the workings of capital on the middle class, rejecting the deliverance promised by her communist friends. As Aaron notes: "Josephine Herbst, who would soon switch to [Mike] Gold's camp and then depart again, sardonically rejected his utopia as well as [Matthew]

Josephson's as late as 1929":

> "All in all, [Herbst wrote] I find the position of Mr. Josephson
> singularly like that of Mr. Gold. Both are hell bent toward a
> banalium, one communistic, the other mechanistic. Both utter hoarse
> cries to loyal cohorts, both point the finger of derision at other
> Pathfinders or rather deny that there is more than one Path. Pathfinder
> Josephson and Pathfinder Gold both paint enviable pictures of the
> promised land. Both have such jolly cohorts, such enthusiastic,
> robustious, forward looking companions in their steady tread toward
> the Soullenium. I can't make up my mind which gent is the better
> bet. Both are undoubtedly sound. There's not a question in my mind
> but that we're all headed toward some sort of bolognyum. Yours for
> the Aluminium. " (134-5)

Herbst's debt to Gertrude Stein, and, significantly, her own
commitment to the dailiness of life, she expressed openly in a quarrel with her
good friend Katherine Anne Porter.   Porter had attacked Stein for an
"irresponsible" fascination with chaos. In a 1948 article in *Partisan Review*,
Herbst answers:

> In her chosen orbit, Gertrude Stein was responsible, and more may be
> learned from her failures than from any number of glittering,
> successful works patterned on models with which we are familiar.
> She was under the spell of the private life that goes on whether there
> is justice or injustice, struggle or ennui, and she hoped by abolishing
> the chronological sequence to express life by its values only. (570)

This sense of the importance of the "spell of private life," if not the
abolition of chronology, is the key to Herbst's most significant work, the
trilogy she produced while thinking through key issues of radicalism within the
communist milieu of the 1930s. In the *Rope of Gold* trilogy Herbst traces the
saga of her own family down to her own radicalization, and in this context a
new strand develops in the warp. *Pity Is Not Enough* (1933), the first in the
trilogy, presents the generation of the autobiographical heroine's antecedents,
the Trexlers. The history, although primarily focusing on the two brothers,
Joseph and David, is feminized in two important ways. First, it is important
to note that while the two brothers are almost completely motivated by money,
the sister, Anne Trexler, mother of Victoria, who will stand in for Herbst

herself, escapes this determining influence. She is able to enjoy evening walks when she contemplates the heavens, to see to the personal lives of her brothers and sisters and generally to become a dominant figure in her own private sphere. While she is certainly interested in money, that money is a means to the end of family comfort and harmony and progress, rather than, as with her brothers, an end in itself.

The second aspect of feminization resides in the fact of the narrative construction. Although the interest is directed to the development of the two brothers, we are reminded by the author herself in an inset passage and by the critic Winifred Bevilacqua that Herbst derived virtually all the material for this story by listening to her mother's stories and reading papers in her mother's attic. The result is a feminized appropriation of what had seemed a male-dominated history. Further, while the opening of the trilogy depicts the founding fathers of the line, it is the feminine line we are following. The crucial figure is not Joe but Anne Wendel, modeled on Herbst's mother. The figure who will carry the brunt of the narrative, upon whom the effects of the men's efforts will be wreaked, is the daughter in the line, Victoria Chance. Thus, although seemingly concerned with the male figures in their own right, the narrative would seem to derive its importance from the effect those men have had in the shaping of Victoria's perspective. The family saga has come to be, like the heirlooms originally given by Uncle Joe, a feminized artifact. It is now a branch of what Luce Irigaray came to call the genealogical continuum, or women's history. It is subject to what women have chosen to preserve and relate about it in the private sphere of conversations around the parlor table and what a female author chooses to reintegrate into the public sphere. Further, the conclusion shows that the material of the family saga has been primarily important for its effect on the main female character, daughter of Anne Trexler Wendel, Victoria Chance, who herself becomes an important radical figure.

Broadly historical in scope, *Pity Is Not Enough* encompasses the period after the Civil War. Joe Trexler is a carpetbagger who goes South and gets involved in a petty railroad swindle that is magnified to such proportions that he must leave. He heads west to the gold mines and there scrambles for a living. In the meantime, brother David, who has had the advantages of education, also heads west and, due to shrewd investment policies, parlays a humble pharmacy into a prosperous banking concern. This is the era of capitalist expansion and the two brothers play out two aspects of this scenario. Where are the women in all this? The focus, in that regard, is on Anne, her financially unfortunate husband, Amos Wendel, and their four daughters.

Anne's main qualities--feminine goodness of soul and generosity of spirit--keep her primarily out of the marketplace and at the same time instill in her younger two daughters a pride in American family tradition that will eventually inspire them to make a life for themselves away from the gender-controlled hearth. Uncle Joe's tea service, bought with embezzled funds, glistens on the parlor sideboard as an emblem of the possibilities of a growing America and not as a symbol of the confining strictures of a masculine world.

In the second volume, *The Executioner Waits* (1934), Victoria, the touchstone figure in the trilogy, takes from her family's middle-class world a sense that opportunities are open to her and that she need not construct the structure of her life in inherited gender-defined terms. In this novel, the keystone of the trilogy, radicalism enters in the person of a relative in the IWW, who intrigues Victoria by his individualism. When Victoria meets Jonathan Chance, renegade from his bourgeois business-world family, she is all ready to join with him in the cause of communist organization.

If the critics were harsh with Herbst's early novels, they tended to warm up with the appearance of the trilogy. To be sure no critic, not even on the left, made the comment I have made that the fault of the early novels resides in the fact that the characters are motivated by monetary rather than human concerns, and that Herbst tends to stand in opposition to anything that could be construed as a feminine or feminist attitude or style. If anything, the criticism was that Herbst had understood her characters as individuals rather than as socially determined. *The Nation* reviewer writing of *Nothing Is Sacred* critiqued the novel as

> The life of a mean, gray, middle-class American family set down in a designedly mean, gray, middle-class American prose. Miss Herbst is as skilful within the limitations of her manner as anyone could possibly be; and she extracts from the petty tragedies of her characters more than one would think conceivable. Fiercely honest as this recent type of realistic writing is, it leads one to suspect its intrinsic artistic importance. . . . At times it seems as if Miss Herbst's carefully flattened style and piteously truncated characters were merely the inventions of a sophisticated intellect that is choosing this more difficult and delicate method in order to express indirectly a sense of complete fatigue. For if we do not consider it as a projection of a personal pessimism, Miss Herbst's novel, admirable and intelligent as it is, is in the end unmoving.[3]

Interestingly enough, women reviewers from the less politically conscious papers of the Midwest tended to be more generous in their welcome of Josephine Herbst. What is interesting about this is that, as Jane Tompkins has pointed out, the female readership even as late as 1929 tended to the sentimentalizing and extolling of the virtues of family life that it was precisely Herbst's mission to subvert. To the contrary, Isabel Campbell, writing in the Oklahoma City Press, reports

> Miss Herbst has accomplished a tour de force. She has given us something new and original and fascinating in the matter of novel technique . . . She uses the pared to the bone, boiled down method that Mr. Hemingway has made popular, but she uses it with a difference. Her method is organic. It fits her material as no other method could. The stumbling, disordered unfinished periods of her dialogue reveal her characters better than any embellishment of style could do . . . . It is inconceivable that people who talk so should have any clear conception of what they want or how to get it. The muddle in which they get themselves, by their own folly makes a sad, pitiful and yet amusing story.

As Katherine Anne Porter pointed out in her review in the New York *Tribune*: "You will not find a trace of sentimental revolt or sentimental hatred or special pleading." Porter also pointed to the central strength of the mother character in *Nothing Is Sacred*, holding the family together by dint of sheer force of personality.

That women--at least women writing in publications--were more sympathetic to the early novels than were men suggests possibly that Herbst's rapier attack on the sentimentalizing of the family thrust home. Male writers--especially leftist men--wanted to see more social determinism and less defeatism. They were happier with the trilogy, but still did not see it in the feminist terms I have been indicating. Even acknowledging the importance of the women's story in *Pity Is Not Enough*, *Saturday Review* critic Basil Davenport, perhaps understandably, tends to see that aspect of the novel through male eyes:

> The story is told largely in terms of the effect on [Joe Trexler's] womenfolk, his mother, his sisters, and the Southern girl whose suitor he had been, and who suffer for him all through his life. Much of his story is presented to us as it reaches the women at home, in a tangle

of counter-accusations, and this is enclosed in another frame, for the whole story of Joe Trexler is given to us as it gradually unfolded itself to the nephews and nieces who never saw him, from the scattered anecdotes told by their mother, his sister. The whole book is written in the homely idiom that would be employed by such women; and the result is a powerful picture of the seamy side of life in drab houses and dreary towns, in the latter half of the last century. . . . For the women in the story, it is true pity is not enough, it will do them no good. And yet in this world God Himself could offer them no more. They love Joe, and Joe is worthless, and all that can be said is that the human tendency to fasten love upon worthless objects is, according to the point of view, the most hopeful and most pitiful thing about mankind.

It must be noted that Herbst's own intention may well have been to do more with theme than style. While her early novels are marked by a stylistic asperity that proves to be their most salient feature, in the trilogy she departs from the mean anti-sentimentalism that had been her early trademark. Here, the work shows the results of her encounter with Marxism and seems marked by an attempt to develop her own point of view on the questions posed by the radical left. Without issuing public documents on the issue of class struggle, Herbst in the trilogy seems to indicate that she has done her own independent thinking, primarily on the question of what constitutes a class force and what will become the agency of social change. She does this in the form of a family saga delineating the plight of the middle class and the forging of a new class force in the merging of interests of the working class and the middle class. This unification would include a solidarity across gender and race. Key to the determination of the direction of this force--toward liberation or disentegration--is the factor of consciousness. If this seems to subvert the essential doctrine of communist-initiated proletarian literature of the time, it does. Herbst's rope of gold, however diverse and indefinable the strands, yet pulls together into the conveying of a social force that may have an effect on the changing of the world in the direction of a humane vision more individualistic but no less beneficial than the force of class struggle alone.

In her discussion of the trilogy, Paula Rabinowitz notes that Victoria's "desire as a radical intellectual is to articulate the psychological and historical forces pushing the waffling middle class into action." (157) As Rabinowitz says, referring to the trilogy,

This weblike structure serves a number of rhetorical functions. First, it implies that one cannot build a monofocal narrative about history; too many contradictory forces shape it. Second, one cannot assume the individuality of a family, which is constantly being shaped by economics, history, and politics. Third, although individuals feel atomized within American capitalism, appearing to drift along disconnectedly, they are interconnected by class. (160)

I would only add a contextual factor. Herbst was voicing her concern with the interconnectedness of class and the indeterminateness of personal and social history precisely at a time and in a milieu that isolated the working class as the primary agent of social change and that tended, if anything, to assert unequivocally that history and materialist factors were all that needed to be taken into consideration in social analysis. As her private letters and notes indicate, Herbst steadied herself on a course that was decidedly her own.

As Walter Rideout's invaluable if perhaps overambitious omnium gatherum suggests with reference to Herbst:

Despite heavy prose and mechanical structure, the over-all scheme [of the trilogy] even if one rejects the doctrine, lends a certain dramatic power to these books. That scheme is clear enough. The middle class, which so long obscured the actual operation of Marxian laws in American capitalism, is fast disintegrating between the hammer and the anvil of the two great antagonistic classes. The lines are now drawn. Class war is out in the open for all to see. (193)

Rabinowitz discusses *Rope of Gold* in the context of Tess Slesinger's *The Unpossessed,* stating, "The female intellectual, like the male proletarian, enters history, but she does so through her desire to connect the language of the personal to the experience of the political." In point of fact, it is more difficult to see how this theory proves out with Herbst's work than with Slesinger's. Slesinger clearly counterposes the world of working-class women having babies and enjoying a solidarity with each other in the maternity ward to the hothouse sterile intellectualism of the left-wing male magazine editors she satirizes. In the case of Herbst, all her characters are personalized, male and female. Certainly, Anne Trexler Wendel, the mother of the piece, operates more intimately outside the male-dominated marketplace than do her brothers. However, as Victoria's exploits indicate, women function at the site of political event as effectively as men. If Victoria's heart is on her sleeve, so is Steve Carson's.

Surprisingly, considering her two major lesbian engagements (delineated by Elinor Langer), Josephine Herbst had very little to say in her private notes and correspondence about feminism or "the woman question." There are some passing references to male chauvinism within the party, but even her attacks on Mike Gold in letters to James T. Farrell characterized Gold not as a sexist but as "anti-intellectual." Her complaints about the inhumanity of CP life tended to discuss general human rather than gender values. In a letter to a friend indicated merely as Kay from Paris in 1935, Herbst, referring to various dispositions in relation to her breakup with Herrmann, laments "When our movement realizes that it cannot expect work from people inhumanly treated, it may be wiser and get closer to what the masses live by."

One of her few references to her own assertive stance as a woman occurs in her draft notes for her memoirs in preparation for the collection published as *The Starched Blue Sky of Spain*. Here, describing the personal excreta she had left behind in her house for those who came after her to find, she waxes nostalgic:

> Or they might feel along the gritty shelf for newspaper clippings with accounts of murders, strikes and fires; nesting habits of birds; what to do about the wasp. Or find the old little magazines and *The Little Review* that I had carried to classes in Berkeley in 1917 when I should have toted, no doubt, a ball of wool to knit a sock for a soldier boy.

Even here, it is not clear whether she is denigrating the ball of wool because it is a symbol of feminine compliance to men in general or compliance to World War I in particular. What is clear is that the issue of memory and how memory constructs consciousness is important to Herbst. In an undated note in her files, she observes:

> Discrepancies and contradictions make no difference at all: they do not matter. Anything that [smacks] of comparative literature is apt to sound pedantic and boring, yet it is hard to resist pointing out that Remembrance of Things Past is also full of discrepancies and contradictions--although one could avoid that literary allusion by simply pointing out that our own memories of our own past are constantly subject to voluntary and involuntary revision, and that the stories of our lives as we rehearse them, unhappily enough, to ourselves are never orderly or final. And it is, of course, precisely

this contemplative revisionist quality, this picking up of an object and turning it over and over again, this diligent inspection of a character, this experimental - in the scientific sense - testing of actuality against hypothesis, that gives F [Farrell?]'s work the importance it has, providing it also, not accidentally, with that power of attraction, that sort of incantation, which triumphs over all manner of obstacles.

In the face of charges that she was a "Stalinist" or attempts to include her in the category of proletarian realists, it is sometimes hard to realize with what difficulty Herbst honed for herself a unique vision, socially conscious but not held to any party dictate. A little of that difficulty can be glimpsed in her correspondence with James T. Farrell, whom she supported in his fight within the Communist Party, but did not eventually follow. Reporting to Farrell from Paris on her way to Berlin in 1935, Herbst relates an encounter with some rather effete intellectuals:

And good work is good work and stands so always which is something for some of the too fervent ranters for proletarian literature at all costs--but what the precious school forgets [is] that great art has to relate to something besides great art, it doesn't hang like an arm to the sky but like an arm to a body and the body is the body of this living world, not some dream place where a few choice spirits genteely bugger each other under violet lights with masses of asters standing at bay.

That Herbst's position could be contradictory can be seen from a 1962 letter to Stanley [Kunitz] which discusses the relationship between the personal and the political in non-gendered terms:

The roots of abstraction in the psyche are important - for abstractions do not move out of a void though they move toward a void. And in rejecting abstract art the Russians were moving toward abstraction of man, himself, just as the whole tendency of the 20th century - alas - is moving here and elsewhere toward impersonal, not individual man. But this central issue is what is exciting to try to see and why a book like Daniel Aaron's on the Left Writers (no mention of writing at all in the book - it is all management, party orders - functionalism as a matter of fact) is so useless. It doesn't explain me in the thirties and I doubt if it explains you.

Herbst continued to wrestle with the philosophical issues implicit in her alliance with communism all her adult life. Her contemplations frequently take on a weighty, ponderous nature but are rarely despairing, even after the revelations of the Stalinist debacle. In her 1960s memoirs, making notes to herself, she indicates some of the lines of thought that had motivated herself and her writing all her productive life. Here, she is writing a brief essay, not for publication, on Berdyayev, Slavery and Freedom.

There is no organic principle, no integrality, no totalitarianism existing in society at all. Society is always partial and to claim integral organic principle for the organization of society is to give a false character of sacredness to things that are relative. The organic in society is an illusion of objectivization. Not only is the totalitarian state [an] enslaving lie, but Tot. soc. is an enslaving lie also. As nature is partial, so is society partial. It is not society that is an organism; it is man that is an organism. The idea of integral man, not of integral society, ought to be laid as the foundation-stone of the organization of society. The organic ideal of society is an enslaving lie. This is the social lure, and it is like the lure of the cosmos. Society is not an organism; [it] is co-operation. The organic idea of society is an illusion of enslaving consciousness; it is a product of exteriorization. A society of free men, not of slaves, ought to be created not on the pattern of the cosmos but on the pattern of the spirit, that is, not on the model of hierarchism but on the model of personalism, not on the pattern of determination but on the pattern of freedom, not on domination of force and of the strong man, but on the model of solidarity and kindliness of heart. Such a society alone would not be servile. The sources of human freedom cannot be in society, but in the human spirit. Everything which proceeds from society is enslaving; everything which issues from the spirit is liberating. The right and true gradation is the primacy of personality over society, its primacy over the state; and behind this stands the primacy of spirit over the world.

It is hard to tell from this how much of what she wrote in her private notes was a matter of items she found interesting in her reading and how much was a statement of her own philosophy at the time. Surely, we can see that to call Herbst a "Stalinist" or a slavish copier of proletarian realist dictate is a gross misjudgment. At the same time, one would have to stretch the terms of the discussion of the relationship between the personal and the political or the public and the private to attribute to Herbst any active involvement in the feminist discussion. The import of the major novels, I suggest, is that they go beyond class, race, and gender to discuss a unity of humankind as the possible locus for hope for a transformation in the social and spiritual order.[4]

Notes

1. For a full discussion of this convention and the effect it had on *Anvil*, see Douglas Wixson's *Worker-Writer in America: Jack Conroy and the Tradition of Midwestern Literary Radicalism, 1898-1990.* Urbana: U of Chicago P. 1994.

2. These quotes are taken from Josephine Herbst's own file of reviews now in the archives at the Beinecke Library. In many cases, page numbers and even precise dates are missing.

3. These reviews are taken from Josephine Herbst's private collection in her archives and frequently give no indication of exact date or page.

4. Portions of this chapter appear as a contribution to the anthology *The Eye of the Reporter,* Deckle McLean and Bill Knight, eds. Western Illinois UP. 1996.

Chapter Eight

Josephine Herbst: Memory Speaks

Curiously, although Josephine Herbst clearly played a crucial role in the break from the Communist Party initiated by what has come to be known as the "New York Intellectuals," who went on to revive and reinvent *Partisan Review,* her name has been all but eliminated from the published record of that venture. The reasons for this may be at least twofold. First, one must consider the biases of the primarily male recorders of that dispute and the fact that somehow no clues led them to the Yale archives where Herbst's lengthy correspondence with James T. Farrell and William Phillips, prime actors in the crucial dispute, is readily available. Second, one considers, from further notes by Herbst herself, that for various constitutional reasons of her own, she was not game for a primary position in a political dispute which was not suited to her political temperament, even if such a position had been available to her, or she simply didn't choose to go public with her views. As it was, the key position I am suggesting she played was as background confidante, sounding board for Phillips and Farrell to develop their strategies and rationales, and she intervened publicly herself on only a few significant occasions. While those occasions--most notably her angry letter to Mike Gold defending Farrell--have been noted in most works on the period, the key correspondence has somehow been overlooked.

According to discussions by Alan Wald, James F. Murphy, and Walter Rideout, the key issue in the dispute was the Communist Party's insistence on proletarian realism as the required mode of expression among acceptable writers and artists. (Murphy, it should be noted, has important new material to add, indicating that the issue of "proletarian realism" was not as central to the dispute as had been previously thought.) Phillips, Farrell and Rahv, the argument goes, wanted acceptance for a more eclectic, more pro-modernist prose. While this is undoubtedly the central issue, what comes through in the correspondence with Herbst is that the *Partisan Review* editors had little respect for the party leadership, especially Mike Gold, and resented being dictated to by them on any terms.

Farrell and Phillips both began their friendships with Herbst at the writers colony Yaddo during the period when she was breaking up with Herrmann. Farrell and Herbst became, for a while, fast friends, Farrell and his wife Hortense offering Herbst sanctuary in their apartment in New York while she was suffering the doldrums of the divorce. At about the same time the dispute was brewing that would lead to the ultimate split of the *Partisan Review* editors from the Communist Party. That Herbst was a principal in that split is clear from the correspondence. What remains an open question is why she did not follow her new friends into their organizational arrangements.

Farrell wrote in a January 2, 1935, letter to Herbst:

> Also the New Masses has been a preponderantly philistine magazine, and I don't think that it has really encouraged the production and the reading and understanding of literature. The argument that its main point is politics is not a reply to this charge, because the New Masses has devoted, weekly, a great deal of space to culture, literary criticism and the rest of it. The trouble has been that it has used this space and used it like philistines, and not at all encouraged writing, and gotten the best that has been written in rev. literature, and not gotten much from younger writers, poets, and short story writers, and so since that [is] so, I hope, but with apprehension, that the Sunday Worker might do something. Well, again we'll see.

What Farrell, Phillips and Rahv failed to take on, was the whole relationship between art and revolution that James Murphy indicates was under discussion at the time between the Soviet Comintern and the international parties, the CPUSA included. Trotsky's position, outlined in *Literature and Revolution*, widely circulated by Max Eastman, was attractive to both Farrell and Herbst, but did not really address the central issue--that of the relationship of artistic creativity to the task of taking power in the name of the working class. Trotsky addresses the questions in terms of what a revolutionary government's position should be once the socialist state has been established.

Then, he concludes, a full flowering of humanistic experimentation and individualistic expression should be encouraged. It would require a reading of the latter-day Frankfurt Utopianist writer Ernst Bloch to translate that philosophy into one that could be utilized in the struggle for socialism under conditions of capitalism. While Phillips, Farrell and Rahv did not seem to concern themselves directly with the relationship of literature to the struggle for workers power, implicitly they seemed to be entering this discussion with the slogan: It is not the function of art to serve the ends of the revolution; it is the function of the revolution to serve the ends of art. Clearly, this slogan would have been judged heretical if overtly expressed--perhaps even by Trotsky.

The two issues that intertwined not always in a way that was easy to discriminate were thus the issue of the efficacy of the insistence on proletarian writing and the point that the *Partisan Review* group--Herbst included--had little use for the party leadership at least as far as its literary policies were concerned. The issue came to a head even before the American Writers Congress where the debate ensued, over the question of Farrell's review in the *Herald Tribune* of Clara Weatherwax's proletarian novel *Marching! Marching!* This novel had won the prize in the literary contest sponsored by the *New Masses* in 1935.[1] Farrell, making no discussion of the feminist aspects of the novel that Rabinowitz was to point out, blasted the novel in the communist press under the heading *Stumbling! Stumbling!* For this he was roundly attacked as a petty-bourgeois decadent. Herbst came to his defense when the warfare between Farrell and the party leadership included Farrell's attack on Clifford Odets. She wrote an angry letter to Mike Gold, which Gold printed in a somewhat bowdlerized version that she had agreed to. The antagonism Farrell felt toward the CP leadership on the question of literature and his own act of deliberately pitting himself against that literature can be seen in the following paragraph written in a letter to Herbst, December 22, 1935:

> I reviewed "Stumbling Stumbling," the New Masses prize novel, and it will appear, my review, in next Sunday's books. Look for it. I attacked the book without mercy. I said it came as a shock since it was a prize novel. Because revolutionary writing in America had attained a considerable degree of maturity, and that in proof, it could claim such works as novels by Josephine Herbst, Henry Roth, Nelson Algren, and Grace Lumpkin, short stories, by Caldwell, Hughes, Godin, plays by Albert Bein, and that this piece was just no good. And I quoted the New Masses heralding it in an editorial paragraph.

The Book Union selected it too.   Well I am not going to be a ballyhoo boys for those guys when they pick a mediocrity like this poor girl, and tell her she is the author of a prize novel that will be the most memorable prize novel of this period.   And so, I'll see how Tracty [Alexander Trachtenberg] and the boys like my attack.

To such Party regulars out in the field as Meridel Le Sueur, the fight seemed to be a class issue (interview).   The intellectuals objecting to working-class writing were seen as petty-bourgeois dilettantes attacking the proletarian nature of the party itself.   While this explains Le Sueur's much-quoted speech at the American Writers Congress in 1935, where the issue came to a head, it only partially serves to explain why Herbst was on the opposite side from Le Sueur on this issue.

Herbst, who by all indications, never herself joined the Communist Party, can be seen as opposed as much to party discipline and dictate as she was opposed to proletarian literature.   As we have seen, her trilogy suggests a sympathy for the working-class characters such as Steve Carson and the implicit proposal that the revolutionary movement can be strengthened by an alliance of the working class with the middle-class intellectuals who are won over to its cause.   The official party response to this proposition (with the exception of the brief period of the Popular Front), not new to Marxist-Leninist discussion, was that the middle-class intellectuals who want to align themselves to the workers' cause must purge themselves of bourgeois decadence and subordinate themselves to the dictates of the proletarian party.[2] An exception to this was made during the Popular Front period when, in its fight against fascism, the CPUSA, following Moscow dictates, courted "name" luminaries to enlist their sympathy to the Soviet aspect of the Allied cause.

In February of 1957, in answer to Edgar Branch, Farrell's biographer, who was obviously inquiring about the Farrell/Herbst correspondence of the thirties, Josephine Herbst wrote a lengthy summation of her relationship to Farrell and the relationship of both of them to the literary dictates of the CPUSA.   As the letter is both comprehensive and succinct, I will quote it almost in its entirety:

James Farrell and I had an extensive correspondence for about two years, from 1935 into 1937, and his letters were usually long and detailed. . . . A good many of the letters came to me in the summer of 1935 when I was in Germany for the New York Post and later in Paris.   When I returned I lived with Farrell and Hortense in their apartment on Lexington Avenue.   My marriage had broken up and their kindness meant a great deal to me. I left in about a month to stay at Yaddo all that winter until I had a Guggenheim in the spring.

But my first meeting with Farrell was at Yaddo the year before, in 1934, when I went up there in early winter to finish some work. They were living in the old farmhouse and Farrell and I stayed up late every night drinking coffee and talking. I read in mss. the Studs Lonigan last volume at that time. It was, and remains for me, an extremely impressive book.

I think it would be important for you in interpreting or understanding Farrell to get as much as you can of the climate of the period, a time extremely different from today. When I first met Farrell he struck me as being an independent person to the point of loneliness. He didn't belong to any cliques and what he had worked out within himself had come, so it seemed to me, pretty independently. The important factor for him was that he had really *lived,* he had lived in his early days in Chicago and had seen through the implications of his experiences with a searching vision that naturally carried him beyond his own personal experience. He was an avowed Marxist and a consistent one, so consistent that he was obligated also to enter very soon into controversies with the [prevailing] social demogogues of the time. I think Farrell's [intransigent] position as it was related to literary matters was important not only to himself but to others also.

As I remember, the letter of mine to which you refer in The [New] Masses had to do with Farrell's criticism of Clifford [Odets]. He was attacked by Mike Gold and some of us combined to sign a letter which I wrote in defense not only of Farrell's position but in general the right of anyone to criticize. It was an extremely important point. The original letter was even more emphatic. For in it I said that an anti-intellectual attitude was basically a fascist position, and therefore any blurring of the issues was catering to attitudes fundamentally fascist. The result was that a meeting was called with some of the editors of the New Masses and an attempt was made to have me withdraw the letter entirely. Philip Rahv who also signed the letter backed me up during this discussion but I was persuaded to take out the word "fascist" as directly referring to Mike Gold. I was willing to do this, partly because I was already tired of these words slung about, and partly because the material itself indicated the actuality. That was a time when the Communists were calling

Norman Thomas a "social-fascist" and this name slinging didn't elucidate anything. I could even ask myself just how much or how little my own use of the word "fascist" meant in the given instance.

The entire episode was very important to me and I am sure to others too. I had been perhaps closer in actual working operations of committees, etc. than Farrell, to the New Masses editors and the whole left movement, but this episode dated my own withdrawal. But in a period like that a withdrawal does not come about overnight. Both Farrell and I were interested in the formation of the League of American Writers, too, and yet I believe that neither he nor I had anything to do with it in its subsequent meanderings.

From the point of view of the literary scene, the Communist role was more and more opportunist, in one sense, and less tolerant in another sense. That is, they began to court anybody with a name, a commercial name, in the big time sense. On the other hand, they were less tolerant to people like Farrell or myself, who weren't big commercial names and had at heart only an interest which would lead to some kind of purification in the realm of criticism; the recognition of good writing, not tied to commercial success. Not that good writing might not be commercially successful, but the distinction of what it meant truly to write well was important. All these aims became blurred. The left press was not very hospitable to the very people trying truly to interpret their times. Mike Gold was sentimentally addicted to any "worker" who might throw down his shovel and take up a pen. The League of American writers had no distinction whatever so far as literature was concerned and lost its original meanings almost immediately.

It was unfortunate too that the left simply foisted the term "proletarian" upon writing of the period. There was no such thing actually, and the name was misleading, not to say abysmally stupid. Farrell understood all of this very well. His development seemed to me to proceed inevitably and steadily from certain thoroughly understood roots. . . .

The left press and certainly the League of American Writers tended to be overawed by that bitch goddess, success, and Farrell was interested in defining the roots from which literature might spring, in defining the actual writing in its own terms. I think he performed valuable services in that period quite apart from his own work. But as a friend he was sometimes hard to take. . . . I say he was hard to take because he was so terribly concentrated and consecrated, and sometimes became obsessive; his literary feuds too wearing to be borne. This has its good side, for him as a writer, but is likely to be devastating to a friend who is too close. . . .

I am not as familiar with his later work as I should be. Nor am I interested in the American Committee for Cultural Freedom with which I believe he has been involved. I am perhaps more suspicious of organizations which tend to discard one kind of totalitarianism for another kind. But I am sure of one thing, so far as Farrell is concerned, and that is that he could never be involved in anything for opportunist reasons, but for deep motives essentially moral. His work is concerned with the moralities and that is what gives it so much authority.

In thinking about the period of the thirties in terms of writing it seems to me that the New Masses and the petty functionaries of the left were making all the mistakes, which on a huge scale the Soviet Union has made, with probably more excuse--although *nothing* can validate such procedure. Farrell was keeping to Marx, who could read Balzac with admiration and despise the little squirts who were producing socialistic tracts under the guise of socialist fiction; he was also perfectly aware that Lenin had good taste, read widely and never presumed to step even on Gorki's literary toes. There is such a thing as writing, simply as writing, and Farrell knew it and hammered away at it. In one sense the left tended to inflate the wrong values of the writing they tended to admire. When they did praise writing like Farrell's, for instance, it was often for the wrong reasons, inflating the wrong reasons and thus warping the intention. But the real heroes in the writing world for the left were not people like Farrell, but somebody or other whom we now no longer even know exists.

The period of the thirties has been a good deal maligned however and much more was in it than the revisionists of the period wish to credit. . . . I think a revaluation of the period is bound to be made, sooner or later. It was for a person living in it far more lively, fresher and exciting than later accounts would indicate. A great deal of fresh lively writing was being done. The thirties actually might have developed into something far better if the Nazi-Soviet pact, the war and the cold war had not evolved. These events ushered in the Southern School and the trend toward personalism and the neurotic hero. I think it is due to break and in the final examination Farrell's writing will be seen to be in a main stream which is going to have more impact than some of the work spurting up in more recent years. With my best wishes for your project.

If Herbst did not play a foreground role in the *Partisan Review* break from official CPUSA politics, she nonetheless retained her own view of the importance of the interrelationship between politics and artistic creativity, as her own work attests. During the years (1934-1937) that the rift was brewing and finally came to a head, Herbst occupied herself with a behind-the-scenes reportage series for the New York *Post* which took her to Berlin during the Hitler era.[3] In Germany, using CP contacts, Herbst ferreted out signs of resistance--strikes and community organizations--that were not getting the notice--or the support--of the anti-fascist world. Curiously, perhaps due to the nature of the contacts she had made through the local Communist Party, the pockets of resistance she unearthed tended to be non-Jewish, labor-oriented and communistic. In that same period, Herbst reported on farm strikes in her native Midwest, filing reports with both *New Masses* and *Scribner's*. Here, too, her attention was focussed on the ordinary responses of rank and file farmers and farmwives rather than on the machinations of organized leaderships. Her assignment in Cuba during the Batista uprising has been recorded by Elinor Langer and elsewhere. But once again, the genius of her reportage was to be her eye for the responses of ordinary people in extraordinary circumstances and the inclusion of the doings of women and children in her accounts.

Nowhere in her correspondence does Herbst criticize Farrell or Phillips for not themselves taking on this sort of single-handed anti-fascist writer's campaign, but at the same time, neither does she blame herself for not having time left over to engage in their internecine battles on the home front. Furthermore, the unique blend of the socially-concerned writer's intelligence with the novelist's individual sensibility was to become quite intentionally her goal not only in the Rope of Gold trilogy, as I have indicated, but in the later posthumously collected and published memoirs as well.

Clearly Herbst was thinking in those terms in very prescient concepts, as can be seen from an undated passage taken from the collection of notes for her memoirs that she was making throughout the fifties and sixties:

> Today too much is put into boxes. Literature is filed in a box and in sub-boxes. Politics is in a box and economics in a box and the sociologists have packaged our very lives. As the psychologists have packaged our egos. What becomes lost is the *flow* for no matter what

your views, any attempt to isolate one from the other can only lead to cancelling out whatever meaning the subject might hold for us. It can only lead to a type of passivity in which man is no more than an object, waiting to be [maneuvered]. In which culture is something not to be lived in and to create but to buy.

In Herbst's later work, including the memoirs, the key to the "flow" between social and artistic categories is memory and sensuality. If her early work is marked--and perhaps flawed--by a too heavy imitation of the sparse and uninflected "Hemingway" school of midwest American refusal to adorn, the note struck in her later work is more satisfyingly and sensually appealing.

Why this change occurred in Herbst's work remains a question about which it is difficult to speculate. Katherine Anne Porter, a consummate stylist, had been a friend for years and had not had much visible impact on Herbst's native style. Herbst's husband, John Herrmann, himself a writer as lean as his good friend Hemingway, may have reinforced Herbst in her early style during the years she was married to him. Then, when Herbst began associating with such sensual woman poets as Jean Garrigue (with whom she had a long-standing love affair, according to Langer) there may have been some effect on her prose style. Memoirists and critics such as Alfred Kazin whom she befriended in the early 1950s may have reinforced this tendency.[4] Certainly, a fascination with the stuff and the effect of memory can be seen throughout the Rope of Gold trilogy. The reason for her late experiments in the development of a more sensual prose style may lie in the simple fact that she grew tired, in the postwar Cold War period of her virtual eclipse. Story after story was written for the commercial market, circulated by her agent and returned with a round of rejections. Similarly, although her two postwar novels, *Satan's Sergeants* and *Somewhere the Tempest Fell* were commercially published, they did not sell well and did little to revive her reputation. Both bear the mark of books written for a commercial market that was hostile to the author's natural social/personal point of view.

In my research, I mark the change in style with the memoir of Nathanael West, fictionalized as a novella under the heading "Hunter of Doves" in 1954. This piece was intended to be one of a series of four on modern writers; one, in manuscript form, is based on Herbst's knowledge of Hemingway. "Hunter of Doves," however, is more than a memoir of Nathanael West thinly disguised. West had been a close friend of Herbst and Herrmann and stayed with them frequently in their cottage in Erwinna, Pennsylvania. With the retrospective view of memory, the novella of West becomes an occasion for an extensive exploration into the question of memory itself and the placing and structuring of the mortality (and possible immortality) of an individual through the memory of another. The situation is seemingly simple. A young reporter, Timothy Comfort, has come to interview Mrs. Heath, a writer, about her deceased writer friend, Noel Bartram. Little actually happens by way of plot, except that in the course of talking about her late friend, Mrs. Heath recreates not only her friend, but herself, intertwines memories of the two and passes those along to the next generation, Comfort, who will presumably outlive her and will retell the tale in his own terms tainted by his own memories and personality. One extended quote will give the flavor of the new method of writing with which Herbst was experimenting:

> She tried to focus on the visitor. Surely, he was *too* youthful. He must have been a mere brat in the 'thirties when Noel Bartram was writing the three short novels that were the sum of his art. Youth was well and good, but did it not seek first of all to serve itself? The eyes--were they actually truthful or only self-consciously determined to look trusting? They gazed at her with almost embarrassing steadiness, offering all, and made her feel infantile, too trusting herself, as she had felt long ago when she held tightly to the hand of her father who was gravely interpreting the expression in the melting eyes of a great dog. "See, he wants to speak," her father had said, and she had placed her own hand on the creature's head, pressing the bony structure beneath the mat of hair. What had the dog been imploring so earnestly? Surely for more than a bone. That her mind was running to doggy analogies made her lips twitch in a jerk of a smile and she brought her hand up to her mouth roughly to rub away the threat. For all his angelic appearance, the young man on the terrace was a gravedigger. But there would be no earthen pots, no beads, no beautiful flasks for the feast of the dead, no solemn cerements with stately folds to give off definite pungent clues to former existence. No, for her friend there would be nothing but a rag bag of recollections culled from a medley of indidviduals, some of whom had barely had a speaking acquaintance with the dead man and who now waxed loquacious simply because they scented a chance to get their own names in print. The huge sheaf of notes on the young man's knee testified to his industry, but to what else? Were they more than rags, to be pinned to her friend's tree of life, to flutter in

the wind and even to conceal the branches and the fruit?

    The vision of an actual tree was suddenly so strong that Mrs. Heath seemed to see it, with all its quivering leaves, and her dead friend stepping softly around it and past it, headed for some high grassed meadow, in his old trousers deliberately shabby for the hunt, weaving his long legs through the tobacco- and rust-colored tufts, the dead thistles shaking stiff purplish manes, the milkweed pods bursting to fatten another summer, and the man himself, with gun slanted, and his dog--ah, always a dog--after the elusive bird that was forever on the wing (310-311).

    The echo clearly emanates from Virginia Woolf's early work *Jacob's Room*. In that work, the character of Jacob Flinders is never approached directly through his own consciousness, but his legacy, after his death in World War I, is a reconstruction in the consciousness of others, and in the imprint he leaves behind in his belongings, his room, and on the memory of his friends and family. Similarly, the "actual" truth about Noel Bartram has been buried with him, if it existed even then. His legacy will be mixed up with dogs and trees in the sensual consciousness of the likes of Mrs. Heath. To see the new line of development Herbst's work took with this memoir, one has only to contrast it with a typical scene of recounting of the doings of Joe Trexler in the Rope of Gold trilogy. While it is safe to assume that some elements of the following passage were derived from letters and photographs in the files Herbst received from her mother, nonetheless, the narrator is absent from the telling, and the events, including those that take place in Joe Trexler's consciousness, are given as actualities unmediated by the extraneous sensual memories of the teller or of the participants:

    [Joe] carried the [family] pictures back to Atlanta with him and showed them around with pride at the compliments they drew. He took them with him on the night he went to see little Nannie but she was too ill to look at them, saw Joe only for a moment, smiling at him above a mass of white coverlets. What had been a bad cold had turned into consumption and she would die. He tried to think of something to say to Mr. Ellis, who went to the door with him as he left the house, standing in a half hearted incompetent manner in loose slippers, with his long straggling mustaches seeming to trickle down his neck beneath his stiff collar. He'd lost all in the war, he said, and now he was to lose a daughter. He said it grudgingly as if she were a possession of value only to him, her father, as if he not Nannie were the loser, so that Joe wanted to knock the old fool down. (*Pity* 52)

The Hemingway memoir, told directly from Mrs. Heath's point of view, falls between the two. It is the kind of summing up and recounting that, while perhaps typical of many memoirs, did not come to life in Herbst's hands as did the Nathanael West piece. In any event, she never felt confident enough of the piece to finish it and attempt to publish it. The opening sample reads:

> Jackson Redding never really got away from his own beginning. He tried very hard to get away and he added very many complicated curleycues to his original self, some of which were admirable, at least in the attempt. But he remained, in spite of himself, the boy up in Michigan who had come close to some quick of life where his spark held true. He was always the boy who had to be brave and he was always a little afraid that he wasn't brave enough. . . . Death was the great test and old age as the approach to death was a test and in lieu of something more active to deal with, a war or an animal, the accumulating years were something to battle with, to meet head on and to van[quish] before they vanquished him. He really sought to devour death as death devoured his hero or his heroine and what he felt about death, what he did with it in his work, how it operated upon him was exactly the element that Constance Heath liked in him in her acquaintance with him during the Paris period and the beginning middle years. He never tried to make it pretty and in that sense he was not typically American for as the republic got away from its early pioneer beginnings it was surely a fact that it tended to ignore death as far as possible, to make it pretty and to rush the corpse off to the cemetery.[5]

Clearly, memory was always important to Herbst's work, especially that proceeding with the development of the trilogy. In the fifties and subsequently this commitment to memory became an abiding passion, virtually her only remaining commitment. The distinction in the move from the recounting of "actualities" from the past, and an exploration of how memory works, such as we find in "Hunter of Doves" may very well be a move toward the feminine, a repossession of the sensual that Herbst had denied in her early work. In Herbst's case, the repossession of the sensual combines with a socio-political awareness to take her prose out of the realm of the neurasthenic individualists she saw coming to literary power in the Cold War period. In her most successful prose of the period of the end of her life--the fifties and sixties--Herbst was to blend memory with socio-political event in a way she had not before attempted to validate both her own life and the period in which she came of age. This is apparent not only in the Nathanael West novella but in her posthumously collected memoirs as well.

Herbst's 1956 article in *The Nation,* "The Ruins of Memory," seems to answer the question Elinor Langer raises at the close of her defense of Herbst in May of 1994[6] as to why Herbst herself never "recanted." As if in reply to this question, Herbst poses the problem as it seemed to her in 1956:

> In a period of demoralization and terror it was no bad thing to try to act, however mistakenly or inadequately, as the conscience of the age. If you can bear to lift the black cloth placed over the thirties by the revisionists, some of whom seem more infatuated with the revelation of their own private sense of guilt than in the situation as it *then existed,* you may be surprised to discover work not entirely marred by "innocence" nor requiring the afterthought of "shame."[7] (*The Nation* 302).

It was to lift this "black cloth," then, that Herbst set about working on her own memories, revitalizing them with the stuff of sensuality and making of them a sensual, not strictly materialistic substance, that could continue to live in the consciousness of a new generation. The result is, in my opinion, as fine as, or even more rewarding than much of her more studied fiction. As Herbert Leibowitz, author of a work on autobiography, *Fabricating Lives,* points out:

> It is entirely logical that because of . . . generic obstacles, autobiography has built up its long common boundary with fiction and that over the last century it has annexed--or had ceded to it--vast tracts of land formerly belonging to novelists. Character in autobiography, as in fiction, is the invented equivalent of men and women, dressed up in words, who move through time and live in a physical world that confines and presses hard on them, whether in the Mississippi Delta or in a leafy New Jersey suburb (xvii).

For Herbst, the task was not an easy one. It occupied her for the better part of the last three decades of her life. One does not want to stretch a point and suggest psychological factors that have not been corroborated by psychoanalytical testimony, but I suggest that part of the difficulty can be illuminated by such studies of women's autobiography as that undertaken by Sidonie Smith, Jean Bethke Elshtain, Nancy Miller, and others. If Herbst had, as I have previously indicated, resisted a feminine persona--certainly a middle-class feminine existence--in her early work, how was she now to attempt to construct and develop a sensual, sensitive, essentially feminine prose style? If she rejected, the "neurotic individualists" of the Cold War period in 1956, how was she now to turn inward herself and still hope to make a connection to a larger social vision? This matter was especially complicated--or facilitated--by the fact that she herself was no longer part of a social movement, maintained a few radical friends, and was all but eclipsed as a writer from the public eye.

What I submit, basing myself on Sidonie Smith's important work, is that the project of writing her memoirs, became, for Herbst if not a recantation, then a substitution for the social movement that had nurtured her in her early years. The memory would reconstitute the actuality. As Smith says: "The autobiographical text becomes a narrative artifice, privileging a presence, or identity, that does not exist outside language." (5) With her autobiographical work, Herbst was forced to gain, in Smith's terms, "confidence in the referentiality of language and a corollary confidence in the authenticity of the self." (5)

The result is that the medium did as much to create Herbst as Herbst did to create the medium. Going beyond an almost slavish faithfulness to the contents of her mother's attic, and her own journalistic dispatches, Herbst produces, first in the Constance Heath of the Nathanael West piece, then in the "I" persona of *The Starched Blue Sky of Spain,* the most eminently satisfying creation of her career. This process can be understood in the terms Smith indicates:

> The autobiographer's effort to capture the quality and to shape the development of her life is problematic to begin with. Trying to tell the story she wants to tell about herself, she is seduced into a tantalizing and yet elusive adventure that makes of her both creator and creation, writer and that which is written about. The very language she uses to name herself is simultaneously empowering and vitiating since words cannot capture the full sense of being and narratives explode in multiple directions on their own. . . . Whatever "truthfulness" emerges resides, not so much in the correspondence

between word and past, but in the imbrication of various autobiographical intentions into form--memoir, apology, confession (46).

I'm not sure it's an absolute, but it is certainly true in Herbst's case that, as Smith points out, "The autobiographer begins to grapple self-consciously with her identity as a woman in patriarchal culture and with her problematic relationship to engendered figures of selfhood" (56). As we shall see, while certainly no less socially conscious, and by no means overtly feminist, Herbst's memoirs emerge as her best realized womanly prose.

If there is such a thing as "Marxian" prose, perhaps Herbst had been employing it and supporting it during her Communist years when she was writing the trilogy. Is such a prose necessarily gendered masculine or "patriarchal"? Does a break from that dogma account for Herbst's emergence as a fully formed woman writer? Elshtain would seem to indicate an affirmative to those questions.

If one's answer to the question "Who is the female subject?" revolves around the centrality of speech, Marx's account poses another major problem. In Marxian thought the eradication of a world of necessity will remove barriers to the full exercise of human powers. Man will be free insofar as his essence is freedom. But where does Marx locate this freedom? What is its substantive content? Marx urges that freedom is realizable in a community of persons who have been restored to themselves as "social beings": it is the positive transcendence of all estrangement. A diffuse species-being will override the particularity of individuals. But how does one substitute generic man for real individuals? . . . Due to the paucity of his references to language and the theoretical thinness of his transcendent future where there is no coherent sense of a speaking subject, Marx ends on a silencing note for that subject, male and female ("Feminist Discourse" 613).

The answer to Elshtain is in a dialectical approach that she fails to give Marx credit for. Just as the commodity is simultaneously generic value and is also specific use-value, so, too, although Marx seems to be speaking of "generic" man, he is, as Terry Eagleton has pointed out, eminently the philosopher of the individualized body. As Eagleton notes in his chapter on Marx:

It would seem that the only fruitful strategy is to go back to the
beginning and think everything through again, but this time from the
standpoint of the body itself. The implicit materialism of the aesthetic
might still be redeemable; but if it can be retrieved from the burden
of idealism which weighs it down, it can only be by a revolution in
thought which takes its starting-point from the body itself, rather than
from a reason which struggles to make room for it. What if an idea
of reason could be generated up from the body itself, rather than the
body incorporated into a reason which is always already in place?
(*Ideology of the Aesthetic,* 196-7).

We can see that while Elshtain is forcing Marx's method of
abstraction into a current gender debate, Eagleton's reading places Marx as the
emergent champion of physicality--sex included--arising from the de-
materialized abstractions of idealism. One would be more likely to get an ear
from Marx for a materialist interpretation of gender and language, one can
assume from Eagleton's argument, than one would from a Plato, Descartes, or
Hegel.

The point that relates to Herbst is that she was not so much making
a break from her early Marxism in order to pursue her arguably gendered,
certainly individualized, memoirs. Since "proletarian realism" versus "neurotic
individualism" was a dichotomy that was never clearly defined--definitely not
in Marxist terms--and Herbst herself never considered herself a party to that
debate on the basis of orthodox tenets, the move she made in developing her
memoirs seems to be precisely on a vector begun in the trilogy of
reparticularizing the individual that Elshtain calls for--this time in intimately
personal language.

The purpose behind Herbst's later work--for we feel thematic intent
is as much present in the memoirs as in the trilogy and reportage--seems to go
beyond the point of autobiography generally, that is, to entertain a bid for a
hope of immortality. (Why else does one write?) Judith Newton and Deborah
Rosenfelt seem to have summed up an intent we may well attribute to Herbst
both for writing the memoirs at all and in decidedly gendering them feminine.
Summing up their discussion of a materialist-feminist film critic discussing a
Cuban filmmaker, they note:

Feminist art and criticism cannot directly change power relations,
cannot alone effect the transformation of relations between public and
private spheres that [is] the goal of feminism. But . . . the greater

self-awareness and imaginative capacity fostered by such art, when linked with a social movement is an essential component of revolutionary change (xxii).

I would now like to follow the image of a loaf of bread through the memoirs to show just how this refeminizing, reparticularizing of the agency of social change manifests itself in Herbst's work. As Langer notes:

> One of the first things [Herbst] noticed was the smell of bread, and throughout her life in foreign cities or alone in domestic ones its aroma would fill her senses the way flowers draw bees and make her think of Mary [her mother], but then again what wouldn't? Mary inhabited her daughter's life as if both were characters in a single story, which in a way they were (23-24).

This may be overstating the case. Certainly there was much on Herbst's mind through all the various stages of her life that did not involve her mother or her mother's values. Nonetheless, Langer is correct to point out the importance to Herbst of the smell of baking bread, its association with mothering, and its pervasiveness in the memoirs.

First turning up in the trilogy as a present-day childhood event, the baking of bread is the keystone in the "Magicians and Their Apprentices" segment now incorporated into the *Starched Blue Sky* collection. Herbst is an adult in this memoir, recollecting. The subject is as much the workings of memory and of memorabilia as it is the stuff of the memories itself. Remembrance of baking aromas past is as important as the tangible loaf, which is never to materialize except in its guise as reminder of mother. Here, Herbst is going through a packet of letters and clippings and stuff left by her mother. Herbst notes:

> As I had fumbled over the batch of oddly assorted papers, so much had been telescoped to swift scenarios of feeling and action that it was almost a shock to realize that the bold handwriting I was confronting was my mother's hand, charging like the black horses of some Roman charioteer across the arena of what had been the blank pages of our old notebooks. . . . One page had a clot of dried paste on it: bread dough. My mother had been "putting the bread to set" before she sat down. . . . The loaves would come out a golden brown, would be coated with butter, and placed in the pantry, for the first

clean slice "across the loaf" to be spread with homemade apple butter (22-23).

For all the loving detail, and the almost palpable aroma and savor, Herbst is ambivalent about her mother as role model, if not as parent of choice. She notes, a little later, that working in the office with her father's tractor parts business "was much better than the kitchen, which, in spite of its delicious smells, could be a trap. If you didn't watch your step, you'd be in a little bungalow, beating eggs for keeps." (26) Clearly, Herbst did not want to eat her fresh-baked bread and grow up to make it, too.

That the memory of the baking serves as apt substitute for the baking itself, in the hands of a writer as skillful as Herbst was to become, is evident in the final episode of the memoirs, the title segment, set during the Spanish Civil War in 1937. Herbst recalls leaving Hemingway in charge of his filming of the front-line shooting and going herself to visit the young Spanish and International soldiers in the outlying areas. One young soldier has confided in Herbst that he has dreamt of a river of blood. To take his mind off, she says,

> I told him I dreamed of bread. It was true. At the [Hotel] Florida I was always having this dream of coming home from school and smelling my mother's wonderful homemade bread. In the dream I would head for the pantry and have time to lift the white towel from the beautiful golden loaves before I heard the thunder. I had to leave the bread to shut the windows so the rain wouldn't come in. Then I woke up. There was no bread and no thunder. Only the noise of the early bombardment (148).

The bread, now shared with the young soldier in the form of a dream as consolation for his more violent dream, becomes a shared image or incarnation of mother, more palpable than a universalized icon of the Virgin would be. It is almost as if the soldiers can taste the luxury of Herbst's mother's homemade bread as surely and as significantly as Herbst herself can. She notes:

> They loved this story, and I had to repeat it several times. There may seem to be something childish in all this, but these were not childish men. It just happens that a kind of childishness, in the sense that the child knows how to savor joyful things, is a source of instinctual happiness, and even in this crucial situation, they had not lost the art or the heart for this kind of search (148).

Nor, we note, was Herbst herself ever to lose the art or the heart for this search.

* * *

If, for reasons Langer indicates, most of Herbst's major reporting junkets were often for the purpose of self-discovery and self-reaffirmation after personal distress, certainly this was true of her Spanish venture, launched while she was still attempting to heal both the hurt of the separation from Herrmann and the loss of faith caused by her joining privately with the anti-Stalinist forces in the *Partisan Review* dispute.

The saga of the Spanish cause was to be for Herbst a healing journey, paradoxically enough, considering that the anti-fascist forces were doomed almost from the start. It was an assertion that there are good causes left, and that it is worth risking one's life to fight for the righteous side, even when that side is alone and underequipped. The Spanish saga was also to be, intentionally or not, Herbst's last word, the final chapter in her posthumously published memoirs. In that respect, it is the answer to those who asked her for a recantation in the face of her lifelong alliance with what turned out to be Stalinist forces.

For all the forays I've made into the literature, I still don't know whether there is a significant difference in the way men and women view the same phenomena. Although I have said Herbst went behind the lines and interviewed women and children, the main actors in the memoir were the young soldiers on the Republican front--and of course Herbst herself in her quest for self-reconciliation.

It is possible to note as does Barbara Brothers, that Sylvia Townsend Warner wrote on the Spanish Civil War from a woman's vantage point:

> through the "pantry window," thus achieving what those running the castle have missed: "an ease and appreciativeness in low company." (163)[8]

Perhaps Warner's view was similar to Herbst's in that, in Brothers' terms:

Not the Marxist theory of history but the possibility of a richer life of the spirit and body for her fellow human beings, which social reform seemed to promise, drew Warner to become a Communist (162).

If Herbst herself was never entirely anti-theoretical, Herbst seemed not, after all, to share Warner's "pantry" sensibility. I will not expatiate on Warner too much, since my subject is Herbst, but I note that her images seem barren, where Herbst's are rich with sensuality. A brief snip from a poem shows the contrast with the image of bread we have already examined:

> And on the hillside
> That is the colour of peasant's bread
> Is the rectangular
> White village of the dead. (Brothers 168)

From the vantage point of Hemingway, as Allen Josephs elucidates, the political triumphed over the personal. "It is true, as David Sanders wrote," Josephs writes, "that Hemingway tended to see the war as a Spanish struggle against foreign aggression." (179) The struggle, in Hemingway's terms, was a matter of fighting for democracy, a man's fight (with women as helpmates). As Josephs says:

> Hemingway at his best was always an antipolitical writer, and in *For Whom the Bell Tolls* he began, perhaps unintentionally, reverting to type. The old man at the bridge had no politics, and as Hemingway told Joseph North and veterans of the Lincoln Brigade who were displeased by the book, he, like Robert Jordan, had no politics. So, it seems reasonable to conclude, *For Whom the Bell Tolls* is nonpolitical. But the Spanish Civil War *was* political (183).

Nonetheless Hemingway was at least engaged in military operations on the Republican side, as is clear from his *Fifth Column* stories and his impassioned speech "Fascism Is a Lie," reprinted in New Masses in June 1937.

For Andre Malraux, the interminable fighting was a necessary concomitant of a military revolution. One character in *Man's Hope* asks

> "Will the revolution be brought about by the proletariat or by the--the Stoics?
>> "Why not by the most humane element of mankind?" asks
> another.

"For the simple reason, my dear fellow, that the most humane people don't stand for revolution. They stand for public libraries and . . . cemeteries. More's the pity!"

The inquirer asserts, "A cemetery doesn't prevent an example from being worth the making. Quite the contrary."

Then comes the rationalization for the fighting: "But meanwhile, we have--Franco!" (211)

For George Orwell, the socialism in practice he observes among the International Brigade on the front lines and the villagers supplying them is what makes the fighting worthwhile:

> Up here in Aragon one was among tens of thousands of people, mainly though not entirely of working-class origin, all living at the same level and mingling on terms of equality. In theory it was perfect equality, and even in practice it was not far from it. There is a sense in which it would be true to say that one was experiencing a foretaste of socialism, by which I mean that the prevailing mental atmosphere was that of socialism (187).

Reporting from behind the lines, where she stayed among peasants, Herbst filed several accounts of the villagers replanting abandoned *latifundias* in order to provision their families with much-needed fruits and vegetables. I have not been able to track down any official CP bulletins denouncing this policy, but informants who were close to the party at the time have reminded me that the Comintern was apparently opposed to the redivision of land due to the fact that they were attempting to forge a popular front with the liberal bourgeoisie, some of whom owned these lands. The Trotskyists, I am informed, supported the redivision efforts. Herbst, without mentioning the international dispute or the popular front policy, reports in 1938:

> The folk on the mountain had not seen this enemy as closely as I had. The enemy came to them mostly at night and the people saw only their dead. They had just made the first beginnings to control the valley that they had worked in as day laborers and poor small landholders. This valley, so beautifullly and intensively tended and cared for, had yielded rich crops but never before for them. Something evil had been at work before the enemy came. Something came between them and all they produced during the long seasons

when water was carefully directed into little ditches and every orchard looked as if each leaf were counted, each olive especially marked for some market. . . . Now they could use their own produce. They could sell it and with the proceeds do a hundred things, buy machinery, extend irrigation, raise tomatoes and artichokes where land had lain fallow through the carelessness of a   landowner. . . . The big landowners no longer controlled the crops with the divine right to pay for labor and for produce what they pleased. No one was in debt to them any more; they had vanished.

Then they suddenly appeared again, in German planes, in the sky. This is the way the people see it as they talk about the crops on their way to the top of the mountain ("Night Comes" 19).

Curiously, this was not the way Herbst herself saw it in her memoirs written twenty years later in the wake of the Cold War. Here the emphasis is on the personalities of individuals and the sensuality of memory. Somehow, the politics that Herbst had almost alone championed in her reportage in the thirties has dropped out and she has taken up the sensuality she perhaps had been warned all along was missing from her work:

There was a big iron kettle outside [the bivouac], from which the men were ladling stew, and they even offered us some. It tasted better than anything we got at the Gran Via, as seemed only fitting. Not far away, in another village, the same thing was going on, and this time the men were exercising on what had been a threshing field, which still held the firm beautiful color of a golden loaf of bread. As they wheeled and turned in the lovely ambient air, the blue and red of their smocks bellied out with the exuberance of little flags. All the color seemed to have drained upon the field, which sparkled with gold and blues, reds, and greens and made the womenfolk, some of whom stood watching on the sidelines, seem like little black withered fig trees. But that was only the superficial view, for though they were in the perpetual black clothes of women always in mourning or always at work, their eyes snapped with an inner fire (161).

The final summation of Herbst's Spanish excursion, like the final summation of her life, can be read in the closing paragraph of the *Starched Blue Sky* memoir, the last published word Herbst left us. Clearly written in the period of post-Stalinist, post-Cold-War, even perhaps, post-modernist dismay, it is yet an assertion, a gentle, non-dogmatic reaffirmation of faith. In response to a Republican townsman's urging to be *"muy inteligente,"* Herbst writes:

> But I was far from understanding everything. About the most important questions, at that moment, I felt sickeningly at sea. As for being *valiente*, who wasn't? If I wrote it down in my journal, it was to put heart in myself, if only to say, Come now, be *muy inteligente*, be *valiente*. Just try (178).

Perhaps many of us could do worse than to try to be as valiant and as intelligent as Josephine Herbst.

Notes

1. For a discussion of this novel see Paula Rabinowitz *Labor & Desire*.

2. That this was as much Trotsky's position as the CPUSA's, even after Farrell joined his cause, can be seen in *In Defense of Marxism* and James P. Cannon's *The Struggle for a Proletarian Party*.

3. This reportage is reprinted in a pamphlet, *Behind the Swastika*, published in 1936 by the Anti-Nazi Federation.

4. See Alfred Kazin's obituary "Josephine Herbst (1897-1969)" in *The New York Review of Books*, March 27, 1969, pp 19-20. I am grateful to Alfred Kazin for granting me an interview in which we discussed some details of his friendship with Josephine Herbst as that was delineated in the correspondence between the two on file at the Beinecke Library.

5. This extract is taken from an unpublished typescript not circulated for publication, from the Herbst archives at the Beinecke Library.

6. See Langer, Elinor, "The Secret Drawer," *The Nation*, May 30, 1994, 752-760. This article is a defense of Herbst against the assertion by Stephen Koch that Herbst and her husband John Herrmann were Soviet agents. As Langer does a competent job of defending Herbst, I will pass over the charge in my commentary.

7. Herbst is referring here to the wave of postwar intellectuals who recanted and renounced their radical youth, including Malcolm Cowley, Philip Rahv, Edmund Wilson, and most especially, in her mention of "innocence" and "shame," to Leslie Fiedler. The point of her article was clearly to dissociate herself from those considered "cold war liberals," who were then attacking the Communist experience of the thirties.

8. The quotes given are from Sylvia Townsend Warner's "Women as Writers: The Peter Le Neve Foster Lecture," *Journal of the Royal Society of Arts*, May 1959, 384.

Chapter Nine

The Return to Nature:

A Cross-Reading

I discovered a remarkable development while preparing the final material for this text: a relationship among the three authors that I had not been aware of when I started out. All three seemed to have turned to nature and to the writing about nature as their final legacy. This seemed, on first investigation, to be a similar, although uncoordinated, response to the Cold War hysteria that had blasted each of them, jeopardizing their very survival. One must also consider that as communists, both affiliated and independent, they must have had some response to the news that started coming out in the 1950s about the purges and the criminal nature of the Stalinist regime. If none of them exactly recanted, neither was any of them involved in a public campaign to defend her beliefs, whatever those beliefs may have been at that time.

For Meridel Le Sueur, nature imagery had always been woven into the weft of her work, as of her life. At the end of her life, as political preachings began to pall, she has relied more and more heavily on the nature imagery of her early Persephone stories, developed now into a totalizing construct, to sustain a natural optimism in a world that looked to many to have gone sour.

Tillie Olsen's only fiction published after the *Tell Me a Riddle* collection is an uncompleted novella, "Requa-I," that may have been begun in the thirties but was not made public until 1980.   At that, it was never collected with her other stories, and remains little known today.   I choose to discuss this piece under the rubric of a return to nature because it is very much about a Depression boy's finding transcendence and revitalization in the natural beauty of a redwood forest.   Conveying effectively Olsen's sense of "goodness" in the human spirit, this story, albeit possibly first outlined in the Depression era of political activism, came to the public at a time when the author had her own difficulties with the Cold War forces and the remains of Stalinism to work out.   In that context, "Requa" is an act of reaffirmation of faith.

Similarly, though separately, Josephine Herbst responded to the Cold War despondency that had cost her her job not only by championing her good friend Harvey O'Connor's case to uphold the First Amendment against the House Un-American Activities Committee[1] and to join some ex-communist friends in attempting to exonerate Alger Hiss but, as a writer, by leaving the legacy of a perfect gem of a book, *New Green World,* the biography of eighteenth-century botanist John Bartram and his son William.   In the recounting of the Bartrams' lives, Herbst delineates a civilized, non-rapacious, non-capitalistic reverence for nature, a nature which we can only assume sustained her on her own on her daily rounds in the environs of her little cottage in Bucks County, Pennsylvania.

I will discuss all three of these responses more fully but first I would like to place them in the context of the Marxist and feminist arguments I have undertaken to address.

For feminism, the issue of nature and woman's relationship to it presents a problem.   Susan Griffin's *Woman and Nature* (1978) offers a rich, poetic, (if not didactically useful) array of mythos culled from history and literature on the ideas men have had about nature and about women and how those ideas have affected women themselves.   The result is an expansion of Simone de Beauvoir's elaboration on the "otherness" of woman in man's eyes.   If women are closer to nature through the reproductive tract, and if nature must be controlled in order for the species to survive, it follows that women must be subject to the same set of controls--kept from invading and thwarting the particularly human intellectual labor it is man's place to pursue.   Griffin quotes witch-torturing broadsides; Wollstonecraft argues with the proto-Romantic Rousseau as to the "natural" place of woman, and de Beauvoir argues with all of history to free woman from the shackles of her indenture to nature.

The Derridean poststructuralist answer to the woman-equals-nature paradigm may not be entirely acceptable. In *Spurs*, Derrida argues with Nietzsche's discussion of the otherness of woman. Derrida's argument is that both feminism and anti-feminism are equally reducible to texts--texts that can be changed by an act of will. Hence, woman is not confined to nature, banned from the intellectual, nor do similar boundaries necessarily limit men. Derrida's statement, the destruction of logocentrism will be the destruction of phallocentrism, joins Freud's "where id was there shall ego be," as a perhaps unwitting liberatory gesture, to link up with the slogan of the *Communist Manifesto*, "Workers of the world unite, you have nothing to lose but your chains." It may not be true, as Derrida suggests, that the world is logocentrally constructed. Witches did actually burn at the stake, and depressed housewives still receive memory-blasting dosages of electro-convulsive therapy. There *is* a reality, a reality that Marx still explains better than anyone else, of guns and jails and unemployment and the circulation of capital and commodities that is only tangentially mitigated or enforced by linguistic factors. If the mythos of nature has held women in bondage, those bonds are not difficult to break by the substitution of new mythologies.[2] Overthrowing or replacing the system of exploitation of labor and the production of surplus value is not so easy a matter. As Derrida indicates, the overthrow of phallocentrism may well be a concomitant of that revolution, but no one can demonstrate that linguistics and rationalism by themselves can lead to a better ordering of the means of production for the betterment of mankind and womankind.

Elizabeth Fox-Genovese, in her discussion of individualism and community in the women's movement, expresses best the curious dialectic that led all three of the women I am discussing to turn to a highly individualized outlook on nature within the context of lives devoted to communality. The first thing worth noting is that the transcendent awe of Emerson became more accessible to these writers as the strict materialistic utilitarianism of Marxism paled. Even so, having devoted their adult lives to the assertion of the primacy of communal values over "anarchistic" individualism, they were not, late in life, searching for ways to turn tail and adopt postmodernist values. The synthesis they found, apparently, was in their writing about nature. This writing allowed them to continue to explore the interaction between individualism and community in terms very similar to those indicated by Fox-Genovese in her recent book. If she does not exactly discuss nature in the terms I am indicating the three writers under discussion do, her references to woman as "other" takes up what Griffin and De Beauvoir have commenced:

This pervasive female experience of being other carries the seed of a special redemption, for deep in female self-awareness lies the awareness of self as rooted in and inseparable from a collective--or, if you prefer, community--life that embraces both men and women. If one's sexuality alone provides justification for exclusion, if one's most basic features as a being in the world dictate one's inferiority, then, for all those who refuse the condemnation, the reappropriation of self can be reappropriation not just for the individual but for the community itself (233).

The Marxist conception of nature starts from a different ethos--perhaps from the uninflected, non-gendered neutrality some modern feminists seek. Nature nonetheless remains the crux, the starting point of the Marxist project. As I have previously indicated, Terry Eagleton has already called our attention to Marxism as the philosophy of "the body." This is not the body of sensuality of Hegel, Nietszche and Irigaray, but rather the package of flesh and bones we are all stuck with that eats, sleeps, fucks, farts and gets wet in the rain. Engels states the case more directly in *Anti-Duhring*, in a paraphrase of the argument he and Marx had put forward in *The German Ideology*. The first part of the argument has been frequently cited: "now a materialist conception of history was propounded, and the way found to explain man's consciousness by his being, instead of, as heretofore, his being by his consciousness." (32) The connection to Nature comes in the following:

> But if the further question is raised: what then are thought and consciousness, and whence they come, it becomes apparent that they are products of the human brain and that man himself is a product of Nature, which has been developed in and along with its environment; whence it is self-evident that the products of the human brain, being in the last analysis also products of Nature, do not contradict the rest of Nature but are in correspondence with it. (42-3)

It stands to reason that the alienation that Marx discusses in his early manuscripts is not only alienation from one's own labor, but, by extension, alienation from nature. The reconciliation of the worker to her product, the end of alienation--communism--will bring about as well the end of the alienation of the species from the forces of nature on which its existence is based.

This may sound utopian, but one must remember that utopianism was often the doctrine of choice among the young idealists competing for attention in Marx's time. From Feuerbach to Shelley and the Romantic poets to the American Swedenborgian transcendentalists, Emerson, Bronson Alcott, and the various utopian communards, the point was to return to nature to alleviate alienation. In this way the missions seem similar to the Marxist one. The difference is that Marx put forward a societal plan good for the whole species, whereas Emerson and the transcendentalists asked each man to find nature in his own soul.

While the Marxist plan seems eminently more realizable (if not easily so), it leaves out the ingredient Emerson was to champion and that so appealed to his American following--including, ultimately, I claim, the three women writers I am addressing. That ingredient is awe or mysticism, a sense of wonder. If all things are knowable--including infinity--in the Marxist canon, a brush with the infinite can yet generate a sensation of transcendence and revitalization in those who seek it, at least according to Emersonian doctrine.

Emerson was able to translate the discourse of religious awe into the discourse of transcendence through Nature by a simple trick of transsubstantiation. The church's communion wafer becomes Whitman's leaf of grass. What remains to transcendentalism that is lost to Marxism is the sense of awe, the sense of wonder, the reverence for the not yet known.

In Freudian terms, this reverence can be seen as an abasement, an alienation of the species before a God who has usurped mankind's own powers through the force of projection--as Freud discusses in *The Future of an Illusion*. Marx, by the evidence of *The Holy Family* and other works on religion, would no doubt agree. However, as I have pointed out, to say that we start from nature, and have before us the task of harnessing it in rational terms, is not necessarily to say that we can have no reverence for nature. The point simply does not figure in the Marxist lexicon. In point of fact the rather paltry treatment traditional Marxism gives to matters of psychodynamic and irrational forces may explain its failure to look into the question of alienation and women's oppression in meaningful terms. Certainly, Marx and Engels never dealt with conditions of "the other" except in the forms delineated in the chapter of *Capital* on the fetishistic character of money--and then the discussion is confined to materialist determinants.

The CPUSA, to my knowledge, never took a stand on nature or nature writing, other than that delineated in the Marxist canon. As for the challenge presented by Meridel Le Sueur--and, importantly, Josephine Johnson--Mike Gold and Alexander Trachtenberg took little notice. Certainly they felt no need to rethink the question of the relationship of Marxism to nature. As for

Emerson, Granville Hicks, in his 1935 *The Great Tradition*, stretches a point to include him in the cavalcade of the progressive American popular front tradition. Noting that Emerson's "mission was the liberation of men from chains that were self-forged and self-imposed" (8-9) he yet suggests that "his optimism blinded him to the obstacles placed in the individual's path, to the handicaps imposed by accidents of nature and injustices of society."(9) Going on to indicate Emerson's anti-commercial social theories, Hicks, in his eagerness to claim Emerson as "one of ours," overlooks completely Emerson's poetic theories and insistence on a self-reliant individuated godliness. Praising Josephine Johnson for avoiding "shabby romanticism" (320) in her Pulitzer-prize winning novel *Now in November* (1934), Hicks completely avoids the almost transcendent quality of Johnson's lyrical association of the tenant farmer family that is her subject with the land they live on and the powerful force played in the novel by nature--both external and personified in the primary characters. Clearly, there were times when the CPUSA--and no doubt Marx and Engels for that matter--simply chose not to see what they did not comprehend or what did not fit into the predetermined dogma. Perhaps, for the sake of those whose work was in some ways oppositional, that may have been just as well.

The combined forces of the Cold War and McCarthyism at home and the betrayal of Stalinism in what was supposed to be the new workers paradise took a heavy toll on the radical left emerging from the dynamic social activist period of the thirties. Often, drifting away from former party ties in a mood of disaffection, people faced the persecution alone in isolation and fear.

Meridel Le Sueur told writer Patricia Hampl, "You couldn't get a job. I couldn't teach a writing class; I couldn't even get a job as a waitress." (66) Banned from establishment presses for her major work, Le Sueur got some cash by writing children's books. But even her book on Lincoln, *The River Road*, was greeted by the *Milwaukee Journal* with the headline, "New Book on Lincoln Has Pink-Tinged Pages" (Hampl 66). Le Sueur kept her spirits up and made a few dollars from the radical press by becoming a listening post. She traveled throughout America, taking down "found" speech and people's stories, which she wrote up for the *Worker* and *Mainstream and Masses*. While these stories are primarily bleak, they do not represent a loss of faith on Le Sueur's part.

As I have been indicating throughout this chapter, it was through a return to nature and nature imagery that key figures, such as Le Sueur, deeply affected by the Cold War and the Stalinist debacle, could yet retain a semblance of faith in an optimistic project. To glimpse the difference between her more utilitarian writing even about nature in the press of the thirties and her heartfelt adoption of nature imagery to voice her own state of being, I will look first at a thirties piece, "Cows and Horses Are Hungry."

Originally published in *American Mercury* in 1934, and reprinted in Jack Salzman's *Years of Protest* (1967) this piece of reportage trades on the familiar pathos of the American farmer and his starving stock in order to score a point about the failure of the capitalist government. Nature here is treacherous, punishing. There has been no rain and the crops have failed. Much of the stock is too bony even to sell for provisions for welfare recipients. The farmers are getting bony themselves. Yet this is a truly natural disaster, not the author-invented hot spell of Olsen's *Yonnondio*. A socialist government surely would do something to alleviate the situation. But under capitalism, "The same old rubbish. Committees and committees and committees. But the farmer will keep on starving. He has been rooked by nature and now he will be rooked by the Federal government" (Salzman 61) There is no question here of nature as a non-material force beyond man's capacity for intervention.

With the thaw in the Cold War, the demotion of McCarthy, and the rise of a newly radicalized generation in the sixties and seventies, Le Sueur began finding a new audience. She published poetry in *Prairie Schooner* and self-published with her son-in-law a collection of poetry, *Rites of Ancient Ripening* (1975). This collection does not dwell on "the dark of the time." Rather it seeks to promulgate optimism and a positive identification with nature, which must be assumed to include human nature. Seeking a deep historical connectedness with native American Indian roots, these poems, while not all modulated or individuated in a way a modern reader might like, yet establish a communality between the universe and the individual seeking affirmation. For example, it is possible to read the following brief piece as a return to connectedness after the uprooting experience of the fifties (when Le Sueur was literally nearly always on a bus).

OFFER ME REFUGE
My prairie people are my home
Bird I return flying to their breasts.
Waving out of all exiled space
They offer me refuge
To die and be resurrected in their
                        seasonal flowering.
My food their breasts

> milked by wind
> Into my starving city mouth. (23)

For Le Sueur, the ability to see cosmic forces, such as those emanating from a kernel of corn and radiating outward, may have given her the capacity to weather the outrageous fortunes she had just endured. Cold War and Stalinism? No more deeply troubling than a siege of drought and famine. Life had endured worse, will again, and in the meantime, returns fecund. To see how such a vision developed into a deeply personal manifesto, one has only to compare "The Origin of Corn," written in the mid-seventies, with Le Sueur's penultimate published work, *Winter Prairie Woman* (1990). As Elaine Hedges points out in her introduction to "The Origin of Corn" section in *Ripening*:

> The style of much of Le Sueur's recent work is a multilayered, multidimensional prose-poetry that communicates not so much through conventional narrative form and causal sequences as through the creation of a matrix of event, symbol, and meaning (251).

The result is a deliberately non-individualized song of the interplay of cosmic forces:

> My hungered people come home to the cob, to the stalk, home root to the great council of cyclonic love, defying Strontium winds, purifying poisons in the ovarian grace and the joyful benediction of sperm (259).

By contrast, Le Sueur, in *Winter Prairie Woman* situates her organicism in the body of an individual woman nearing death. (Le Sueur herself was nearing ninety when she wrote it.) The result is that the lyrical naturalistic voice of Le Sueur's early writing becomes the private testament sustaining a richly living woman on her way to death. There is a delicious bit of memory well worth the reading of Le Sueur's "found speech" style, this time placed in the memory of the unnamed woman centered on women's talk about each other's birth-giving ability during the farm life of the character's youth. Primarily, however, the piece is a soliloquy involving the old woman, her memories, and her struggle to maintain her faith in a tenacious relationship to nature. For example:

Her lips smiled for the pleasure of so many seasons and in her the memory of heat and the sun's returning, all returning. How dear to her the long bone slowly rising in the drying flesh and in her, like a seed, remembering to rise again all memory in the seed (10).

The character takes note of drought, depression, war, but "Out of the broken spirits came the blossom" (16).

Indeed the persistence of the seed, of the spirit, of life itself, seems almost to have derived from modern theories about the dominating persistence of DNA. The woman herself becomes a vessel through which nature enacts its tragedies and farce. The final scene, in which the woman has died and a wolf has entered through an open door and feasted on her flesh seems a fitting rather than a tragic end. Just as Walt Whitman urged us to look for him under our bootsoles, so the woman, just as she would have wanted, will eventually fertilize new seeds as she passes through the wolf's intestinal tract. The neighbor who discovers her desecrated flesh is not himself appalled. The woman has always put on a good feed for the farm hands; she has always fed the hungry and homeless. Her last act is to become herself a meal for nature's creature. The act does not seem a desecration, but a continuation. The final lyrical passage is not so much an abstraction delivered to the cosmos, but could be a eulogy for the consecration of the life of an individual:

She was not silent, the sound of a seed splitting in one instant, unfurling, opening to the pit baring the center, unwinding, beyond hearing. Radiance of birth and blood of closure and zero weather, husks weathered into cobs of corn, the burnt barn. Heads and molten rain remembered seeing nothing in the fire, movement toward birth seasons upon seasons, no disappointment (23).

* * *

There is some dispute as to when Tillie Olsen actually produced the text of "Requa-I." Burkom and Williams may be right in their claim that she began writing the unfinished novella in 1962. (79) Other interviews with Olsen indicate that the original text of the novella was included in the box Jack Olsen found in the attic along with *Yonnondio* and shipped off to his wife at the Macdowell Colony after she had already made her breakthrough with "I

Stand Here Ironing." In any event, Olsen worked in the early sixties on shaping her final novella and brought it into print in 1970 in *Iowa Review*. The following year it was selected for inclusion in Martha Foley's *Best American Short Stories*.

The worst of the Cold War period had passed by that time. Olsen, who in the fifties had been denounced over San Francisco radio while participating as a parent leader in school situations, could now publish almost anything she chose. She chose to find redemption, reassertion of faith in the value of human connectedness, and even transcendence through nature. Blanche Gelfant's reading emphasizes the restorative powers of human connectedness in this piece. I want to add to that an investigation of the almost transcendent power of nature itself.

Requa is a native American place name just inside the Oregon border in Northern California. It is high on a hill, looking down on the mouth of the Klamath River and the split rock Oregos, traditionally sacred to the Yurok Indians who lived in the area. The prime character is a boy of thirteen, Stevie, whose mother has just died. Her brother Wes has come to get Stevie and bring him from Southern California up to Requa among the redwoods to work with him at a junkyard in an effort to restore Stevie's well-being and bring him out of mourning. The time is 1932 and jobs are scarce and money tight.

It is the combination of the primeval natural setting and his uncle Wes's reluctant compassion that finally brings Stevie around. In this way Stevie experiences the healing factors of both aspects of nature that both Engels and Emerson discuss. The first is the healing power of natural forces, more important to Emerson's philosophy than to that of Engels. The second is the healing quality of human nature that, despite capitalist circumstance, can call forth communality and caring. Both factors are necessary to the continuation of the human species, as both philosophers in different ways take note, and both are paramount in Olsen's own vision of the powers of "goodness" and beneficence she persistently promulgates in the face of postmodernist despair. Indeed, set in the Depression, with the primal scene a junkheap, the novella seems to test our capacity for optimism beyond even anything postmodernist angst can deride.

When we first meet Stevie, he is a sniveling, vomity kid with no will even to hold up his head. Wes impatiently tosses him a mackinaw in the truck to keep him warm. Stevie rejects nature, pulls the mackinaw tight around him to ward off the rays of the healing sun and retreats into his own sphere. The first sign he will come out of it is when he wakes up early in the morning at a camp in the woods:

Across the creek, just like in the movie show or in a dream, a deer and two baby deers were drinking. When he lifted his head, they lifted theirs. For a long time he and the doe looked into each other's eyes. Then swift, beautiful, they were gone--but her eyes kept looking into his (112).

Stevie's ability to commune with natural creatures, to take from the doe's gaze what we can only assume to be a restorative glance from his mother incarnate, is the first indication we get that he will himself be able to come to a restoration of life and well-being in the wake of his intense grief. In a way, Stevie's mother's presence haunts the whole story much in the same way as does the doe's silent gaze. She had been everything for Stevie, his whole life. The pathetic mementoes he keeps of her, vulgar ashtrays and sodden curio pillows, bits of jewelry, snips of snapshots, form part of the materialistic effluvia that it will become his business to sort through. Olsen seems to counterpose this material stuff to the naturalistic signs of the oversoul, the eyes of the deer, the power of the mighty redwood, the uncle's fishing and hunting, that are the natural gifts of creation. Grief, the ability to mourn, to feel love and its loss are part of that natural endowment.

As Elaine Orr notes:

Stevie's journey begins at the personal level and expands toward a vision of universal quest through imagistic association with animal and plant worlds and the significant relations of this life. The longer light of spring, accompanying the boy's quest for a place and for the knowledge that he is connected with others by life, points to the metaphysical depth of the story. Through the settings of junkyard and cemetery, journeying becomes a metaphor not only for the living but for the hopes of the dead, whose memory sparks the present search for meaning and for a feeling of continuity (171)

That Olsen's concern reaches beyond the Depression era in which *Yonnondio* was written and "Requa" is set is suggested by Orr's comment:

In her notes, Olsen has written, "In the human being is an irrepressible desire for freedom that breaks out century after century." In her fiction she shows that desire to be not merely for freedom *from* want, hunger and fear, but freedom *for* fulfillment, expression, and community. Using women's, children's and working-class perspectives Olsen transforms the vision of human longing from solitary to community questing (172)

When Stevie arrives at the boarding house where he will stay at the ancient Indian camp, he carries the effluvia of his mother's paltry possessions. In comparison with the grief of humanity, the grief of mortality that the Indian camp represents, the material conditions of Stevie's life, even of Wes's, seem trivial, especially in the context of the timeless continuity of the deer, the salmon and the redwood. Nature, overwhelming in the northern California redwood forest, is a dominating force, here, a restorative force.

Uncle Wes, with his sometimes gruff proddings, is a life vector. He allows Stevie to drop out of school and come to work with him in the junkyard. Then there is the junkkyard itself, repository of the detritus of civilization. Gelfant points out that junkyards were frequent sites for Depression narratives (61). At the same time, if we note that this novella was written in the sixties we can assume a suggestion that the whole glut of commodities that signalled the postwar consumerist phase of capitalism is also at stake in this story.

If in *Yonnondio* capitalism has deprived the oppressed of the very means of subsistence and turned good men like Jim Holbrook into rapists and wife-beaters, writing of the same period thirty years later, Olsen sees that capitalism has made of our national heritage a junkheap. This idea is nowhere so clear as in the juxtaposition of images on the day when Stevie first comes on the job with Wes to lend him a hand in the scavenging among the dross for usable kernels.

At last it works, gleaning through capitalism's rubbish allows Stevie to feel deep in his bones that he has gained Wes's respect, that he is himself a worthwhile member of creation. Again, we turn to Emerson (in his "Illusions" essay) rather than to Engels:

> We fancy we have fallen into bad company and squalid condition, low debts, shoe-bills, broken glass to pay for, pots to buy, butcher's meat, sugar, milk, and coal. 'Set me some great task, ye gods! and I will show my spirit.' 'Not so,' says the good Heaven; 'plod and plough, vamp your old coats and hats, weave a shoestring'; great affairs and the best wine by and by.' Well, 'tis all phantasm; and if we weave a yard of tape in all humility and as well as we can, long hereafter we shall see it was no cotton tape at all, but some galaxy which we braided, and that the threads were Time and Nature (1121).

The final relief is a glut of grieving. Stevie and Wes have hollered and slunk at each other for two months at the junkyard. Slowly, Stevie has been coming around. At least he goes every day and tries to answer Wes's demands. Finally, Mrs. Edler, Wes's landlady, takes Stevie on Memorial Day on a round of cemeteries to visit graves and listen to the guns boom. There is nothing maudlin about this scene. Stevie treats the ancient stone markers as he would the stone bears on the bridge--emblems of a time gone by. No tears now, though he is a snot-nosed kid and the scene closes on that note. While he is not overtly thinking of his mother or paying homage to her, she still hovers in the background, in the gravesite of a young mother with child. The encounter is ultimately restorative:

> How warm it felt down there in the weeds where nobody could see him and the wind didn't reach. The lamb was sun warm too. He put his arm around its stone neck and rested. . . . The smell was sweet like before they set the burn pile; even the crackling flags sounded far away (132).

The effect of merging the natural order, of sun-warmth, of ocean sounds against the redwoods, with the fact of mortality and the remembrance of his mother's death has been unexpectedly salutary:

> What did you do to him? Wes asked Mrs. Edler. When I heard where you went, I expected sure he'd get back near dead, bad as in the beginning. But he's been frisky as a puppy all day, Chased me round the junk heaps. Rassled went down to the river on his own throwed skimmers sharped a saw perfect. Paid attention. Curled up and fell asleep on the way home (132).

In its delineation of human communality and natural restoratives as the essential curative forces, "Requa-I" marks Olsen's most decisive break with formulaic proletarian writing with which she was associated when *Yonnondio* was published. While "Requa-I" is still well within the bounds of realism as against the fabulism of Kafka or Donald Barthelme, say, its deciding factors are not primarily material. We may say that Jim Holbrook beats Anna, almost to death, and that Anna in turn beats the kids due to the fact of their poverty and the degradation of mill, mine and packinghouse work--as well as housework under conditions of material deprivation. With the exception of the dandelion-picking, perhaps, and possibly the peach-canning, there is no

Thoreauvian work-ethic in *Yonnondio*. Work, all forms of it, except perhaps that on the ill-fated farm that had to be abandoned, is always drudgery and oppression--Jim's work as well as Anna's. It quite literally fouls the atmosphere, nearly to the point of nausea.

In "Requa-I," work, the exertion of labor, becomes an aspect of the restorative resolution of vectors that bring Stevie back to functionability. The stuff of capitalist existence is reduced to a gleanable junkheap defiling the natural setting. One can almost imagine that Wes and Stevie would be better off if they fished for salmon and hunted bear. Surely, a school education, so important to Anna, has little to offer Stevie at this point. What triumphs in "Requa-I" is what is intimated in *Yonnondio* and developed in the later stories in the *Tell Me a Riddle* collection--the twin factors of the power of the human capacity for caring and the reverent awe demanded by the transcendent power of all that is meant by natural forces--from human capacities to the creation of the universe itself.

* * *

The puzzle in considering Olsen's and Herbst's late addresses on the problem of man and nature is that they both indeed center around men rather than women. Barbara Foley, in her important, compendious reading of the proletarian literature of the thirties, *Radical Representations* (1993), argues against the widely held interpretation that women writers in the milieu of the CPUSA were "burrowers from within against the 'official' doctrines of the 1930s left." Instead, she argues, they were the left's "visionary conscience" (246). I suggest, however, that taking the entire lives' works into consideration allows one to see these authors in a continuum of individuated literary sensibility. If they had operated under the constraint to cater to party masculinism in the thirties, why continue or even exaggerate that masculinism when they are on their own, party influence a dead issue? Perhaps it is difficult for women critics of the new generation to conceive that a woman writer may consider herself a writer first, a chronicler of the entire species condition, and a woman secondarily. One does not cease to be a woman because one writes, surely, but neither does one cease to be a human being because one is a woman.

The problematic it seems to me Josephine Herbst addresses in her marvelous little book *New Green World* (1954)--at least the problem that continues to interest a modern audience, women as well as men--is precisely its challenge to Engels's formulation "being determines consciousness; consciousness does not determine being." The question arises in manifold forms in our times as to whether this is a necessary condition of the human situation, or whether there is such a thing as free choice. If there is free choice, is it possible to ameliorate social conditions merely by deciding to do so, or must we wait for the millenarian crisis that will alter "being" in a way to alter "consciousness."

Certainly, this question has validity for the women's movement of today, as for all marginalized movements and for all those dissatisfied with conditions under capitalism. The question is not new. As I indicated at the beginning of this book, it was contained in the challenge Crystal Eastman presented to Alice Paul's liberal reformist Women's Party in 1920. Is it possible to alleviate the worst injustices of the capitalist system so as to make a comfortable life possible for an important percentage of the previously marginalized sector or do we want to start talking about how to alter the very foundation of the system of exploitation in Marxist--or other--terms?

For my own part, I find the liberal solution of pushing one's way into key positions within the capitalist system to be unsatisfactory. This is the solution of many feminists--Betty Friedan's new book most notably proposes it. I have both theoretical and personal reasons to prefer the mixed camp of men and women who are opposing the system itself to the cause of those women who would "make it" within the system as is.

I have been working more or less steadily, what with school and a brief hiatus for childcare, since I was sixteen. I have been a factory worker, a typist, an editorial associate, and, most recently, a college teacher. During this thirty-five-year time span, I would say approximately ninety percent of the people I have worked for have been women in varying capacities of supervisory positions. I know that personal experience may not count for much in the context of the feminist/Marxist discussion, but I offer my observation, corroborated by colleagues, that women like those I have worked for have been if anything more exacting, less sympathetic and more demanding of personal caretaking favors than men in the same positions. Further, let me draw the conclusion that does seem pertinent here that it is not one whit more pleasurable to have one's surplus value extracted by a woman than it is by a man. Exploitation is just as alienating when conducted by a woman as by a man. Men at my level working for these same supervisors tended to agree. The point is it is the position, not the biology that takes over. Perhaps women's extra-zealousness is motivated by gender-determined anxiety to please a boss in a position in which they are uncertain. That's their business. Mine is to point out that the economy establishes the characteristics that make more profits possible--in worker, supervisor, and employer alike. And that holds across racial and sexual lines. The eighties and nineties have seen a previously unprecedented clamor of frequently marginalized peoples to "make it" within the structure of class exploitation. What Marx points out by dint of his depersonalized, deracinated abstract model of capitalist production is that this is not outside the realm of possibility. The system of exploitation of labor can work just as well if the controlling class is made up entirely of third world lesbian women of color and the exploited class is entirely white Anglo-Saxon males under the age of forty-five. What it is incumbent upon the previously marginalized, as well as all those in gray flannel suits feeling the effects of alienation of labor and intelligence, to do is to make a choice. In my mind, from both my experience and from my reading, the choice has only one set of parameters. Does one want to perpetuate the system of exploitation of labor for the purpose of extracting surplus value, or can we start working together to come up with a viable alternative? Certainly "working together" is a loaded term in a deck that has always been stacked against women and people of color; however, for as long as we all occupy the same planet together and have been plunged willy-nilly by the inexorable laws of imperialist expansion into the terms of more or less the same socio-economic dimension, I see no way to avoid addressing the key questions to the whole human race. I note that this is a stance that has been only rarely taken since the thirties feminism of Le Sueur, Herbst, and Olsen, and in the conclusion of this chapter I will attempt to show how they made this question implicitly part of their abiding lives.

The question of choice as I have posed it deliberately and directly challenges my perhaps oversimplified statement of Marx and Engels's social determinism. This question of choice is very much implicit in most of Herbst's work and nowhere so explicitly as in her penultimate book, her biography of the botanist John Bartram and his son William.

Perhaps it doesn't pay to make too much out of Herbst's choice of subject. She lived in the cottage in Bucks County, Pennsylvania, now on her own, Herrmann long gone. She had been blacklisted, she could not publish her commercially-oriented stories, her two postwar novels hardly sold, but things now, in the mid-fifties were changing. She had two sets of friends. Financial support was more likely to come from those she had known in her Communist days, such as Jessie O'Connor and Elinor Ferry (Mrs. George Kirstein).[3] Kirstein had come from a wealthy liberal socialite family that included Elinor's brother-in-law Lincoln Kirstein, whose acquaintance Herbst was eager to make. Through those connections and through such friends from Yaddo as Alfred Kazin and others, Herbst added another, more socially acceptable, aspect to her field of endeavors. Records from the Herbst archives and from personal testimony, however, suggest that it was her radical friends who were more likely to contribute to her financial support.

In any event, the radical movement, such as it was in the mid-fifties would be hard put to make much of *New Green World*, even though, by my reading, it goes clearly to the heart of her anti-capitalism. Herbst was looking for a subject, Bartram had lived and worked in her neighborhood, she shared his enjoyment of and scientific reverence for nature. The subject was a natural. What comes through in Herbst's narrative is not only a beguiling account of the Bartrams, father and son but also an ultimately disarming conviction "that it might be possible to comprehend the universe by devotion to the minutest creatures whose laws of life might shadow the greater design." (4)

What is noteworthy about John Bartram--and Herbst time and again takes note of it--is that although he must make a living to support a household that includes a wife and ten children, he does not succumb to commercialism. He provides wealthy lords in England with botanical oddities for their collections of exotica but only to finance his own heartfelt mission, the categorization and continuation of the rare plants in the new world. As Herbst notes, in a statement that may well express her post-communist ideology: "the Bartrams understood that changes were due in the world. But such an idea was not soul-shattering. Had they not observed the mutations in a plant?" (5)

The element of choice comes into play in Herbst's narrative as repeatedly she points out that Bartram had a chance--and possibly even a necessity--to make an enterprise out of his endeavor, to become rapacious and capitalistic. He had the customers; many throughout the New World and the far-reaching preserves of imperialism would--and did--jump at the chance.

As I indicated in previous chapters, the question of the individual's ability--necessity--to make rational choices about her relationship to social forces was perhaps the single most important abiding theme of all Herbst's work. This work, set in the eighteenth century, placed in a natural setting, may not seem to have the importance of her thirties novels that take on questions of war and revolution, of poverty and gender. Here, in her statement in what Le Sueur has called "the Dark of the Time," Herbst finds both a challenge to mechanistic Marxism and an affirmation of faith in the possibilities of benevolent life:

It was a time not yet given to boasting of man's control of Nature. Before the Industrial Revolution, Nature's laws were the clue to the order of the universe and compelled awe. Though the vast promise of the unexplored wilderness excited some to dark deeds, some to greedy aggrandizement, to a few like Bartram, the swamps and thorny hillsides, the gloomy woods and fragile wild flowers, were not to plunder or even to civilize, but to see and receive devotion (21).

I have not made a study to pursue the male authors of the thirties into the fifties and sixties, except for a few casual glances at Nelson Algren, James T. Farrell and others. Harvey Swados seems to have been unique in the fifties and sixties in carrying on a personally lived proletarian tradition. Perhaps I am making too much of the identification of these three women with nature. My point has been to show that in a world that turned volte face to defeatism and decadence and nihilism, these women found a means to express the optimism and faith in the goodness of both human nature and planetary grace that I hope I have shown brought them to the communist vision in the first place.

Notes

1. The pamphlet Herbst authored and signed in behalf of O'Connor's case is available in the Herbst archives at the Beinecke Library at Yale.

2. For an intriguing account of how male-dominated logocentric mythologies can be altered by women inventing their own mythos to alleviate childbirth see Martin, Emily, *The Woman in the Body.* Boston: Beacon. 1992.

3. I am grateful to the late Elinor Ferry, a good friend of mine and a valued comrade since 1957, for many taped interviews elucidating her relationship with Josephine Herbst, especially in connection with their mutual efforts to exonerate Alger Hiss.

Works Cited

Aaron, Daniel. *Writers on the Left: Episodes in American Literary Communism.* New York: Columbia UP. 1992.

Baker, Houston A., Jr. *Long Black Song: Essays in Black American Literature and Culture.* Charlottesville: U of Virginia P. 1990.

Bauer, Helen Pike. "'A child of anxious, not proud, love': Mother and Daughter in Tillie Olsen's 'I Stand Here Ironing'." In Mickey Pearlman, ed. *Mother Puzzles: Daughters and Mothers in Contemporary American Literature.* Westport: Greenwood P. 1989.

Bebel, August. *Woman Under Socialism.* New York: New York Labor News Press. 1904.

Bevilacqua, Winifred Farrant, *Josephine Herbst.* Boston: Twayne. 1985.

Boucher, Sandy. "Tillie Olsen: The Weight of Things Unsaid." *Ms.* Vol. III. No. 3. Sept. 1974. 26-30.

Brothers, Barbara, "Through the 'Pantry Window': Sylvia Townsend Warner and the Spanish Civil War, in Frieda S. Brown et al., eds, *Rewriting the Good Fight: Critical Essays on the Literature of the Spanish Civil War.* E. Lansing: Michigan State UP. 1989. 161-174.

Burkom, Selma, and Margaret Williams. "De-Riddling Tillie Olsen's Writings." *San Jose Studies* 2 (1976) 65-83.

Campbell, Isabel. "'Nothing Is Sacred' Is Story of Trouble Over Son-in-Law." Oklahoma City. Nov. 25, 1928.

Cavan, Ruth Shonle, and Katherine Howland Ranck. *The Family and the Depression: A Study of One Hundred Chicago Families.* New York: Arno. 1971.

Chodorow, Nancy. *The Reproduction of Mothering: Psychoanalysis and the Sociology of Gender.* Berkeley: U of California P. 1978.

Coles, Robert. "Reconsideration: Tell Me a Riddle by Tillie Olsen." *The New Republic.* Dec. 6, 1975. 29-30.

Cook, Blanche Wiesen. *Toward the Great Change: Crystal and Max Eastman on Feminism, Antimilitarism, and Revolution.* New York: Garland. 1976.

Davenport, Basil. "Pity 'Tis, 'Tis True." *The Saturday Review.* June 3, 1933.

Davis, Angela Y. *Women, Race & Class.* New York: Vintage. 1983.

Derrida, Jacques. *Spurs: Nietzsche's Styles.* Trans. by Barbara Harlow. Chicago: U of Chicago P. 1978.

De Witt, Karen. "From De Von to LaDon, Invented Names Proclaim 'I Am'." *New York Times,* January 9, 1994. E3.

Duncan, Erika. "Coming of Age in the Thirties: A Portrait of Tillie Olsen." *Book Forum.* Vol. 6. No. 2. 1982.

Eagleton, Terry. *The Ideology of the Aesthetic.* Oxford: Basil Blackwell. 1990.

Elshtain, Jean Bethke, "Feminist Discourse and Its Discontents: Language, Power, and Meaning." *Signs,* 1982, vol 7, no. 3 603-621.

———. *Public Man, Private Woman: Women in Social and Political Thought.* Princeton, NJ: Princeton UP. 1981.

Emerson, Ralph Waldo. "Illusions," in *Essays & Lectures* New York: Library Classics of America. 1983.

Engels, Frederick. *Anti-Duhring: Herr Eugen Duhring's Revolution in Science.* New York: International. 1972.

Erikson, Erik H. *Identity: Youth and Crisis.* New York: Norton. 1968.

Ferraro, Joseph. *Freedom and Determmination in History According to Maarx & Engels.* New York: Monthly Review Press. 1992.

Foley, Barbara. *Radical Representations: Politics and Form in U.S. Proletarian Fiction. 1929-1941.* Durham: Duke UP. 1993.

Fox-Genovese, Elizabeth. *Feminism Without Illusions: A Critique of Individualism.* Chapel Hill: U of North Carolina P. 1991.

Gale, Zona. *Friendship Village.* New York: Macmillan. 1936.

———. *Preface to a Life.* New York: D. Appleton and Co. 1926.

Gelfant, Blanche H. "After Long Silence: Tillie Olsen's 'Requa'" *Studies in American Fiction* Spring 1984, vol. 12, no. 1. 61-69.

Gillmore, Inez Haynes, "The Classmates." *The Masses,* March 1911. 13-14.

Ginger, Ray. *The Bending Cross: A Biography of Eugene Victor Debs.* New Brunswick: Rutgers UP. 1949.

Griffin, Susan. *Woman and Nature: The Roaring Inside Her.* New York: Harper & Row. 1978.

Hampl, Patricia. "Meridel Le Sueur." *Ms.* August 1975. 62.

Healey, Dorothy, and Maurice Isserman. *Dorothy Healey Remembers: A Life in the American Communist Party.* New York: Oxford UP. 1990.

Herbst, Josephine. "Counterblast." *The Nation,* vol. cxxxii, no. 3427, March 11, 1931. 275-6.

——— (as Carlotta Greet). "The Elegant Mr. Gason," *Smart Set,* (July 1923), 35-39.

————. "Embalmer's Holiday." *Accent*. Winter 1941, 85-93.

————. *The Executioner Waits*. New York: Warner. 1985.

————. "The Farmers Form a United Front." *New Masses*. January 2, 1934. 20-23.

————. "Farmers' Holiday." *Scribner's*, vol ci, no. 1. January 1937. 105-7.

————. "Iowa Takes to Literature," *The American Mercury*, VII (April 1926), 466-470.

————. "Miss Porter and Miss Stein." *Partisan Review*. May 1948, 568-572.

————. *Money for Love*. New York: Arno P. 1977.

————. *New Green World*. New York: Hastings House. 1954.

————. Night Comes to the Valley." *Direction*, Vol 1, no. 4. April 1938, 18-20.

————. *Nothing Is Sacred*. New York: Coward-McCann. 1928.

————. "A Passport from Realengo 18." *New Masses: An Anthology of the Rebel Thirties*. Joseph North, ed. New York: International. 1969. 155-9.

———— (with John Herrmann). "Pennsylvania Idyl." *The American Mercury*. Vol. XVI, no. 61, Jan. 1929. 52-59.

————. Pity Is Not Enough. New York: Warner. 1985.

————. *Rope of Gold*. Old Westbury, NY: Feminist Press. 1984.

————. *Somewhere the Tempest Fell*. New York: Scribner's. 1947.

————. *The Starched Blue Sky of Spain*. New York: Harper Collins. 1991.

Hicks, Granville. *The Great Tradition: An Interpretation of American Literature since the Civil War*. New York: International. 1935.

Horkheimer, Max. *Critical Theory: Selected Essays.* New York: Herder and Herder. 1972.

Jacobs, N.M. "Olsen's 'O Yes': Alva's Vision as Childbirth Account." *Notes on Contemporary Literature.* No. 1, Jan. 1986. 7-8.

Jaggar, Alison M., ed. *Living with Contradictions: Controversies in Feminist Social Ethics.* Boulder: Westview P. 1994.

Jones, Margaret C. *Heretics & Hellraisers: Women Contributors to* The Masses, *1911-1917.* Austin: U of Texas P. 1993.

Josephs, Allen. "Hemingway and the Spanish Civil War or the Volatile Mixture of Politics and Art," in Frieda S. Brown et al., eds., *Rewriting the Good Fight: Critical Esssays on the Literature of the Spanish Civil War.* E. Lansing: Michigan State UP. 1989.

Kamel, Rose. "Literary Foremothers and Writers' Silences: Tillie Olsen's Autobiographical Fiction." *Melus: Society for the Study of the Multi-Ethnic Literature of the United States.* Fall 3. 1985. 55-72.

Kazin, Alfred. Introduction, *Call It Sleep,* by Henry Roth. New York: Noonday. 1991. ix-xx.

Kelly-Gadol, Joan. "The Social Relations of the Sexes: Methodological Implications of Women's History," *The Signs Reader: Women, Gender & Scholarship,* Elizabeth Abel and Emily K. Abel, eds. Chicago: U of Chicago P. 1983.

Langer, Elinor. *Josephine Herbst: The Story She Could Never Tell.* New York: Warner. 1984.

Leibowitz, Herbert. *Fabricating Lives: Explorations in American Autobiography.* New York: Knopf. 1989.

Le Sueur, Meridel. *The Girl.* Cambridge, MA: West End Press. 1978.

―――. *Harvest Song.* Albuquerque: West End Press. 1990.

————. *I Hear Men Talking: Stories of the Early Decades.* Minneapolis: West End Press. 1984.

————. *Ripening: Selected Work, 1927-1980.* Old Westbury: The Feminist Press. 1982

————. *Rites of Ancient Ripening.* Minneapolis: Vanilla Press. 1975

————. *Salute to Spring.* New York: International Press. 1989.

————. *Winter Prairie Woman.* Minneapolis: Midwest Villages & Voices. 1990.

Lukacs, Georg. *History and Class Consciousness: Studies in Marxist Dialectics.* Cambridge: MIT Press. 1971.

Madden, David. *Proletarian Writers of the Thirties.* Carbondale: Southern Illinois UP. 1968.

Malraux, Andre. *Man's Hope.* New York: Modern Library. 1983.

Marx, Karl. *Capital: A Critique of Political Economy.* New York: Random House. 1906.

————and Frederick Engels. *The German Ideology.* New York: International. 1970.

McElhiney, Annette Bennington. "Alternative Responses to Life in Tillie Olsen's Work." *Frontiers.* 2 Spring 1977. 76-91.

Murphy, James F. *The Proletarian Moment: The Controversy Over Leftism in Literature.* Urbana: U of Illinois P. 1991.

Newton, Judith, and Deborah Rosenfelt, eds. *Feminist Criticism and Social Change: Sex, Class and Race in Literature and Culture.* New York: Methuen. 1985.

Nilsen, Helge Normann. "Tillie Olsen's 'Tell Me a Riddle': The Political Theme." *Etude Anglaises, T.* XXXVII. no. 2 (April-June 1984). 163-169.

Olsen, Tillie. "Requa-I." *Granta* 1980. 111-132.

———. *Silences.* New York: Delacorte. 1978.

———. *Tell Me a Riddle.* New York: Dell. 1960.

———. *Yonnondio: From the Thirties.* New York: Dell. 1974.

Orr, Elaine. "On the Side of the Mother: *Yonnondio* and *Call It Sleep*," *Studies in American Fiction.* Vol. 21, no. 2 (Autumn 1993). 209-225.

———. *Tillie Olsen and a Feminist Spiritual Vision.* Jackson: UP of Mississippi. 1987.

Orwell, George. "From *Homage to Catalonia*" in *The Orwell Reader.* New York: Harcourt, Brace Jovanovich. 1956.

Pearlman, Mickey, and Abby H.P. Werlock. *Tillie Olsen.* Boston: Twayne. 1991.

Porter, Katherine Anne, "The Family." New York *Tribune.* October 7, 1928.

Pratt, Linda Ray. "Woman Writer in the CP: The Case of Meridel LeSueur." *Women's Studies.* 1988. Vol. 14, pp. 247-264

Rabinowitz, Paula. *Labor & Desire: Women's Revolutionary Fiction in Depression America.* Chapel Hill: U of North Carolina P 1991.

Rideout, Walter B. *The Radical Novel in the United States 1900-1954.* New York: Columbia UP. 1992.

Rosenfelt, Deborah, "From the Thirties: Tillie Olsen and the Radical Tradition." *Feminist Studies* 7, no. 3 (Fall 1981) 370-406).

Roth, Henry. *Call It Sleep.* New York: Farrar, Straus & Giroux. 1991.

Ruddick, Sara. *Maternal Thinking: Toward a Politics of Peace.* New York: Ballantine. 1989.

Ruhle, Jurgen. *Literature and Revolution: A Critical Study of the Writer and Communism in the Twentieth Century.* Trans. Jean Steinberg. New York: Praeger. 1969.

Schneider, Isidor, "The Fetish of Simplicity." *The Nation,* vol. 132, no. 3424, Jan. 18, 1931. 184-5.

Sennett, Richard, and Jonathan Cobb. *The Hidden Injuries of Class.* New York: Norton. 1972.

Showalter, Elaine. *A Literature of Their Own: British Women Novelists from Bronte to Lessing.* Princeton: Princeton UP. 1977

Smith, Sidonie. *A Poetics of Women's Autobiography: Marginality and the Fictions of Self-Representation.* Bloomington: Indiana UP. 1987.

Staub, Michael. "The Struggle for 'Selfness' Through Speech in Olsen's *Yonnondio: From the Thirties."* *Studies in American Fiction.* Vol. 16. No. 3 1988. 131-139.

Stimpson, Catharine R. "Three Women Work It Out." *The Nation.* Nov. 30, 1974. 565-568.

Tompkins, Jane P. *Sensational Designs: The Cultural Work of American Fiction 1790-1860.* New York: Oxford UP. 1985.

Trotsky, Leon. *Problems of Everyday Life, and Other Writings on Culture & Science.* New York: Monad. 1973.

Zetkin, Clara. *Lenin on the Woman Question* in *The Emancipation of Women: From the Writings of V. I. Lenin.* New York: International. 1966.

Index